ORGANIZATIONAL
Linkages
UNDERSTANDING THE PRODUCTIVITY PARADOX

Douglas H. Harris, Editor

Panel on Organizational Linkages
Committee on Human Factors
Commission on Behavioral and Social Sciences and Education
National Research Council

NATIONAL ACADEMY PRESS
Washington, D.C.   1994

NATIONAL ACADEMY PRESS · 2101 Constitution Avenue, N.W. · Washington, D.C. 20418

NOTICE: The project that is the subject of this report was approved by the Governing Board of the National Research Council, whose members are drawn from the councils of the National Academy of Sciences, the National Academy of Engineering, and the Institute of Medicine. The members of the committee responsible for the report were chosen for their special competences and with regard to appropriate balance.

This report has been reviewed by a group other than the authors according to procedures approved by a Report Review Committee consisting of members of the National Academy of Sciences, the National Academy of Engineering, and the Institute of Medicine.

This work relates to Department of the Army grant MDA 903-89-K-0074 issued by the Defense Supply Service Washington. The views, opinions, and findings contained in this report are those of the author(s) and should not be construed as an official Department of the Army position, policy, or decision, unless so designated by other official documentation.

The United States government has at least a royalty-free, nonexclusive, and irrevocable license throughout the world for government purposes to publish, translate, reproduce, deliver, perform, dispose of, and to authorize others so as to do, all or any portion of this work.

Library of Congress Cataloging-in-Publication Data

Organizational linkages : understanding the productivity paradox /
    Douglas H. Harris, editor ; Panel on Organizational Linkages,
    Committee on Human Factors, Commission on Behavioral and Social
    Sciences and Education, National Research Council.
        p. cm
    Includes bibliographical references and index.
    ISBN 0-309-04934-2
        1. Industrial productivity. 2. Industrial productivity—United
    States. 3. Organizational effectiveness. I. Harris, Douglas H.,
    1930– . II. National Research Council (U.S.). Committee on Human
    Factors. III. National Research Council (U.S.). Panel on
    Organizational Linkages.
    HC79.I52074   1994
    338.5—dc20   94-29475
                                                                      CIP

Printed in the United States of America

PANEL ON ORGANIZATIONAL LINKAGES

DOUGLAS H. HARRIS (*Chair*), Anacapa Sciences, Inc., Charlottesville, Va.

PAUL A. ATTEWELL, Department of Sociology, City University of New York

JOHN P. CAMPBELL, Department of Psychology, University of Minnesota

JEROME I. ELKIND, Lexia Institute, Palo Alto, Calif.

PAUL S. GOODMAN, Center for Management of Technology, Carnegie Mellon University

SARA B. KIESLER, Department of Social and Decision Sciences, Carnegie Mellon University

ROBERT D. PRITCHARD, Department of Psychology, Texas A&M University

WILLIAM A. RUCH, Department of Decision and Information Systems, Arizona State University

BENJAMIN SCHNEIDER, Department of Psychology, University of Maryland

D. SCOTT SINK, Virginia Productivity Center, Virginia Polytechnic Institute and State University

GEORGE L. SMITH, JR., Department of Industrial and Systems Engineering, Ohio State University

DAVID A. WHETTEN, Department of Business Administration, University of Illinois

iii

Contents

Foreword   vii

Preface   ix

1   INTRODUCTION   1

2   INFORMATION TECHNOLOGY AND THE
PRODUCTIVITY PARADOX   13
Paul Attewell

3   INDIVIDUAL AND ORGANIZATIONAL PRODUCTIVITY:
LINKAGES AND PROCESSES   54
Paul S. Goodman, F. Javier Lerch, and *Tridas Mukhopadhyay*

4   WHAT IS ENOUGH? A SYSTEMS PERSPECTIVE ON
INDIVIDUAL-ORGANIZATIONAL PERFORMANCE
LINKAGES   81
Benjamin Schneider and *Katherine J. Klein*

5   MEASURING AND MANAGING INDIVIDUAL
PRODUCTIVITY   105
William A. Ruch

v

6 THE INFLUENCE OF ORGANIZATIONAL LINKAGES
AND MEASUREMENT PRACTICES ON PRODUCTIVITY
AND MANAGEMENT 131
D. Scott Sink and *George L. Smith, Jr.*

7 DECOMPOSING THE PRODUCTIVITY LINKAGES
PARADOX 161
Robert D. Pritchard

8 MODELS OF MEASUREMENT AND THEIR IMPLICATIONS
FOR RESEARCH ON THE LINKAGES BETWEEN
INDIVIDUAL AND ORGANIZATIONAL PRODUCTIVITY 193
John P. Campbell

9 COORDINATION AS LINKAGE: THE CASE OF
SOFTWARE DEVELOPMENT TEAMS 214
Sara Kiesler, Douglas Wholey, and *Kathleen M. Carley*

10 PRODUCTIVITY LINKAGES IN COMPUTER-AIDED
DESIGN 240
Douglas H. Harris

11 ORGANIZATIONAL-LEVEL PRODUCTIVITY INITIATIVES:
THE CASE OF DOWNSIZING 262
David A. Whetten and *Kim S. Cameron*

12 CONCLUSIONS 291

INDEX 302

Foreword

The Committee on Human Factors was established in October 1980 by the Commission on Behavioral and Social Sciences and Education of the National Research Council. The committee is sponsored by the Air Force Office of Scientific Research, the Army Research Institute for the Behavioral and Social Sciences, the National Aeronautics and Space Administration, the Air Force Armstrong Aerospace Medical Research Laboratory, the Army Advanced Systems Research Office, the Army Human Engineering Laboratory, the Army Natick RD&E Center, the Federal Aviation Administration, the Nuclear Regulatory Commission, the Naval Training Systems Center, and the U.S. Coast Guard. The principal objectives of the committee are to provide new perspectives on theoretical and methodological issues, to identify basic research needed to expand and strengthen the scientific basis of human factors, and to attract scientists inside and outside the field for interactive communication and performance of needed research.

Human factors issues arise in every domain in which humans interact with the products of a technological society. To perform its role effectively, the committee draws on experts from a wide range of scientific and engineering disciplines. Members of the committee include specialists in such fields as psychology, engineering, biomechanics, physiology, medicine, cognitive sciences, machine intelligence, computer sciences, sociology, education, and human factors engineering. Other disciplines are represented in the working groups, workshops, and symposia organized by the committee. Each of these disciplines contributes to the basic data, theory, and methods required to improve the scientific basis of human factors.

The National Academy of Sciences is a private, nonprofit, self-perpetuating society of distinguished scholars engaged in scientific and engineering research, dedicated to the furtherance of science and technology and to their use for the general welfare. Upon the authority of the charter granted to it by the Congress in 1863, the Academy has a mandate that requires it to advise the federal government on scientific and technical matters. Dr. Bruce M. Alberts is president of the National Academy of Sciences.

The National Academy of Engineering was established in 1964, under the charter of the National Academy of Sciences, as a parallel organization of outstanding engineers. It is autonomous in its administration and in the selection of its members, sharing with the National Academy of Sciences the responsibility for advising the federal government. The National Academy of Engineering also sponsors engineering programs aimed at meeting national needs, encourages education and research, and recognizes the superior achievements of engineers. Dr. Robert M. White is president of the National Academy of Engineering.

The Institute of Medicine was established in 1970 by the National Academy of Sciences to secure the services of eminent members of appropriate professions in the examination of policy matters pertaining to the health of the public. The Institute acts under the responsibility given to the National Academy of Sciences by its congressional charter to be an adviser to the federal government and, upon its own initiative, to identify issues of medical care, research, and education. Dr. Kenneth I. Shine is president of the Institute of Medicine.

The National Research Council was established by the National Academy of Sciences in 1916 to associate the broad community of science and technology with the Academy's purposes of furthering knowledge and advising the federal government. Functioning in accordance with general policies determined by the Academy, the Council has become the principal operating agency of both the National Academy of Sciences and the National Academy of Engineering in providing services to the government, the public, and the scientific and engineering communities. The Council is administered jointly by both Academies and the Institute of Medicine. Dr. Bruce M. Alberts and Dr. Robert M. White are chairman and vice chairman, respectively, of the National Research Council.

Preface

Since its inception in 1980, the Committee on Human Factors of the National Research Council has issued more than a dozen reports regarding the state of knowledge and research needs on topics deemed important by the committee and its sponsors. Some projects undertaken by the committee have been suggested and funded directly by its sponsors: others have been pursued on the committee's initiative. This report is the product of a committee-initiated project.

The initial prospectus for a study on productivity was prepared in 1986 by committee members Jerome I. Elkind, Douglas H. Harris, Thomas K. Landauer, Thomas B. Sheridan, and Stanley Deutsch, the committee study director at that time. The ultimate focus of the study, organizational linkages, resulted from a working paper and study plan I prepared in 1988 and a planning meeting conducted in February 1989. Meeting participants were Jerome I. Elkind, Miriam M. Graddick, Oscar Grusky, Joel Kramer, Grant E. Secrist, George L. Smith, Jr., Barry Staw, and myself (chair). Committee staff attending were Harold P. Van Cott and Beverly M. Huey.

By November 1989, the study plan and study panel had been approved by the National Research Council, and the initial steps in the study had been undertaken. Over the next three years the panel addressed organizational linkage issues during three working meetings, through the development and discussion of numerous concept papers, and finally through the preparation, critique, and revision of the chapters of this report. The principal work of the final meeting, held in

February 1992, resulted in the conclusions of the panel that are presented in Chapter 12. Paul S. Goodman and D. Scott Sink contributed extensively to the preparation of Chapters 1 and 12.

Jean Shirhall, through skillful editing of the entire manuscript, contributed substantially to its readability. The presentation of the volume owes much to her suggestions for consistency and clarity.

Appreciation is extended to Harold P. Van Cott, committee study director, for his participation in the working sessions of the panel; Beverly M. Huey, panel study director, for her coordination of working-session and publication logistics; and Evelyn E. Simeon and Maria M. Kneas for their administrative and secretarial support.

Douglas H. Harris, *Chair*
Panel on Organizational Linkages

1

Introduction

Why do the hundreds of billions of dollars spent annually in the United States on technology to improve the productivity of individuals and groups appear to have so little impact on the productivity of the organizations in this country? Why are increases in individual productivity not reflected in measures of organizational productivity? These and related questions frame the productivity paradox addressed by this report. The position of the Panel on Organizational Linkages, a study panel convened by the National Research Council, is that the answers are to be found in a better understanding of the linkages among individual, group, and organizational productivity.

THE PRODUCTIVITY PARADOX

The ability of nations, and organizations within nations, to enhance the standard of living of the world's growing population depends on continued increases in the productivity of the systems that provide goods and services. In an increasingly competitive global economy, productivity growth is also essential for maintaining or advancing economic opportunities for individuals and societies. Moreover, it is apparent as never before that the peoples and institutions of the world are highly interconnected and that, as a consequence, each nation has a vested interest in the productivity of other nations. A nation might be able to gain short-term advantage over a marginally productive competitor, but over the long term all nations lose from slow productivity growth regardless of where it occurs. Thus, a productive nation is desirable for the contributions it makes not only to the quality of life of its people but, ultimately, to the quality of life of those in other nations as well. Some management theorists have identified productivity growth, particularly in knowledge and service workers, to be the greatest challenge now facing the developed countries of the world. They predict that it will determine the fabric of society and the quality of life in every industrialized nation and that without productivity growth the world will face increasing social tensions, polarization, and radicalization (e.g., Drucker, 1991).

Trends of Productivity Growth in the United States

The United States has experienced more than 25 years of declining productivity growth. Between 1965 and 1985, for example, the U.S. position in the international automobile, steel, shipbuilding, and textile industries deteriorated significantly. More recently, the U.S. position in electronics, computers, robotics, and biotechnology has slipped (Johnson and Packer, 1987; Wohlers and Weinert, 1988). The U.S. labor force does not appear to be making the contribution it once did to the productivity of the world economy.

In a more recent analysis of U.S. productivity growth, the Urban Institute (Sawhill and Condon, 1992) reported that between 1973 and 1990 the hourly output of an American worker grew only 0.7 percent a year. In contrast, the annual rate of growth between 1948 and 1973 was 2.5 percent. According to this analysis, if worker productivity—the basic determinant of wages—had continued to grow at the same rate after 1973 as it did before, the typical family's income in the United States in 1990 would have been $47,600 instead of $35,300.

The Paradox

What is the problem? Has the United States not been investing in productivity growth? There are indeed areas (e.g., infrastructure and education) in which inadequate investment may be inhibiting U.S. productivity. On the other hand, the United States has actually been investing heavily in advanced technologies to enhance productivity growth. The returns, however, do not appear commensurate with the investments. For example, one analysis showed that the data processing budgets for U.S. corporations increased by about 12 percent a year over the previous decade. Productivity increases from those investments, however, averaged less than 2 percent a year (Weiner and Brown, 1989).

In Chapter 2, Attewell reviews a number of investigations of the impact of investments in information technology (IT) on organizational productivity. Such investments are of particular interest because, for many years, they have accounted for a very large proportion of the U.S. industrial investment. As discussed in Chapter 2, however, the huge annual private sector investments in computers and related technologies (an estimated $154 billion in 1990) have had no apparent effect on measures of organizational productivity. Although specific applications of IT have made positive contributions to productivity, the overall investment does not seem to have improved industrial productivity in the United States.[1] This and similar evidence presents a paradox: Why have the enormous investments in IT not resulted in clear-cut increases in organizational productivity? It is clear from the analyses reviewed in Chapter 2 that enhancing productivity is a major national challenge and that this productivity paradox must be understood. As a nation, we need to understand better the factors that influence the productivity of our organizations and the methods for addressing the facilitators and inhibitors of organizational productivity.

ORGANIZATIONAL LINKAGES

Focus and Assumptions of Previous Research

The question that has been addressed by most research into the productivity of work units can be framed as follows: How can the productivity of X be increased? X might be an individual, group, or larger organization. To this end, research has examined a variety of interventions and their impact on the productivity of X. They include the design and implementation of new technology; the application of techniques for the selection, training, and motivation of personnel; the design and redesign of jobs and tasks; innovations in organizational development and management methods; and the introduction of new compensation and incentive systems. Traditionally, researchers have focused on a single level of analysis—improving performance at the individual, group, or organizational level. Interventions are made and, in some cases, measurements are made to determine the impact of the interventions, invariably at the same level at which the intervention was made. The linkage between an intervention at one level and the impact on productivity at another level has largely been ignored.

In attempting to increase productivity, human factors specialists,

---

[1]See also *Information Technology in the Service Society: A Twenty-First Century Lever* (Committee to Study Computer Technology and Service Sector Productivity, 1994) for a more in-depth investigation of this particular issue.

industrial engineers, industrial and organizational psychologists, and others, have largely followed the pattern of focusing on a single level of analysis. The principal level has been that of the individual, but groups and higher organizational units are being given increasing attention. Human factors specialists, for example, have attempted to enhance individual and group performance by matching improvements in technology with the capabilities and limitations of operators. The emphasis of this approach has been on increasing productivity by improving the design of the task and job. The goal has been to fit the task to the requirements of operators and, in doing so, to maximize the speed and accuracy of performance and to minimize other measures, such as learning time, work load, and accidents (Sanders and McCormick, 1987). Industrial engineers, on the other hand, have focused on the work system, often in alliance with human factors specialists and industrial and organizational psychologists. They have attempted to integrate people, technology, and methods to improve the performance of systems, with emphasis on quality and productivity. They have assessed the results of their efforts through such measures as efficiency, timeliness, and defect rates (Sink and Tuttle, 1989).

Industrial and organizational psychologists have attempted to enhance productivity principally by improving the capabilities of the individuals performing the work or through interventions in groups or organizations. Their approaches have included matching individuals to jobs and tasks, training individuals in job skills and knowledge, changing the structure of groups, and motivating individuals and groups toward job objectives. The effects of these efforts have been measured mainly in terms of the facility with which tasks are learned, self-reports of job satisfaction, ratings by others of job performance, indicators of group output, and other behavioral indices (e.g., absenteeism and turnover) presumed to be related to organizational effectiveness (Campbell, Campbell and Associates, 1988). A principal assumption underlying these efforts has been that increases in individual or group productivity will ultimately contribute to increases in the productivity of the enterprise. However, as discussed in Chapter 2, there appear to be factors or processes that inhibit the extent to which changes in individual productivity are reflected in changes in the productivity of aggregates of individuals—groups and organizations.

The Question Addressed in This Report

The question addressed in this report is, given an increase in the productivity of X, under what conditions will there also be an increase in the productivity of Y? Y might be a work unit of one or more people at the same or different level of analysis—the group or the organization. Hence, this is a study of organizational linkages. In this report, a *linkage* is a change (or hypothesized change) in the performance of one work unit as the result of a change in the performance of another. Say, for example, that the introduction of new computer-based workstations results in an increase of productivity averaging 10 percent across the individuals in a work group. The question of interest here then becomes, under what conditions will the productivity gain of the work group as a whole be the same, less, or greater than 10 percent?

This question is addressed from the views of many different disciplines—psychology, engineering, information technology, and others. As a consequence, the report does not speak with a single voice in answering the question, nor does it examine from a single perspective the various influences that inhibit or facilitate productivity linkages in organizations. It is, rather, constructed as a series of essays. At the present state of understanding, this diversity seemed both necessary and useful. The final chapter summarizes the common themes and findings of the report and presents the conclusions that emerged from the panel's analyses and deliberations.

No claim is made that every possible problem involving organizational linkages has been addressed. There are certainly problems specific to work domains, organizational levels, and so on not examined by the panel. However, the panel believes that the interdisciplinary approach resulted in the identification and examination of the key issues in organizational linkages. Moreover, the panel believes that the findings and conclusions relative to these issues can be generalized to linkage problems that are not specifically addressed in this report.

Linkages and Influences

The unique perspective of this report on productivity is that it addresses the productivity linkages among different levels of analysis—individuals, groups, and organizations—and the factors (processes and mechanisms) that influence those linkages. The goal is to explicate the conditions under which linkages can be positively influenced. How can an organization promote the facilitators and diminish the inhibitors? Once that is understood, the organization can create the circumstances under which new technology can be introduced and the productivity of the organization increased as the expected gains in individual productivity are realized. The important influences on linkages are likely to be found in the nature of the relationships that exist between work units, differences in the states and structures of different work units, and differences in the processes that operate on the organizational linkages.

In Chapter 3, Goodman, Lerch, and Mukhopadhyay examine linkages, processes, and influences. Their goal is to develop a set of conceptual tools that will aid the analysis of linkages and promote the understanding of processes that influence linkages. To that end, they introduce and examine five processes that facilitate changes in individual and organizational productivity: (1) coordination, (2) problem solving, (3) focus of attention, (4) organizational evolution, and (5) motivation. In addition, they present a set of important concepts and definitions, an analytic strategy that addresses linkage inhibitors and facilitators, and a set of hypotheses about organizational linkages.

Linkages and influences are addressed to some extent in each chapter, which provides different perspectives on the issues identified. Some chapters focus on understanding the inhibitors and facilitators of linkages; others are more concerned with addressing the measurement issues raised by linkage concepts. Across all chapters there is a mix of theoretical considerations, interpretation of research findings, and exploration of linkage issues and processes in specific work domains. In addition, because the panel believes that understanding organizational linkages will require additional research, each of the chapters makes recommendations for research that derive from the discussion in that chapter.

Multiple Levels of Reciprocal Linkages

The concept of organizational linkages provides a useful framework within which to examine the productivity paradox. It has led the panel to conclude that one contributor to the productivity paradox is the common attempt to initiate change through the introduction of a single intervention (technology) at a single level in the organization (the individual). In Chapter 4, Schneider and Klein state this conclusion explicitly:

Changing a single aspect of an organization almost never results in a substantial change in organizational performance. Organizations are too complex, their performance too multidetermined, and their inertia is great for a single innovation at the individual level to have a substantial impact on organizational performance.

Schneider and Klein address organizational linkages in the domain of office automation—the application of information and communication technology to tracking, monitoring, recording, directing, and supporting information in the workplace. The launching point for their analysis is the report of the study ordered by the U.S. Congress to de-

termine why office automation has not yielded the improvements predicted (Office of Technology Assessment, 1985).

There are several reasons why innovations such as office automation can fail to yield improvements in organizational productivity. The
introduction of new systems may not contribute to productivity at any
level because the systems are not successfully implemented. Even if a
system is successfully implemented and used as intended, it may do
little to enhance, and in fact may impair, individual productivity. Finally, even if the system does in fact augment individual productivity
there may be no resulting improvements in organizational productivity. This leads to the requirement for an organizational systems framework to clarify the multiple reciprocal linkages that determine organizational productivity.

An understanding of important processes that affect productivity,
within the complexity of organizational linkages, can also be gained
from decomposing the productivity paradox—identifying and examining the factors that produce the paradox. This is the approach taken
by Pritchard in Chapter 7. He identifies three main types of factors
that might account for the paradox: structural characteristics of the
organization itself, intervention side effects (unintended consequences
of the intervention), and problems associated with the measurement of
organizational performance.

A number of structural factors associated with multiple levels of
reciprocal linkages are identified and addressed in Chapter 7 and in
other chapters of this report. An example is time lag. Because of the
way the task is structured, improvements at one level can sometimes
take considerable time to show up as improvements in the combined
outputs at a higher level. Other examples of structural factors include
slack in the process, the degree of centrality of the task to the process,
and the degree of interdependence of work units.

An example of an intervention side effect is changing the focus of
the effort, inappropriately, from one unit of analysis to another—the
introduction of computers might result in low task interdependence when
high task interdependence is required. Individual productivity might
increase as a consequence, but the output of the group as a whole might
decrease. Other side effects might be descriptions in communication
patterns and the socialization process, or the generation of resistance
to change as a consequence of the way in which the intervention is introduced.

Measurement Issues

Measurement issues have been a principal concern of the study panel.
The productivity paradox could, of course, be explained by the inad-

equacy of the measures and processes used to assess organizational productivity. Moreover, the study of productivity linkages among multiple levels of analysis would surely require measurement methods of considerable complexity and sophistication to provide the required validity and sensitivity. Thus, this volume addresses measurement from two important perspectives—as an explanation of the productivity paradox and as a critical tool in the understanding of organizational linkages.

Defining Productivity

The panel deliberated at length about the appropriate concept and definition of productivity within which to address measurement issues, but without satisfactorily resolving the issue. Perhaps the panel is not alone in being unable to arrive at a consensus. In a review of the literature on productivity, Pritchard (1991) found that the term *productivity* was used to encompass constructs as diverse as efficiency, output, motivation, individual performance, organizational effectiveness, production profitability, cost-effectiveness, competitiveness, and work quality. Further, productivity measurement was used interchangeably with performance appraisal, production capability assessment, quality control measurement, and the engineering throughput of a system.

Most panel members held one or the other of two positions regarding the concept of productivity. Some wanted to define productivity as the ratio of outputs to inputs, in line with the original definition of the term by labor economists. They believe that this is the only definition that is unique to the concept. Others argued that this definition is too restrictive. They believe that productivity must encompass concepts such as quality and effectiveness to be meaningful. The panel's solution was to adopt the systems model of organizational performance (described by Sink and Smith in Chapter 6). In this model, productivity is but one of seven interrelated and interdependent criteria of organizational performance. The seven criteria, each of which is operationally defined in Chapter 6, are productivity, effectiveness, efficiency, profitability, quality, quality of work life, and innovation.

Within this model, productivity provides just one part of the total performance picture. The total picture requires the examination of all seven criteria, each of which might necessitate several different measures. The approach advocated in Chapter 6 is to consider the seven criteria as variables that explain variation in performance. Variables can be included and excluded from the analysis to determine which ones explain variation in performance for a particular work unit relative to a specified objective. In Chapter 6, Sink and Smith address measurement issues and the design of measurement systems within the framework of this model. They conclude that the paradox of unrealized productivity improvements results from incomplete systems thinking and from failure to understand the nature of linkages among the individual, group, and organizational levels.

Measuring Individual Productivity

The characteristics of measures of individual productivity determine the extent to which the measures can be aggregated or related to higher levels of analysis. These characteristics—the definition and scope of individual productivity, the measurement systems employed, and the specific measurement metrics—are the focus of Chapter 5. In that chapter, Ruch introduces a variety of concepts, such as goal alignment, that put these measurement issues in perspective. Goal alignment is the ideal in any system that is assumed to be driven by goal-based measures. In such a system, individual productivity depends on the extent to which individual measures are in line with organizational goals and the extent to which those goals form a logical hierarchy across organizational levels. He also presents two models that provide alternative views of factors affecting individual productivity. The models encompass such variables as individual characteristics, psychological factors, sociological factors, technology, and the characteristics of systems and organizations. He then extends his analysis to examine four key measurement issues to be considered when individuals become groups—complexity, input factors, aggregation, and goal alignment.

Measurement and Its Implications for Research

In Chapter 8, Campbell addresses models of measurement and their implications for research on the linkages between individual and organizational performance. His central argument is that effective measurement depends on the substantive specification of productivity in the specific domain of interest, such as a specific aspect of IT. In support of this approach, he provides a hierarchical measurement model for research application that is consistent with the models provided in Chapters 5 and 6.

Domain-Specific Examinations of Linkages

The chapter authors provide many examples in an attempt to clarify the concepts and ideas they introduce. To reduce further the level of abstraction in this report, some chapters examine linkage issues within a specific domain. The objective is to determine how linkages, and the processes that influence them, actually work within operational organizations. The panel considers this exercise to be a reality check on the formulations that emerged from its individual study and group deliberations.

Coordination in Software Engineering

Software engineering is the domain of Kiesler, Wholey, and Carley's examination in Chapter 9 of the role of coordination in the linkage between individual and group productivity. The technical project team approach employed in software engineering is actually a paradigm for how various types of technical work are now accomplished. Organizations create a project team when the required technical tasks transcend the assigned functions or capabilities of individuals. A project team can range in size from two to several hundred members, and the membership of larger teams is relatively diverse. The interdependence of tasks and jobs make coordination—those activities required to support group work—a critical factor in team productivity.

In Chapter 9, Kiesler, Wholey, and Carley discuss what is known about coordination in groups and apply that knowledge to the problem of coordination in software development teams. They show that the traditional model of coordination, with its emphasis on sharing ideas through direct communication, is not applicable because of the complexity, uncertainty, and interdependence that characterize software engineering. They emphasize team design and team communications as positive approaches to enhancing the linkages between individual and group productivity, and they provide a set of hypotheses relative to each approach. In addition, they present a set of stimulating research problems and directions, the pursuit of which will enhance understanding of linkages.

Productivity Linkages in Computer-Aided Design

Computer-aided design (CAD) has been introduced into engineering organizations with the expectation of increasing the productivity of the organization by increasing the productivity of individual designers. The principal output of a design effort is a set of design specifications that meet agreed design objectives, guidelines, and constraints. Thus, the core definition of productivity within this domain is the ratio of design-specification output to the input of resources, mainly labor. Productivity gains are anticipated from the capabilities of CAD to automate routine functions, enhance the accuracy and efficiency of design tasks, promote the exchange of information, facilitate the performance of sophisticated design tasks, and integrate better the design and production processes.

In Chapter 10, Harris examines productivity linkages and influences within the CAD domain. Many of the issues discussed in earlier chapters are relevant to this type of information work. They are examined in Chapter 10 as they relate to linkages among designers, design teams, and engineering design organizations. The central question Harris addresses is, when CAD technology increases the productivity of individual designers, under what conditions will those increases lead to increases in the productivity of the design team and, in turn, the design organization? Among the influences he discusses are the degree of physical isolation of designers, the extent of task specialization in the design team, the mode of team supervision, the nature of controls on the flow and access of information, the burden of design support and coordination, the manner in which technology is implemented, resource management, and system quality and reliability. Each of these influences is examined relative to its impact on organizational linkages.

The Case of Downsizing

Organizational downsizing has been one of the major initiatives undertaken by firms in the United States during the past decade to increase productivity. Downsizing encompasses shrinking, retrenching, or consolidating the organization, principally by reducing the number of employees and hierachical levels. However, according to the evidence in Chapter 11, the anticipated effects have not been realized. The mounting evidence that downsizing initiatives do not yield commensurate gains in productivity is another form of the productivity paradox. It is a particularly troublesome version of the paradox because removing sizable amounts of overhead slack from an organization would be expected to lead directly to increased organizational productivity. Using the perspective of organizational linkages, Whetten and Cameron examine this productivity paradox within the domain of manufacturing organizations. They report the results of their analyses in the form of a set of myths regarding the best way to design and implement a downsizing program. The prevalence of these myths was verified by a survey of 909 businesses in the United States. The extent to which downsizing programs have been based on these myths helps explain the productivity paradox associated with downsizing. Whetten and Cameron further examine organizational linkages by comparing two approaches to downsizing and their impact on organizational productivity.

In Chapter 12, the panel summarizes the principal themes and common issues that run through the various chapters. These themes and issues encompass the productivity paradox and organizational linkages. In this chapter the panel also presents the broader conclusions it reached. As noted, the more specific conclusions and recommendations for research are provided at the end of each chapter.

REFERENCES

Campbell, J.P., R.J. Campbell and Associates
  1988   *Productivity in Organizations.* San Francisco: Jossey-Bass.
Committee to Study Computer Technology and Service Sector Productivity
  1994   *Information Technology in the Service Society: A Twenty-First Century Lever.* Computer Science and Technology Board, Commission on Physical Sciences, Mathematics, and Applications. National Research Council. Washington, D.C.: National Academy Press.
Drucker, P.E.
  1991   The new productivity challenge. *The Harvard Business Review* November-December:69-79.
Johnson, W.B., and A. Packer
  1987   *Workforce 2000: Work and Workers for the Twenty-First Century.* Indianapolis, Ind.: Hudson Institute.
Office of Technology Assessment
  1985   *Automation of America's Offices.* Washington, D.C.: U.S. Government Printing Office.
Pritchard, R.D.
  1991   Organizational productivity. In M.D. Dunnette and L.M. Hough, eds., *The Handbook of Industrial and Organizational Psychology,* 2d ed. Palo Alto, Calif.: Consulting Psychologists Press.
Sanders, M.S., and E.J. McCormick
  1987   *Human Factors in Engineering Design,* 6th ed. New York: McGraw-Hill.
Sawhill, I., and M. Condon
  1992   Bidding war—or growth? *The Washington Post* February 27.
Sink, D.S., and T.C. Tuttle
  1989   *Planning and Measurement in Your Organization of the Future.* Norcross, Ga.: Industrial Engineering and Management Press.
Weiner, E., and A. Brown
  1989   Human factors: The gap between humans and machines. *The Futurist* May-June:9-11.
Wohlers, E., and G. Weinert
  1988   *Employment Trends in the United States, Japan, and the European Community: A Comparative Economic Study.* New Brunswick, N.J.: Transaction Books.

2

Information Technology and the Productivity Paradox

Paul Attewell

At first glance, it would seem impossible that anyone could argue that information technology (IT) has been ineffective in the U.S. economy. Over the past 25 years, microelectronics has revolutionized many services and products, the way goods are produced, and the life-styles of consumers. Advances in medicine, from computerized axial tomography (CAT) scanners to ordinary laboratory equipment, are totally dependent on microelectronics. The round-the-clock availability of automatic teller machines (ATMs) and the capability to send facsimiles of documents thousands of miles in seconds also attest to the impact of microelectronics. And more somberly, the intact but empty facades of government buildings in Baghdad are reminders of the power of microelectronic "smart bombs" to destroy their targets with surgical precision.

Despite these and numerous other examples of the power of IT, a growing body of scholarly research indicates that the information revolution has failed to deliver in one important respect. That is, for all its accomplishments over the past quarter century, IT has not improved the productivity of the U.S. economy or U.S. firms.

As discussed in Chapter 1, the term *productivity* can take on several meanings. In this chapter it refers to the ratio of output (e.g., goods produced or total sales) to inputs (labor, capital, raw materials) for a firm or for an entire economic sector. This ratio is sometimes called *throughput productivity*, and it is measured in physical or monetary terms. The expectation for microelectronics was that it would enable

13

factories and offices to produce more productively—that the ratio of output per unit of input would increase.

Several scholars who have attempted to measure the benefits of computer technology in the U.S. economy in a systematic fashion were unable to find overall productivity improvements due to IT. Some used government data on the productivity of the economy as a whole. Others examined specific industrial sectors, such as services. Still others collected data on representative samples of firms within one industry and found little or no payoff, even in industries that have invested very heavily in IT, such as the banking and insurance industries. A few researchers did find a positive contribution of IT, but sometimes of such small magnitude that it underlines rather than contradicts the concerns of other researchers regarding productivity. It is the combination of such evidence (detailed below) that leads to the belief that there is a productivity paradox regarding IT.

In this chapter I review the emerging literature on the IT productivity paradox and discuss the major studies. I also identify a series of mechanisms that explain how the potential productivity payoffs of IT are attenuated or negated. Some of the mechanisms have been well documented; others are more speculative—hypotheses with partial evidence. Taken together they begin to chart the causes of the productivity paradox. But before undertaking those parts of the chapter, I frame the discussion by explaining why the productivity paradox is so profoundly puzzling to scholars and why it should also be taken very seriously by the public at large and, especially, the computing community.

BACKGROUND

The computer revolution would appear to have been extremely successful. Initial improvements in electronics unleashed a wave of innovation, and computers rapidly diffused across an enormous range of industries. Today, computers are indispensable parts of all manner of enterprises, from multinational corporations to mom-and-pop groceries. Further, there have been dramatic improvements in the productivity of the basic technology. Microprocessors continue to provide improvements in the processing power per dollar for central processing units on the order of 20 percent a year.

Almost everyone expected the next step to be a marked improvement in productivity in the broad range of industries that had adopted computers. The need for such a productivity breakthrough was acute: Since the late 1960s the productivity of U.S. factories, service industries, and offices had been virtually stagnant, while that of the nation's international economic competitors had been rising. Firms in the United

States were losing market share, in part because of their higher cost structure (National Academy of Engineering, 1988).

The promises made for IT were lavish and typically centered on productivity payoffs. Vendors of the technology, from office automation to computer-aided design to computer-aided software engineering, assured buyers that the technology would increase productivity by requiring fewer workers to perform a given amount of work or by allowing expensive skilled labor to be replaced by cheaper semiskilled labor.

American industry believed the promises. The levels of investment in IT have been staggering. In 1990 alone, U.S. businesses invested about $61 billion in hardware, about $18 billion in purchased software, and about $75 billion in data processing and computer services (U.S. Department of Commerce, 1991). (These amounts exclude investment in telecommunications per se, beyond computers.) Within a U.S. corporation today, IT often accounts for a quarter or more of the firm's capital stock, the total value of its equipment and plant (Roach, 1988b, 1991).

For two decades IT has consumed an ever-increasing proportion of the investment dollar in U.S. industry. Overall industrial investment, however, has been roughly constant over the same period, which implies that investment in other types of machinery and equipment, as well as investment in employee training and other "soft" investments, has been lessened or deferred in favor of IT. This pattern differs from that of the nation's major international competitors. While they too have put large sums into IT, their investment in computing (especially in white-collar automation) falls far behind that of the United States (Picot, 1989).

In one sense then, U.S. industrialists have taken a huge gamble on IT, in terms of the success of their individual firms and, most especially, the nation's competitive standing. It is in the context of international competitiveness that the apparent lack of productivity gains is so shocking. It begins to look as if the gamble is failing. Thus, those who believe in the productivity paradox do not argue that computers are a bad thing. Nor do they disregard the important improvements in goods, services, and the quality of life that have resulted from IT. Rather, they are profoundly disquieted by the fact that IT does not appear to have fulfilled its most important promise, that of increasing economic productivity and thereby improving the competitiveness of U.S. industry.

The challenge is to understand the basis of the productivity paradox, to unravel the reasons why IT investments as a whole have not paid off. Has the investment gone into the wrong applications? Are some applications productive while others are not? Are there positive productivity contributions of IT that are being offset or frittered away by psychological, sociological, or organizational dynamics within firms? To what extent do design and technological factors contribute to the paradox? Only when the nation gains an understanding of the dynamics of IT and productivity inside economic organizations and answers these questions can it expect to reverse the productivity paradox and realize the productivity potential of IT.

PRIOR RESEARCH

Research Designs

The studies that suggest a paucity or lack of productivity payoff from IT are of three types, each of which involves a different level of aggregation, a different unit of analysis. The first type analyzes productivity levels and IT investments in an entire economic sector, such as services, for a period of years. The expectation is that increases in IT investment over time will be reflected in improvements in sectoral profitability or productivity over time (albeit with lags).

A second type compares productivity and IT investment across several industries. The expectation is that those industries with greater penetration of IT will show greater productivity increases over time. If no relationship between IT intensity and productivity change is found, there is a prima facie case that IT is ineffective in terms of increasing productivity.

A third type focuses on representative samples of firms within one industry and looks at whether those firms with higher levels of IT investment have higher productivity or profitability (net of other factors) than similar firms with less IT. By specifically controlling for differences in size, capitalization, and other plausible determinants of productivity, this kind of study most effectively isolates the contribution of IT investment to increases in productivity.

A fourth type exists, studies of single firms, but is not discussed here. Individual case studies can be very useful in identifying mechanisms underlying productivity, and they are used for that purpose in Chapters 9-11. But one cannot determine from a collection of individual case studies whether productivity is improving in the economy as a whole. For that, one needs representative samples of firms or sector-level data. (For a synopsis of case studies of IT and productivity in individual firms, see Crowston and Treacy, 1986.)

Each of the first three approaches above has strengths and weaknesses, but in combination they are most powerful because the analytic strengths of one approach tend to offset the weaknesses of the others.

For example, confronted with sectoral evidence that increased expenditures on IT over time have coincided with stagnant productivity, Bowen (1986) suggested that without the currently high level of IT investment, the productivity trend might have been even more dismal. This is a perfectly tenable rejoinder to sectoral studies, but it fails to explain why in interindustry studies, industries with higher levels of IT investment tend to have lower levels of productivity improvement than industries with far less IT investment, or why in several studies of firms within one industry, IT-intensive firms perform no better than low-IT firms. Thus, findings on IT and productivity that hold across all three levels of analysis should be more convincing than findings limited to one type of study design, and theoretical objections to findings from one level of analysis should be viewed with caution unless they also negate findings from other levels of analysis.

Findings

Sectoral Analyses

Roach (1983, 1984, 1986, 1988a-c, 1991; Gay and Roach, 1986) has conducted a series of studies of the relationship between IT investment and productivity within the service sector. Conditions in the early 1980s did not seem auspicious for a dramatic leap in productivity in this sector. The rate of growth of the nation's capital stock had slowed from the 1960s to the 1980s, which did not augur well for investment-driven productivity growth (Roach, 1983). Nevertheless, in the early and mid-1980s, Roach expected that as the information sector became more capital intensive, its productivity would surge (Roach, 1984). That did not happen, however. Investment in white-collar work did indeed catch up: By 1983 the amount of "high-tech capital" per information worker achieved parity with the amount of "basic industrial capital" per production worker in manufacturing (Roach, 1986:13). But despite this infusion of capital, white-collar productivity in the service sector grew at a miserly rate of 0.7 percent a year between 1982 and 1987.

Roach is aware of the many possible causes of the nation's productivity slowdown, but he has become increasingly critical of investments in computers and other IT. He has documented the very large investments in IT in service industries over the past two decades and the extent to which those industries have become highly IT dependent. For example, he reported that 38 percent of the entire capital stock of insurance carriers is invested in IT; 26 percent for banks, and 53 percent for the communications industry (Roach, 1988b). Yet productivity has been falling in the finance and insurance industries since 1973, and the greatest drop has occurred since 1979. The communications industry has experienced modest productivity growth, but that growth has been slowing over time, despite continuing IT investment. Even with the infusion of 84 percent of the nation's multibillion dollar IT investment, "the level of white-collar productivity in 1987 was actually no higher than it was in the mid 1960s" (Roach, 1988c:1).

Roach (1988b) has suggested that executives in charge of IT investments have been "rolling the dice" (i.e., spending large sums on projects whose productivity and profitability outcomes are uncertain while tolerating internal measurement systems that are incapable of telling them whether their investments are really paying off). He points out that the investment in IT has occurred in a period when total investment has been stagnating. In this zero-sum situation, precious investment capital has been committed to a low-payoff technology.

In contrast, the goods-producing sector in the United States has experienced a significant increase in productivity, despite its relatively low investment in IT. The implication is that IT investment in the service sector has been excessive: In Roach's (1988a:6) words, "We have over-MIP'd ourselves" (refers to a computer's capability to process millions of instructions per second). Such sentiments produced a flurry of comment in the business press (*Business Week*, 1988; Roach, 1988a), but that apparently did not affect IT investment. In 1988, IT absorbed 42 percent of total corporate outlays on capital equipment, and the proportion is still climbing.

A dramatically different sectoral approach to assessing the value produced by IT investments is to be found in Bresnahan's (1986) study of the financial services sector. Bresnahan used a welfare economics framework that has been applied to several other technological innovations (Mansfield, 1977). Within this framework economists conceptualize advances in one sector as providing spillovers in the form of reduced costs or extra value to downstream users of the product of that innovation. For example, advances in computer design and manufacturing techniques spill over from computer manufacturers into benefits for the immediate user of less expensive computers (the financial services sector) and the customers of that sector.

What is striking about Bresnahan's approach is that he did not measure changes in output or productivity in the downstream sector (here, financial services) in order to assess the value produced by computers in that sector. Instead he inferred "the value of the technology from the adopters' willingness to pay." More specifically, "the value spilled over [is] inferred from the demand curve of the downstream sector for the output of the advancing sector [computer manufacturing]" (Bresnahan, 1986:742). Thus, by analyzing the relationship between the quality-adjusted price of computers in 1958 and 1982 and the demand for them (expenditures) by financial services in those two years, Bresnahan obtained a *derived demand curve*. The area under the curve is then conceptualized as a welfare index—the value of the spillover. Using this technique, Bresnahan concluded that between 1958 and 1982, the value of mainframe computers to the financial services industry and its customers was at least 1.5 to 2 times the expenditures on those computers. There is "a very large social gain to computerization" (p. 742).

Bresnahan drew on models that are widely accepted by economists of innovation but highly problematic for other scholars. Treating productivity and related benefits as a direct function of the demand curve for computers enabled him to bypass the thorny problem of empirically determining the magnitude of productivity changes. Moreover, the possibility that a sector could make large (and increasing) investments in a technology without obtaining benefits is ruled out by the theoretical assumptions under which Bresnahan and his colleagues work.

Bresnahan's most important assumption is that the volume of computer purchases at a given price (the demand curve) is a function of the actual value produced by computers for the buyer (rather than a function of the buyer's hopes or expectations of produced value). To the extent that purchases of a new and complex technology are like a "jump in the dark," in which productivity or profitability benefits are hoped for but not known in advance, the welfare approach is suspect. Thus, it is prudent to treat Bresnahan's findings as estimates of what benefits would obtain from computers under stringent, but questionable, theoretical premises, rather than as measures of the actual historical payoff from computers.

A striking contrast to Bresnahan's research is to be found in Franke's (1989) analyses of computerization in the financial services sector (insurance and banking) based on government time series data on industry inputs and outputs from 1958 to 1983. Capital intensity has grown very steeply in this sector since the early 1960s, largely because of the introduction of computer technologies. Disaggregating trends over time in capital productivity versus labor productivity, Franke found that while labor productivity has risen modestly, the productivity of capital has dropped precipitously since the mid-1950s. Through regression analysis, he linked changes in capital productivity to specific technological innovations, for example, magnetic ink character recognition (MICR), second-generation mainframes, and ATMs. In general, these innovations were associated with drops in capital productivity: They lowered the return on investment (ROI), rather than improving it, to the point that capital productivity in 1983 was only 22 percent of its 1957 peak.

Franke's models provide some reasons for optimism about the future, however. Microcomputers and fourth-generation computers appear to be improving productivity somewhat, although ATMs are reducing it. Thus, Franke interprets the productivity paradox as an essentially transitional phenomenon, albeit one that has resulted in three decades of declining capital productivity in financial services. He expects productivity improvements in future decades.

Interindustry Comparisons

Osterman (1986) examined productivity using government data on employment and capital stock in 40 two-digit Standard Industrial Classification (SIC) industrial groups and survey data on the computer stock of each industry (a two-digit industrial group aggregates a number of different products). His focus was the effects of computers on managerial and clerical employment between 1972 and 1978, net of changes in output and wages. He observed a positive and statistically significant effect of computers on clerical productivity: For each 10 percent increase in computer stock, clerical employment decreased by 1.8 percent between 1972 and 1978 (net of changes in output). He also found a similar, but smaller, effect for managerial productivity.

Osterman's findings indicate that computers do have measurable productivity effects, but one must be cautious in reading them as a direct refutation of Roach's findings. Osterman's analyses included manufacturing and service industries. In order to address Roach's findings directly, one would have to know whether the productivity effect was created primarily by manufacturing or whether computers also displaced labor in service industries. It is also hard to gauge the size of the productivity effect from Osterman's measures. He described the displacement of clerks as "substantial." But whether a 1.8 percent reduction in clerical labor per 10 percent increase in computer stock is substantial depends on how much investment in IT is necessary to produce that 1.8 percent shift. Unfortunately, the measures as reported do not permit a practical assessment of the size of the effect.

Berndt and Morrison (1991) used a combination of government data sets to examine the effects of IT investment, defined broadly (computers, communications equipment, photocopiers, and the like), on profitability and productivity for a sample of 20 two-digit SIC manufacturing industries from 1976 to 1986. In most of the industries, IT's share of investment increased dramatically during the period.

Berndt and Morrison carried out a variety of econometric analyses—within-industry, across-industry, and pooled models. Their major finding on the profitability of IT was that there was "no significant relationship," although they found a "modest but significant" positive effect in one pooled analysis. In terms of labor productivity, they found a consistent pattern indicating that IT "has not been labor saving, but is instead correlated with increases in labor intensivity and decreases in average labor productivity" (p. 28). They found a similarly negative effect when studying the impact of IT on multifactor productivity: IT investment had degraded rather than enhanced productivity during the period.

Multifirm Analyses

Strassmann (1985:159-162) presented data collected by the Strategic Planning Institute in a pilot study of 40 large firms. Although published details of the study are very sketchy, he reported that there was no correlation between IT costs and his measure of productivity.

In a subsequent analysis, Strassmann (1990) elaborated on his earlier study. First, he examined data sets that linked financial performance (long-term shareholder return) to an index of computer intensity for two industries, food and banking. In neither industry did he find any relationship between amount of IT investment and financial performance. He then plotted computer intensity against financial performance for some 100 manufacturing and service-sector firms, using survey data published by the magazine *Computerworld*. In neither the service nor manufacturing firms was financial performance correlated with computer use. Survey data from *Information Week* produced similarly unfruitful results.

Strassmann did not interpret all these null findings as indicating that computers did not have an impact. Rather, he decided that better measures of firm performance and computer use were needed. He developed a methodology for calculating several value-added measures of performance, which he demonstrated were good predictors of more traditional firm-level performance measures but which were, he argued, superior. Using the PIMS (profit impact of market strategies) approach (Buzzell and Gale, 1987), he surveyed some 292 predominantly manufacturing businesses to obtain value-added measures of performance and detailed information on IT. With these custom-designed measures, he found the following: (1) There was no relationship between IT expenditures and his productivity measure: "Over-achievers deliver their results with a level of [IT] spending equivalent to below-average performers" (Strassmann, 1990:138). (2) In most firms, IT expenditures on management information systems (MIS) dwarfed IT expenditures on operations, on the order of 18 to 1. (Applications in operations include point-of-sales, order-entry, and decision support systems.)

(3) Superior firms, in terms of productivity, spent less than average-performance firms did on IT (p. 139). (4) Some superior performers tended to spend proportionally more of their IT investment on operations than on MIS.

In sum, even with a methodology and data collection tailored to the purpose, Strassman found no correlation between IT expenditures and superior productivity. He found limited evidence that low performance was related to where firms deployed their IT: Stinting operations on IT and spending a lot on MIS appeared to undercut productivity. This idea of misallocation of IT investment recurs in research reviewed below.

Loveman (1988) examined the productivity effects of IT investments on 60 U.S. and European manufacturers from 1978 to 1984. The data refer to business units (predominantly large manufacturing divisions of Fortune 500-sized firms). The data set includes quite detailed information on IT and non-IT investments and stock, as well as information on output, market share, wages, and so on. He defined productivity as the increase in output from an incremental increase in IT, net of other changes (in wages, non-IT investment, organizational structure, and so on).

Loveman used a range of econometric models, but he found that "the data speak unequivocally: In this sample, there is no evidence of strong productivity gains from IT investments" (p. 1). In most of the models, the productivity gain from IT investment was zero. Despite efforts to find IT effects for subsamples (e.g., for high-IT investors) and careful assessment of model biases and their magnitudes, Loveman could not find a statistically significant or a substantively significant effect of IT investment on productivity for the manufacturers.

Weill (1988) studied 33 strategic business units in the valve-manufacturing industry. He examined the impact of IT investment from 1982 to 1987 on return on assets (ROA) and other performance variables in 1987. He found no significant relationship between total IT investment and any performance measure, despite testing for various lags or time periods. This parallels Loveman's results. Weill, however, took his analysis an additional step by dividing IT investment into three qualitatively different types: (1) strategic IT, intended to increase sales or market share (e.g., an inventory system allowing sales staff to give accurate delivery time estimates); (2) transactional IT, such as accounts payable and order entry; and (3) informational IT, including electronic mail (email), accounting, and other infrastructural purposes. His analyses then revealed that transactional IT investment was related to better performance in terms of improved ROA and lowering nonproduction labor adjusted for sales. In contrast, strategic IT investment was not associated generally with performance (and in the short term appeared to lower performance on two measures). Informational IT was not related in any way to any performance measure. Thus, Weill's findings suggest that the 22 percent of IT investment directed into transactional activity had some impact on performance, but the remaining 78 percent of IT investment did not. Unfortunately, he did not report the size of the transactional IT effect, only the fact that it was statistically significant (i.e., positive and nonzero).

Turner (1983) studied a representative sample of 58 mutual savings banks of diverse size. Although he documented different patterns of computerization among banks (often a function of size), he observed that "unexpectedly, no relationship is found between organizational performance and the relative proportion of resources allocated to data processing" (p. 1).

Cron and Sobol (1983) examined 138 medical supply warehousing firms and linked the extent of computer use (determined primarily by number of software uses) and several performance measures. Analysis of variance did not reveal a significant relationship between computer use and performance measures. In fact, extensively computerized firms exhibited a bimodal distribution in performance: They performed either very well or very badly. Cron and Sobol noted that the two groups (high versus low performance) differed on dimensions such as size and growth rate, but they did not attempt a multivariate analysis controlling for such variables. They concluded, despite the bimodal findings, that "extensive and appropriate use of computer capabilities is most likely to be associated with top quartile performance" (p. 178).

Bender (1986) looked at the financial impact of information processing on a sample of 40 firms in the insurance industry. In a cross-sectional analysis, he found that IT was related to performance, defined as a firm's ratio of expenses to premium income. However, the relationship was curvilinear: Those firms with very little IT expenditure and those with a lot were worse performers than those in between. Investment in applications software was not related to performance, but investment in hardware was positively related. Bender presented a series of bivariate relationships between a performance measure and one aspect of computerization. He did not assess the combined effects of the various IT aspects (e.g., through regression) on performance, nor did he control for size, market share, type of insurance, or other possible sources of spurious correlation.[1]

---

[1] Companies providing different kinds of insurance had very different values on Bender's dependent variable (operating expense ratio), which suggests that this should be controlled for when assessing the effect of IT (Harris and Katz, 1988:127).

Harris and Katz (1988) analyzed the same insurance industry data set of 40 firms. They found that high-performance firms were spending considerably more on IT than less successful firms. Although suggestive that IT was helping performance, their analysis, by their own account, was not a causal analysis. They did not control for other likely predictors of performance, such as size.

Significance

In looking at these studies overall, what is striking is the fact that despite very large investments in IT, productivity payoffs are elusive. Several of the empirical studies reviewed did not find any productivity or other performance payoff from IT investments. Others provide evidence for some payoff, but either used research designs that did not control for important sources of spurious correlation or did not document the size of the productivity payoff. No study documents substantial IT effects on productivity. It is this lack of a clearly observable and substantial IT payoff, given the very large investments in IT, that raises the question of a productivity paradox.

EXPLANATIONS AND MECHANISMS

Methodologic and Data Problems

It is possible that the negative findings on productivity are artifacts, that is, they stem from inaccurate data or methodologic problems, rather than from a shortfall in IT effectiveness. For example, the analyses by Roach and Osterman reviewed above are based on government data series on output. Measurements of output and productivity, however, are fraught with difficulties, which are compounded in the service sector by problems in counting nontangible outputs (Bailey and Gordon, 1988; Kendrick, 1988; Mark, 1988).

Mishel (1988) analyzed one key government statistical series on U.S. output and productivity. He argues that an erroneous downward adjustment made to the series in 1973 resulted in a widely held misperception of substantial growth in U.S. manufacturing output since 1973: Forty percent of the reported growth in manufacturing output between 1973 and 1985, according to Mishel, was due to this 1973 adjustment. Equally disturbing is his comparison of two major government series on productivity growth rates at the level of two-digit SIC industries, which shows extraordinary divergences between the two series: "The two series are only within 25 percent of one another (plus or minus) in seven of twenty-one manufacturing industries" (Mishel, 1988:103).

Denison (1989) was no less critical of these government data. He reported that a major distortion results from the accounting method used by government statisticians to deal with the remarkable improvements in speed and power of computers in recent decades. Statisticians have treated these improvements as indicating spectacular increases in the productivity of production in the computer-manufacturing sector. This, along with an overweighting of computers in total output, means that the productivity increases reported in recent years for U.S. manufacturing as a whole are in large part a statistical artifact of productivity increases attributed to computer manufacturers. The government series therefore greatly overstate increases in output and productivity.

The scholars who have questioned the accuracy of the government data are well versed in the details of government accounting systems. A systematic assessment of the implications of their criticisms for the findings of Roach and Osterman would require rerunning analyses with alternative government series and comparing the results, a very time-consuming task. Until such checks have been performed, the studies of Dennison and Mishel and work by the Office of Technology Assessment (1988) leave one unsure of the accuracy of all industry-level and sectoral analyses of recent U.S. productivity trends. But this does not invalidate the basic idea of a productivity paradox; if anything, it strengthens it. For if government data series have overstated productivity gains, the payoff of computers may have been even lower than indicated by those statistics.

Firm-level studies such as those of Strassmann, Loveman, and Weill cited above are not dependent on government data, but they are vulnerable to other methodologic objections. Findings that parameter estimates are not significantly different from zero must be assessed in light of the statistical power of the sample. Small samples (e.g., 40 cases) can produce estimates of zero or nonsignificant estimates for IT, not because IT has no effect, but because the sample size is so small. Unfortunately, most companies guard their investment and performance data from survey researchers and thus few firm-level data sets are available.

Another methodologic point, raised by Barua et al. (1989), Cron and Sobol (1983), and Strassmann (1985), is that IT has quite different effects on productivity in high-performance firms compared with low-performance ones. They suggest that the introduction of IT into poorly run firms does not increase productivity, whereas the introduction of IT into well-run firms pays off. The implication is that there is a bimodal distribution of productivity outcomes: Firms cluster at two extremes, either doing well or doing poorly. The fact that current research practice assesses the impact of IT on representative samples of firms, including good and poor performers, means that any positive IT impact in good firms is balanced by IT's negative effect in poorly run firms. The overall (and misleading) impression is, therefore, that IT has no effect.

Social scientists are unlikely to abandon the use of statistically representative samples of firms in favor of using only high-performance companies because the loss in terms of generalizability would be too great. The theoretical point is to assess the payoff of IT to the economy as a whole, an economy that includes both well- and poorly managed firms. However, scholars can test for this effect by searching for subsets of firms within their representative samples whose experience with IT is markedly better than the norm. This approach was taken by Loveman (discussed above), who was, however, unable to find any bimodal performance effect. But the issue is amenable to additional empirical inquiry.

These methodologic and data difficulties provide some grounds for skepticism about the existence of a productivity shortfall from IT investments, although they do not appear to warrant dismissing the paradox as a statistical mirage. The uncertainty will only be resolved as more studies accumulate. For the present, it is fruitful to give tentative credence to the productivity paradox, based on the above studies, and to ask what mechanisms might explain the lack of payoff from IT.

Individual-Level Mechanisms

The Shift to Slower Channels of Communication

Speaking, gesturing, writing, drawing, and demonstrating by doing are all ways of communicating information; they use different sensory channels and distinct kinds of cognitive information processing. Each of the channels differs in regard to the speed with which information is transmitted, the accuracy of transmission, and the difficulty of interpretation.

As a first approximation, productivity, when applied to communication, can be measured as the speed of production of messages, for example, words per minute. When engineering estimates are made of the productivity gains from, for example, word processors, the typical contrast is within one channel, in this case the written word. If word processors are faster (in words produced per minute) than typewriters, one assumes (as a first approximation) that they will improve personal productivity (Card et al., 1982).

The introduction of a new IT, however, not only changes activity within the same basic channel (e.g., from writing or typing to word processing), but can also shift communication from one channel to another channel. For example, a manager decides to compose a memorandum using email rather than dictate it. Different channels have quite different speeds of transmission—speech is potentially five times faster than writing or typing (Gould and Boies, 1983:274). Thus, a new technology may simultaneously improve productivity in terms of speeding communication within a channel, and degrade productivity if it shifts communication from faster to slower channels. (This is the implication that can be drawn from a series of experimental studies by Gould (1980, 1981, 1982) and Gould and Alfaro (1984), although it is not so stated by the authors.)

The Formalization of Human Communication

Another level of complexity must be considered for the actual comparison here is not between saying certain words into a microphone and typing the identical words using email. The same semantic content will be phrased differently using different channels—a face-to-face communication may be less wordy than an email message.

To explain this phenomenon, sociolinguists use the concept of *indexicality*, which refers to a property of language having to do with the degree of knowledge that one expects of one's partner in a communication (Garfinkel, 1967). In a highly indexical conversation, two conversationalists assume a lot of shared background knowledge of each other, and they can speak in a terse way because of this shared knowledge. Less has to be said. In contrast, less-indexical conversation is more elaborate: Everything is explained, because less shared background knowledge is assumed to exist.

The degree of indexicality can differ markedly across communication channels or modalities. Face-to-face communication is often, but not always, highly indexical. Consequently, a shift away from speaking to another channel can change the speed of communication, not only because of the physical limitations of the media involved (speed of tongue in speech versus fingers in typing), but also because of the different degree of indexicality used for each channel. For example, Gould and Boies (1978, 1983:291) compared speaking a message into a voice-mail system, where one expects the receiver to listen to one's voice, with dictating a message, which one expects will be typed and then read by the receiver. In both cases the purpose of the message is identical, and both use the same channel (speech). But the subjects who spoke and expected their message to be heard communicated considerably faster (more indexically) than those who dictated a message to be typed and read.

Until very recently, IT investment focused on the written (typed) medium. Even as IT was (arguably) improving speed and productivity within that medium, it may have been slowing the overall speed of communication by drawing messages that might previously have been conveyed face to face, or telephoned, into the less indexical and therefore slower channel of writing. This is one potential explanation, at the individual level, of why IT has not improved productivity.

Systematic quantitative data are lacking on how much IT has shifted communication between channels, but there is no dearth of ethnographic examples. In one office observed, employees sent email messages to colleagues sitting a matter of yards away, rather than speak (Attewell, 1992b). Office etiquette had evolved to the point that it was considered intrusive to interrupt a colleague with a nonurgent spoken message. In a more elaborate example, Markus (1984) described managers sending messages by email and later conversing by telephone while looking at the same email documents on their terminal screen.

The process of shifting the communication mix toward a slower and wordier (i.e., less indexical) written/typed medium is referred to here as *the formalization of communication because of IT*. It is occasionally a coercive process: If everyone else uses email, a person feels obligated to follow suit. More typically, formalization occurs because people value the added clarity (lessened ambiguity) of written communication (as in the Markus example), or because senders place a value on not interrupting a colleague and thus use an asynchronous medium rather than speech (the first example). In either case, formalization represents a trade-off between maximizing speed of communication and some other value.

An analogous kind of formalization of communication occurs when IT is applied to shop-floor manufacturing. Large numbers of communications that were once conveyed informally by voice or signals are now being drawn into complex computer systems used for job scheduling, parts ordering, and so on. One striking example of this is provided by comparing the Japanese use of just-in-time manufacturing with an IT-intensive American counterpart (Warner, 1987). The Japanese typically use noncomputerized signaling (i.e., colored balls) to indicate that more materials are needed or that a job is complete. This requires little recordkeeping or elaboration of the messages. An IT-intensive counterpart found in many U.S. firms is manufacturing resource planning (MRP) software, which "decides" when and where parts are to be produced and moved based on a myriad of data inputs, from keyboarded reports of inventory to scans of the bar codes on parts and subassemblies.

The MRP approach is more powerful than signaling with balls (although several commentators have argued that it is overly complex and error prone; see Anderson et al., 1982; Warner, 1987), but it is a more formalized and demanding method of communication than its noncomputerized alternative. Aggregated across thousands of organizational communications, this formalization of communication, facilitated or driven by IT, may cut into potential productivity improvements and counterbalance the positive contributions of IT. However, there is as yet no quantitative evidence with which to assess the magnitude of this effect.

The Quality Versus Quantity Trade-off

A trade-off between the quantity and the quality of output also affects the productivity gains realized from IT. For many white-collar jobs, the introduction of IT seems to alter preexisting balances between the quality and quantity of task performance by tempting individuals to improve quality. Often the change in quality is primarily a matter of improvement in the aesthetic aspects of output rather than in its substance. But whether "real" or superficial, improvements in quality are achieved either by a slowing of work speed (a decrease in output per hour) or, more commonly, by using any time freed by IT to enhance the quality of documents.

In workplace ethnography, one observes employees devoting time and concern to formatting attractively and illustrating the most mundane of communications. Much time is spent reediting text and using spelling checkers to remove every last typographical and spelling error, even if those errors might have a minimal impact on comprehension. And a degree of attention is given to type fonts and print quality that would have been unheard of a few years ago. Among programmers, one sees untidy but workable code being reworked to obtain a cleaner, more elegant, or otherwise more satisfying product. And among managers, one observes reworking of spreadsheet models, presentational graphics, and the like.

The shift toward quality is an expression of pride in one's work and as such is a positive gain for individual employees. It also reflects the fact that the appearance of documents is important in many bureaucratic settings because it affects the authority of the message. Whether this shift improves efficiency is doubtful, as the following studies demonstrate.

In a controlled study, Card et al. (1982, 1984) found that writers composing on a word processor made nearly five times as many modifications and corrections as those writing by hand. Some of the differences between word processing and handwriting were attributable to correcting errors and some to changing margins, type fonts, and so on. But the largest differences stemmed from refining the text. Independdent composition experts evaluated the latter refinements and judged that fewer than half improved intelligibility. Overall, the quality of documents created by word processor was no better than equivalent documents produced by hand.

Pentland (1989) studied more than a thousand Internal Revenue Service (IRS) auditors who used laptop computers. He obtained measures of productivity (e.g., average time per case) and measures of quality of work, and he was able to compare subjective measures (agents' assessments of their work) with objective measures obtained from case files.[2] He also regressed outcome measures on measures of the use of various software applications and on demographic and experience variables.

Looking first at the self-report data, Pentland found that productivity was unrelated to the use of various software applications but that subjective sense of quality was significantly related to the use of almost all applications. In other words, from their own reports, agents' use of computers was not enabling them to work faster, but it did enable them to do better-quality work.

Pentland found striking discrepancies between the self-report findings and analyses of objective measures of the same agents' work. None of the computerized features was associated with increased productivity measured objectively, and several were associated with lower productivity. The implication is that agents' efforts at improving quality through computers undermined their productivity.

Nor was there a "real" effect of computer use on objective quality of work. Pentland found a widespread belief among the IRS staff that use of word processing was more authoritative and would lead taxpayers to accept an unfavorable audit result. But this belief proved unfounded when tested with objective data. Agents used more word processing in big cases and in contested cases, in order to bolster their sense of professionalism and credibility, but it had no effect on the outcome.

The studies of document preparation and of the IRS indicate the ways in which computing becomes important in user impressions of quality, credibility, and self-image. Users sacrifice quantity for quality. The research also suggests that users' impressions of enhanced quality may not be borne out in terms of objectively determined measures of product quality. The quality versus quantity trade-off is thus a mechanism whereby potential gains from IT become lost.

---

[2]Pentland's terminology was changed to match the terminology used in this chapter. He used the terms *efficiency* (equivalent to productivity or quantity) and *effectiveness* ("the quality of work done using the computer").

Operator Skill and Complexity

A popular explanation for a lack of productivity payoff is that employees and organizations have not yet learned the requisite skills for using IT software and hardware efficiently. The implication is that once a few more years have passed and the computer revolution matures, the IT-using work force will have improved its skills and raised productivity.

Although appealing, this explanation neglects some important aspects of the information revolution that today turn skill development and retention into a chronic (rather than transient) problem for organizations and individuals (Attewell, 1992b). First, the very dynamism of the information revolution, the creation of a stream of new or improved products, creates a serious problem of skill obsolescence. The working knowledge that employees have painstakingly accumulated can be rendered useless if the company changes hardware or software. It is not unusual to find organizations that, in the prior 5 to 10 years, have had clerical support workers first doing text editing on, for example, Wang machines, then shifted to personal computers (PCs) with Wordstar software, then restandardized again with WordPerfect. Each change of software rendered a substantial body of prior working knowledge useless—not just a knowledge of keyboard commands, but also of strategies for getting various kinds of documents produced and for shifting data or text from one piece of software to another. Even within one brand of software, operators have to deal with software updates, the inconvenience of going from documents typed using one version of the software to those typed in another, and so on.

Skill obsolescence is not a problem solely of word processing: Software applications from accounts receivable to inventory control to financial and statistical modeling have been undergoing periodic replacement. In a study of 187 firms in the New York area, the average age of current applications was only three to four years (Attewell, 1992b). There seems little end in sight: Today's workers are having to assimilate local area network (LAN) and Windows versions of their favorite software and to master new telephone systems, email, and so on. Thus, new learning demands are repeatedly thrust onto employees whose major responsibility is to do work, not to learn about IT.

The environment of constant IT change is fueled more by the competitive dynamics of software vendors, and the behavior of in-house office IT buyers, than it is by hard-headed productivity considerations. Software manufacturers want to sell new software to established customers, and a product upgrade is an easy way to achieve that. They also dread having product reviewers rate their product as "behind the times."

Within IT-using firms, Salzman (1989) documented that the people who make decisions about adopting software are rarely those who actually use the software. Because purchasing managers are often unaware of how hard or easy the software is to use, they tend to focus on *features*, the numbers of things a piece of software can do. This leads to a situation in which competing software houses look for more and more features with which to dazzle potential buyers. As a result, software programs become ever larger and more complex.

From the perspective of the IT operator, skill development can take on the nature of the myth of Sisyphus: No sooner has one pushed the boulder (of learning) to the top of the mountain, than it rolls back to the bottom—all at the direction of senior management who insist on a software change. Operators who attempt to avoid skill obsolescence by sticking with software they are already skilled in using tend to be stigmatized or overruled by managers, who invoke the need for company-wide standardization as an antidote to those who would cling to old software and skills. Or managers claim that cherished productive software must be abandoned because hardware manufacturers will no longer support it on their new generation of machines.

Software developers are not unaware of the burden that new and ever more complex programs place on end users. They have made great efforts to improve interfaces for greater ease of use and to enhance documentation for trouble-shooting (e.g., help screens and pop-up advice). They have also automated various human tasks, such as spelling correction. But these attempts to lighten the learning and work burdens for users often displace rather than eradicate the productivity problem. They have resulted in much larger, more complex software programs, which require faster computers, more disk space, faster access times, and so on. They also require more sophisticated setup and maintenance work. Thus, there is the irony that a business letter that could once have been written rapidly and effectively on a personal computer with 64 kilobytes (K) of random access memory (RAM) and one or two floppy disk drives now is written on a 386-K machine with several megabytes of RAM and a plethora of related memory-management, disk-caching, LAN, and other software.

It seems plausible, then, that much of the potential productivity gains from IT have been absorbed by the process of change itself and its impact on skill and performance.[3] Users find themselves with obsolete skills and new programs or procedures to learn. Technical support personnel face ever-higher degrees of software and hardware complex-

---

[3]For a model of the diffusion of IT in which knowledge or skill acquisition plays a central and sometimes limiting role, see Attewell (1992a).

ity, which create new layers of productivity-wasting problems, from "interrupt conflicts" to "memory crowding." Strassmann's (1985) injunction that computerization pays off only if accompanied by a drastic simplification of work processes and procedures is violated by the incessant movement toward greater complexity.

There is no reason to assume that the skill-obsolescence and learning burdens of IT are only start-up or transient phenomena. They have already lasted two decades, and there are no indications that the speed of change of software or hardware is abating. All one sees in computerized workplaces is more and more change. The cost of that change must be balanced against the promise of productivity gains. But that is unlikely to occur when those who prescribe the changes are not those whose work is primarily affected by them.

Group-Level Mechanisms

Computers Generate More Work

Even if IT makes employees individually more productive, that does not necessarily translate into improved productivity for groups of individuals or the organization as a whole because information technologies are embedded in a web of political and social processes within firms (Bikson et al., 1987; King and Kraemer, 1985; Kling and Iacono, 1984, 1988; Markus, 1984). Those interpersonal, group, and organizational dynamics come into play and can absorb or redirect individual efforts and alter the goals toward which new technologies are directed.

One possibility is that employees are using IT tools to increase their output, but that their extra output is largely unproductive because it does not result in more goods and services being sold by the firm. An example would be applying the bulk of IT investment to extra paperwork and administration without realizing any ultimate payoff in terms of greater or more efficient production. Clearly, this is not what was envisioned by IT designers or expected by scholars of office automation and transaction processing. On the contrary, Leontief and Duchin (1986) and other experts believed that IT applied to white-collar work would greatly increase productivity and shrink administrative overhead. By entering engineering estimates of productivity improvements from IT into input-output analyses of the economy as a whole, they predicted 11 million fewer jobs by 1990 and 20 million fewer by 2000 as a result of automation.

The predicted displacements of clerical and administrative workers have not come to pass, however (see below). And one reason that administrative staffs have not greatly shrunk is that IT appears to be associated with a rapid increase in paperwork and its electronic equivalent. The study of New York area firms mentioned above, (Attewell, 1992b) assessed the changes in employment and work load resulting from the introduction of specific IT applications. Some examples of an IT application, defined as a computerized work task or combination of tasks associated with particular employees, are (1) a computerized system for processing accounts payable and receivable; (2) a system for entering orders, querying inventory, and generating shipping slips; and (3) a system for analyzing loan risks.

The employment changes associated with the IT applications were far less dramatic than would have been anticipated by Leontief and others. Only 19 percent of the applications studied led to shrinkages in employment on those tasks, 20 percent led to increases, and 61 percent showed no change. Some of the job shrinkages were quite dramatic. However, the overall effect is what is analytically important, that is, the sum of losses and gains across all applications in all firms. In total, the job losses were equivalent to 1.7 percent of the total employment of the sample firms. Job gains were equivalent to a 3 percent increase. The overall effect was an expansion in employment of 1.3 percent.

The reason why the overall employment changes were small is that in the very applications in which productivity improvements were most marked, there was an equally striking increase in work load after the application was implemented. Thus, in a sample of 489 applications for which there were complete employment and productivity data, managers reported that mean output per worker rose by 78 percent compared with the immediately prior technology—a substantial productivity effect. In those same applications, however, the volume of work also jumped by 76 percent, effectively absorbing almost all of the potential productivity gain.[4] (Kraut et al., 1989, found a similar increase in the volume of work in their study of computerization.)

There are several distinct explanations for the marked expansion of paperwork or information output that follows computerization. Economists note that as the unit cost of a good falls, the demand for that good increases. For example, as word processors make editing more convenient, the number of drafts a document goes through increases. Similarly, as computer-aided design makes certain aspects of drafting and design work easier, the number of drawings produced before a design is settled upon also increases (Salzman, 1989).

An expansion in the information output of computers requires an

---

[4]Another, albeit indirect, indication of the increase in information work load following computerization is to be found in office consumption of paper, which since 1979 has grown at twice the rate of the gross national product. Manifestly, IT has not created the once-predicted paperless office (Fisher, 1990).

increase in the amount of processing being done and, thus, an increased need for computers and for processing power. Thus, while the unit cost of information processing is falling, the resulting demand for processing may grow even faster, such that the total volume and cost of processing in the organization can reach new highs (Bailey and Chakrabarti, 1988:97). (In economic terms, the price elasticity of demand for IT is greater than one.) This effect is exacerbated by the fact that computing is heavily subsidized in most firms. End users rarely pay the full cost of mainframe time, software support, LAN maintenance, and so on. This spurs the demand for IT.

Although the economist's language of *cost* is appealing, and the falling unit cost of processing certainly explains much of the IT expansion, focusing on cost can obscure another important aspect of the phenomenon. Within an office, what most employees experience is not cost (to the organization) but effort (for the individual). It is the fact that costs are relatively invisible, while personal effort is quite tangible, that gives computer technology some of its counterproductive sting. It takes little effort to make several extra copies, but it does cost. It takes minimal effort on the part of the originator to send copies of an email message to several colleagues, but that places a substantial burden on the recipients to read that message (Bowen, 1986). It may take less time for an executive to compose and edit a memorandum on his or her PC than to assign the work to a secretary. But in cost terms, given their relative salaries, that may be a less efficient approach.

In sum, IT has been designed to lower the effort burden for an individual user, and it often succeeds in doing so. In each case the benefit is tangible, but the cost becomes invisible because IT links people's work in subtle rather than obvious ways (through data bases and email instead of face-to-face contact). This can make it harder to tell whether actions that help one person's job performance rebound unfavorably on someone else's productivity down the line. The cost also becomes invisible because IT is increasingly shared and IT expenses are removed from the immediate view of the user. The traditional secretary could have a fairly immediate sense of consumption of typing paper, the cost of repairing a typewriter, and so on. The costs and other consequences of using a departmental laser printer for drafts of documents, or of leaving large amounts of old messages or data on fast-access disk storage devices, are far less obvious.

Economists would view these phenomena as examples of "principal/agent problems" within organizations, that is, the gap between what is rational for the individual employee and what is rational for the firm. Agency problems are chronic features of organizations, but IT can exacerbate them. Information technology makes the production process ever more capital intensive. It widens the gap between the interests of employees, who use IT to improve the productivity of their labor (while largely ignoring capital and other costs), and the interests of the organization, which tries to optimize its total factor productivity—capital as well as labor.

Burgeoning Administrative Overhead

Much of the productivity payoff from automating lower-level jobs and relatively routine tasks has subsequently been expended in hiring new, higher-paid employees. The most obvious reason for the extra employment is that new technical skills are required to support computer systems. Employment in computer specialties (systems analysis, programming, and so on) had grown to over a million persons by 1989. In addition to those formally assigned to computer-related jobs, researchers have noted the existence and importance of informal computer experts (computer "mavens," "gurus," "power users"), many of whom fill staff positions but whose work as computer experts may equal their formal staff responsibilities (Bikson et al., 1990). The amount of employment represented by informal computer experts "hidden" in operating departments is not known.

The issue of IT and administrative overhead goes well beyond the expansion in the number of technical experts, however. Government data series document that the administrative component of private sector firms has been growing for several decades. Figure 2-1 shows that administrative overhead, far from being curtailed by the introduction of office automation and subsequent information technologies, has increased steadily across a broad range of industries.

Although there is a widespread perception that the growth in administration implies employment of more clerks and secretaries, analyses of government statistics indicate otherwise. Based on data from Klein (1984) and the Bureau of Labor Statistics (1989), for example, the number of managers employed in the United States increased from 7.3 million in 1972 to 14.2 million in 1988. Managerial employment growth, not clerical growth, is driving current administrative expansion (see Figure 2-2).

It seems likely that some significant part of the recent growth in managerial employment within firms reflects the growth in information systems and the complexity of managing them. Certainly, some case-study data suggest a direct link. Figure 2-3 shows data on employment shifts for a leading insurance firm that introduced email and extensive office automation in an attempt to control administrative overhead. Many clerical jobs were lost, but numerous new managerial jobs were created.

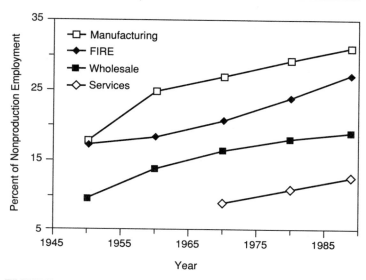

FIGURE 2-1 Growth in administrative employment in selected industries. NOTE: FIRE = finance, insurance, and real estate. SOURCE: Bureau of Labor Statistics (1989).

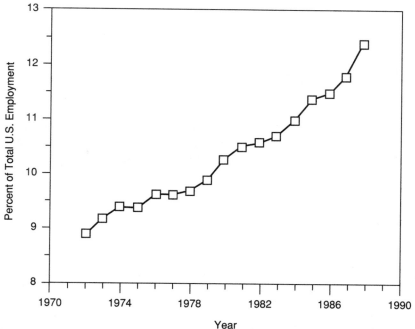

FIGURE 2-2 Growth of U.S. managerial employment, 1972-1988. SOURCES: Klein (1984); Bureau of Labor Statistics (1989).

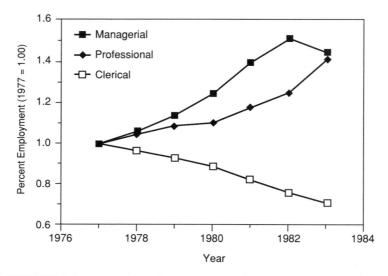

FIGURE 2-3 Occupational change in an insurance company following the introduction of information technologies. SOURCE: Unpublished company data, from Paul Attewell.

Bailey and Chakrabarti (1988:86-101) have offered a rather different argument regarding increased employment and the productivity paradox. They hypothesize that the efficiency gains of IT may have been spent on increased employment in marketing, sales, and service staff necessitated by the intensification of domestic and international competition. They developed a microeconomic model to simulate the loss of productivity gains through such employment. However, empirical data on the growth of sales and related occupations in various (nonretail) industries suggest that their explanation is wide of the mark. The growth in sales employment has been much smaller in absolute numbers than that of managers. It is not a major component in the growth in administrative overhead detailed above. Figure 2-4 presents data for three sectors (manufacturing; finance, insurance, and real estate; and services) that illustrate these trends.[5]

---

[5]In Figure 2-4, the logic for studying composition within industries, rather than across the economy, is that it avoids effects due to the relative expansion of one economic sector versus another. The period 1982-1988 was used because a change in occupational classifications made data collected before 1982 not strictly comparable with data collected after 1982; 1988 was the most recent year for which data were available.

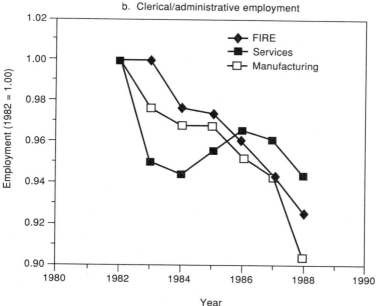

FIGURE 2-4 Occupational changes within U.S. industries, 1982-1988. NOTE:
FIRE = finance, insurance, and real estate. Services exclude private household
services and wholesale and retail trade. SOURCE: Bureau of Labor Statistics
(1989).

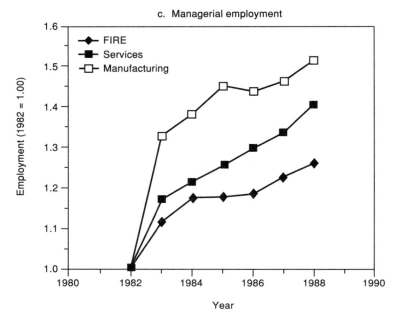

c. Managerial employment

FIGURE 2-4   Continued

Information and the Managerial Taste for Control

To understand why the infusion of IT appears to have resulted in the expansion of managerial ranks requires consideration of the role of managerial information systems and the dynamics of control and power in the modern enterprise. Although many employees believe their bosses are immensely powerful, the experience of top management is often the reverse: Executives often find it very difficult to change the organization's course, and their policy initiatives can become bogged down, ignored, or even reversed lower down the organizational pyramid. This leads, according to organizational sociologists, to an incessant quest for tighter control by top management. Executives alternate among instituting new rule systems, productivity measurement, and direct surveillance by supervisors in unceasing attempts to gain control over their subordinates and thus over firm-level performance (Blau, 1955; Gouldner, 1954; Merton, 1940). This quest is rarely successful: Attempts to control backfire, are blunted, or result in dysfunctional adaptations by employees. Nevertheless, this does not stop each generation of managers from pursuing greater control over subordinates (Beniger, 1986).

Several recent developments have tied this taste for control to an enthusiasm for quantitative information. Intellectual advances in operations research, microeconomics, and managerial science, combined with the dissemination of these disciplines in an occupation increasingly populated by masters of business administration (MBAs), have convinced many managers that rigorous decision making is possible if only one can obtain numerical data on aspects of a firm's performance and apply quantitative analytic methods. This has encouraged a culture that seeks to "manage by numbers." Executives who emphasize management by numbers (or by "facts"), who demonstrate intellectual prowess in memorizing or penetrating dense financial and performance data presented by subordinates, are lionized in business publications (e.g., Pascale and Athos, 1982:92-97).

Thus, after being initially applied to routine transaction processing in the 1960s, IT in the 1970s and 1980s was harnessed to the task of providing management with quantitative performance data. Management information systems, decision support systems, and executive support systems reflect a massive investment in elaborate reporting and control systems for management. The direct cost of such systems—hardware, software, and systems staff—is very large. Weill (1988) estimated that "informational IT" constituted 56 percent of total investment in IT in his particular industry. Strassmann (1990:120) estimated that 64 percent of total IT costs was spent for managerial as opposed to operational purposes. To this must be added the indirect costs, in managerial hours spent studying MIS data, of decisions made using these data, and of new staff and managerial positions opened for persons who enter or analyze such data.

There is a widespread feeling among managers that MIS data indeed help them manage their jurisdictions better. Many report being better informed and feeling more in control (Attewell, 1992b). But there is no proof that these feelings correspond to actual improvements in managerial decision making, and there is even less evidence that the marginal improvement in managerial decision making made possible by computerized information systems justifies the very large cost of those systems.

A series of studies of decision support tools, especially the "what-if" scenarios on spreadsheets, illustrates these effects (Davis and Kottemann, 1992; Kottemann and Remus, 1987, 1991; Kottemann et al., in press). In experimental settings, managers and MBA students were asked to make a decision regarding a production scheduling. Some used a Lotus spreadsheet's what-if capacity, which enabled them to simulate alternative decisions; others worked unaided. The researchers found that the decision makers using what-if approaches made decisions that were no better than those of the unaided subjects. This mirrors a larger research literature indicating that what-if modeling is sometimes worse than (Kottemann and Remus, 1987, 1991), sometimes no different from (Fripp, 1985; Goslar et al., 1986), and sometimes better than (Benbasat and Dexter, 1982; Sharda et al., 1988) unaided decision making. However, their most striking finding, which was replicated in several studies, was the degree to which managers and MBA students believed that they make better decisions using what-if spreadsheet models, despite the fact that their performance was no better (and in some experiments worse) when they used such methods. The researchers called this overestimation of the effectiveness of this computer technique *the illusion of control* and *cognitive conceit*. The effect was widespread and apparently resistant to disconfirmation from experience: Subjects continued to overvalue the what-if technique even when told of its practical limitations.

Computerized MIS and tools such as what-if spreadsheet scenarios have become a routine feature of large corporations, and there is little likelihood that any firm would forgo them. Managerial culture has become habituated to managing by numbers, even though it may be counterproductive (Attewell, 1987; Levy, 1989). The management-by-numbers culture places new work burdens on managers: In several firms I studied almost any request for new machinery or investment had to be accompanied by a rationale entailing spreadsheet models of cost and payoff based on MIS data, often illustrated by pie charts and other graphics. Today's managers spend many hours (often at home) preparing such proposals. An earlier generation might have made the request in a simple memorandum.

Since the "information culture" within firms is driven by managerial desires, it is rarely opposed. But it has enormous costs, in terms of hardware, software, and labor time spent in collecting and analyzing data, which are rarely balanced against its benefits. Some critics have suggested that management by numbers actively contributes to productivity decline. Perhaps the most eminent is W. Edwards Deming (1986:76), the father of statistical quality control, who noted the following:

To manage one must lead. To lead one must understand the work that he and his people are responsible for. . . . It is easier for an incoming manager to short-circuit his need for learning and his responsibilities, and instead focus on the far end, to manage the outcome—get reports on quality, on failures, proportion defective, inventory, sales, people. Focus on outcome is not an effective way to improve a process or an activity . . . management by numerical goal is an attempt to manage without knowledge of what to do, and in fact is usually management by fear. . . . Anyone may now understand the fallacy of "management by numbers."

Firm-Level Mechanisms

Competition Versus Productivity

In the 1960s, information technologies were primarily conceived of as methods for lowering the unit cost of processing various kinds of highly routinized paperwork (e.g., transaction-processing systems). In the 1980s, computer systems were characterized as "strategic information systems," competitive weapons to wrest market share from rival firms. While the two uses of information systems are not mutually exclusive, they have quite different implications for productivity.

A firm that uses IT as a strategic weapon seeks to increase its market share, and thereby its profits, at the expense of its competitors. This will typically mean that the successful firm expands to accommodate the increased market share. But the firm need not necessarily improve its productivity (output per unit of input) to increase its profits: An increase in output/sales at the old level of productivity will still generate increased profits. Thus, profitability is divorced from productivity. Nor will the productivity or profitability of the industry as a whole be improved through this strategic use of IT: The firm is redistributing market share, not creating more wealth with less input. In such a situation there is a disjuncture between what benefits an individual firm and what benefits an industry or economy. Increased market share clearly benefits individual firms, but the economy at large benefits only if productivity or quality is also increased (see Bailey and Chakrabarti, 1988).

If this hypothetical situation was common, one would expect to find large investments in strategic IT yielding increased market share (but not increased productivity) for some successful firms but with negligible impact on industry-wide productivity or profitability. This industry-level outcome is consistent with Roach's findings (see above), and one can find illustrative evidence (not proof) in some of the most lauded firm-level examples of strategic information systems.

American Hospital Supply (AHS) Corporation has been portrayed as an outstanding example of successful IT use. It is widely used as a case study in business school curriculums (e.g., Harvard Business School, 1986). By installing order-entry terminals in the purchasing departments of its hospital customers, and later providing inventory management software to them, AHS made it easier for its customers to order medical supplies and speeded its response to orders. Based on this innovative use of IT, which required large investments in hardware, software, and systems personnel, AHS was able to develop an enviable degree of customer loyalty, and its sales and market share zoomed.

Table 2-1 presents the performance ratios of AHS during a decade of investment in IT and rapid growth in market share. Sales and profits boomed. But several indices of productivity—gross profit as a percentage of sales, operating expenses as a percentage of sales, operating earnings as a percentage of sales—showed no improvement at all, or had decreased, at the end of the period. This did not hurt the firm: It was growing and generating more profits, even though it was no more efficient than before.   This becomes a cause of concern, however, when translated into an industry-wide or economy-wide phenomenon. For if IT investment is focused on the strategic goal of increasing market share and is shunted away from productivity-enhancing areas, costs may increase and productivity will stagnate. In the long run, this could leave those industries in which strategic IT investment dominates highly vulnerable to competition from firms that maintain a cost-lowering strategy.

IT and the Service Approach

Although American Hospital Supply illustrates the effects of strategic investment in IT, it is also an example of the use of IT to gain customers through improved service. In recent years a powerful current among American managerial theorists has extolled the importance of customer service for the overall success of a business (e.g., *In Search of Excellence*). IT is often used to actualize this philosophy—computerized inventory systems enable salespeople to give accurate assurances about availability of products, order-entry systems are used to speed delivery times, and so on.

American companies have allocated substantial proportions of IT investment to service activities in the hope of winning customer approval and market share. If IT investments in service succeeded in attracting market share or allowed prices to be raised to reflect the improved service component, there would be a payoff at least to those who first adopted the technology. And, as discussed in the prior section, firms like AHS did just that. But one can also identify forces that make it rather difficult to earn profits from IT-assisted service provision.

To capture profits, firms need (1) a period of time during which investments in a new service give them a temporary monopoly, thereby differentiating them from the competition, and (2) a willingness on the part of customers to pay a premium for the service-enhanced product. Such conditions have occurred for certain IT services, for example, airline reservations systems. But other IT pioneers have found themselves with a very short period in which to capture market share and capital-

TABLE 2-1 Performance Ratios of American Hospital Supply Corporation, 1974-1984

Year	1974	1975	1976	1977	1978	1979	1980	1981	1982	1983	1984
Sales ($ million)	915	1,065	1,238	1,363	1,619	1,928	2,261	2,660	2,965	3,310	3,448
Net earnings ($ million)	42.4	50.2	58.5	70.1	81.3	100.0	117.1	133.5	170.0	211.9	237.8
Performance Ratios:											
Gross profit/sales (%)	34	34	34	34	34	34	34	34	34	34	34
Operating expenses/sales (%)	25	25	25	25	25	25	25	25	25	25	25
Operating earnings/sales (%)	9.1	8.5	8.8	9.4	8.7	8.3	8.1	8.4	9.2	9.8	8.6

NOTE: These performance figures cover the period during which the ASAP computerized inventory and ordering system was first implemented and subsequently elaborated and expanded. Net earnings are post-tax. Performance ratios are based on pre-tax figures.

SOURCE: Harvard Business School (1986).

45

ize on IT investment. The introduction of ATMs by banks proved enormously popular with customers. However, it took relatively little time for other banks to follow suit. Moreover, although no consumer bank can hope to survive today without having them, ATMs have not generated large new profits for banks. On the contrary, the highly competitive environment in banking has made it difficult to charge customers for ATM service.

Nor have ATMs enabled banks to cut costs by employing fewer tellers (Haynes, 1990). Available evidence suggests that customers use them for transactions they would not have made before. For example, they take out smaller sums of money at more frequent intervals.

There is nothing new to the idea that technological innovation gives the first-comer a short-term advantage that is soon lost as the industry as a whole adopts the technology. Karl Marx, for example, noted the phenomenon in his comments on nineteenth-century textile manufacturing in Britain. What is new is the rapidity with which IT-based service innovations can be copied by competitors, the short window for recouping one's investment in the innovation, and the apparent reluctance of customers to pay for service improvements compared with their willingness to pay for better tangible goods. Taken together, these developments place an unusual burden on IT investors. More and more industries (like the banks with ATMs) have to make large IT investments to "stay in the game," whether or not an improvement in firm-level profitability or productivity results.

Consumers, and thus society at large, clearly benefit from the below-cost provision of IT services. The phenomenon looks less benign, however, when viewed from the perspective of corporations. Having to invest in IT in order to stay in the game and suffering poor returns on IT investment as a result detracts from capital accumulation. This would not be serious, except for the fact that it occurs during an era of intense competition and productivity stagnation, when investment should be productively deployed.

Interorganizational Processes

Information technology has led organizations to place greater demands on their suppliers and customers for information. Such demands can often only be met by further investments in IT. For example, in the early 1970s, insurance companies that processed medical insurance claims began to install costly mainframe-based interactive claims payment systems. There were several reasons why the companies chose to shift from manual or batch processing of claims to interactive computerized processing, but two are relevant here. At the time, the installation of computers in hospitals and doctors' offices for generating bills had resulted in a dramatic increase in the number of duplicate bills being generated by such computers and presented by clients for payment. This placed extraordinary burdens on manual claims processors, who had to avoid paying for the same medical service twice. Claims payment had to be computerized to deal with this double-billing assault from others' computers.

Simultaneously, firms that paid for group health insurance for their employees began asking the claims payment companies for ever more detailed breakdowns of how each dollar was expended—on what medical procedures, for which covered person, and so on. Detailed reports had not been feasible, and had therefore not been provided, when recordkeeping was entirely manual. But with the advent of on-line claims processing, those insurance companies that had not developed computerized systems capable of analyzing payments found themselves losing clients to highly computerized competitors.

In these examples one can see the truth in Ellul's (1954) macabre vision of technology, in which technologies create needs that only more of the technology can fulfill. The possibility of computerized data has enabled government to demand more and more detailed information from hospitals, military contractors, banks, and so on. It has stimulated bank customers to expect 24-hour information on their accounts, and users of overnight delivery services to expect rapid tracing of their packages. Whatever the long-term implications of such phenomena for profitability and economic growth, in the immediate term computers are placing greater burdens of information work upon organizations. In highly competitive environments, or when faced with legally mandated demands, firms may have no way of capturing the cost of this investment. Their provision of information therefore reduces, rather than increases, their efficiency.

CONCLUSION

The relationship between investment in IT and productivity is paradoxical. Research suggests that the strong productivity gains that were expected from IT have not manifested themselves—in the economy as a whole, in particular industries, or for representative samples of firms. The empirical evidence on the question is mixed, and this review has considered issues of data and methodology that might "explain away" the paradox. While more research on this question is clearly needed, the preponderance of evidence suggests that the shortfall of productivity payoff from IT should be treated as credible and that the next step— looking for forces that are undermining or attenuating potential gains from IT—should be taken.

Pointing to a productivity paradox does not mean that IT investments have been ineffectual. In this chapter the focus has been specifically on productivity, not on other important goals or areas of impact, such as increasing market share, improving service, or improving quality. Market share is critical for the competitiveness of individual firms, and quality and service are important to consumers and for economic competitiveness.

Nevertheless, one should not shrug off the importance of a productivity shortfall because of market share, quality, service, or other potential benefits of IT. To reiterate an earlier point, increases in productivity are central to keeping unit costs down and, thus, to enabling firms to compete successfully in the international arena. Increased productivity is also a major source of salary increases for the industrial labor force. If firms can produce more per person, they can afford to pay higher wages. Anemic progress in productivity has been a prime cause of two decades of stagnant wages for a large proportion of the working U.S. population. Conversely, generating higher productivity is the key to higher living standards in the future. If IT is to achieve its promise, then, it must enhance productivity as well as quality and service.

Going beyond the evidence suggesting a productivity paradox, this chapter sought to identify several mechanisms that undercut or attenuate the potential productivity payoffs from IT in organizations. Some of the mechanisms identified are firmly grounded in research, others are more tentative. All would benefit from additional empirical scrutiny.

The general pattern that emerged from the discussion of mechanisms is that IT creates a series of trade-offs at various levels of an organization. The potential benefits of the technology may be channeled into alternative directions—either doing the original work more efficiently (productivity enhancing) or doing a different kind of activity or the same activity more often. Such trade-offs were identified at different levels, from the individual to the organizational. At the individual level, various researchers have found that employees may channel the technology's potential into improvements of quality and appearance, rather than quantity of work. Initial evidence suggests that employees often favor the former, thereby attenuating potential productivity gains. At the group level, IT can result in an expansion of the work to be done or its complexity, rather than accomplishing the original amount of work with fewer inputs. A great deal of IT resources are also invested in managerial information systems and management by numbers, rather than in automating direct operations. According to data from Weill (1988) and Strassmann (1985, 1990), this trade-off seems to be associated with lower performance. Finally, at the organizational level, IT is sometimes channeled toward strategic, competitive, or service activities that, while laudable in their own right, may be achieved at the expense of potential productivity gains.

The next step is to document, through additional research, the magnitude and full implications of these trade-offs and to study the articulations of levels: how individual-level, group-level, and firm-level processes intertwine and affect one another such that productivity improvements at one level do not simply translate into productivity improvements at higher levels. Several of the chapters that follow focus on assessing productivity dynamics across levels of an organization.

REFERENCES

Anderson, J.C., R.G. Schroeder, and S.E. Tupy
  1982   Material requirements planning systems: The state of the art. *Production and Inventory Management* Fourth Quarter:51-66.
Attewell, P.
  1987   Big brother and the sweatshop: Computer surveillance in the automated office. *Sociological Theory* 5(Spring):87-99.
  1992a   Technology diffusion and organizational learning. *Organization Science* 2(4):1-19.
  1992b   Skill and occupational changes in U.S. manufacturing. Ch. 3 in P. Adler, ed., *Technology and the Future of Work*. London: Oxford University Press.
Bailey, M., and A. Chakrabarti
  1988   *Innovation and the Productivity Crisis*. Washington, D.C.: The Brookings Institution.
Bailey, M., and R. Gordon
  1988   Measurement issues, the economic slowdown and the explosion of computing power. *Brookings Papers on Economic Activity* 2:347-430.
Barua, A., C. Kriebel, and T. Mukhopadhyay
  1989   A New Approach to Measuring the Business Value of Information Technologies. Unpublished manuscript, Graduate School of Industrial Administration, Carnegie Mellon University, Pittsburgh.
Benbasat, I., and A.S. Dexter
  1982   Individual differences in the use of decision support aids. *Journal of Accounting Research* 20(1):1-11.
Bender, D.
  1986   Financial impact of information processing. *Journal of Management Information Systems* 3(2):232-238.
Beniger, J.R.
  1986   *The Control Revolution*. Cambridge, Mass.: Harvard University Press.
Berndt, E., and C. Morrison
  1991   High Tech Capital, Economic Performance, and Labor Composition in U.S. Manufacturing Industries: An Exploratory Analysis. Unpublished manuscript, National Bureau of Economic Research, Cambridge, Mass.
Bikson, T.K., B. Gutek, and D.A. Mankin
  1987   *Implementing Computerized Procedures in Office Settings*. Santa Monica, Calif.: RAND.
Bikson, T.K., C. Stasz, and J.D. Eveland
  1990   *Plus Ça Change, Plus Ça Change: A Long-Term Look at One Technological Innovation*. Santa Monica, Calif.: RAND.

Blau, P.
  1955   *The Dynamics of Bureaucracy.* Chicago: University of Chicago Press.
Bowen, W.
  1986   The puny payoff from office automation. *Fortune* (May 26):20-24.
Bresnahan, T.
  1986   Measuring spillovers from technical advance: Mainframe computers in finan-
         cial services. *American Economic Review* 76(4):742-755.
Bureau of Labor Statistics
  1989   *Handbook of Labor Statistics.* Bulletin 2340. Washington, D.C.: U.S. Depart-
         ment of Labor.
Business Week
  1988   The productivity paradox. Special report. *Business Week*, June 6:100-102.
Buzzell, R.D., and B.T. Gale
  1987   *The PIMS Principles.* New York: Free Press.
Card, S.K., J.M. Robert, and L.N. Keenan
  1982   On-line Composition of Text. Unpublished manuscript, Xerox Palo Alto Re-
         search Center, Stanford, Calif.
  1984   On-line composition of text. Pp. 231-236 in *Proceedings of Interact '84. First
         IFIP Conference on Human-Computer Interaction.* New York: North Holland
         Publishers.
Cron, W., and M. Sobol
  1983   The relationship between computerization and performance. *Information and
         Management* 6:171-181.
Crowston, K., and M. Treacy
  1986   Assessing the impact of information technology on enterprise level performance.
         Pp. 299-312 in *Proceedings of the Seventh International Conference on Infor-
         mation Systems.* San Diego, Calif.: International Conference on Information
         Systems.
Davis, F.D., and J. Kottemann
  1992   User Misperceptions of Decision Support System Effectiveness: Two Produc-
         tion Planning Experiments. Unpublished manuscript, School of Business Ad-
         ministration, University of Michigan, Ann Arbor.
Deming, W.E.
  1986   *Out of the Crisis.* Center for Advanced Engineering Study. Cambridge, Mass.:
         MIT Press.
Denison, E.F.
  1989   *Estimates of Productivity Change by Industry: An Evaluation and an Alterna-
         tive.* Washington, D.C.: The Brookings Institution.
Ellul, J.
  1954   *La Technique ou l'Enjeu du Siecle.* Paris: Librarie Armand Colin. English
         translation published as *The Technological Society.* New York: Vintage.
Fisher, L.
  1990   Paper, once written off, keeps a place in the office. *New York Times* (July 7):1.
Franke, R.
  1989   Technology revolution and productivity decline: The case of U.S. banks. Pp.
         281-290 in T. Forester, ed., *Computers in the Human Context.* Cambridge,
         Mass.: MIT Press.
Fripp, J.
  1985   How effective are models? *International Journal of Management Science*
         31(1):19-28.
Garfinkel, H.
  1967   *Studies in Ethnomethodology.* Englewood Cliffs, N.J.: Prentice-Hall.

Gay, R., and S.S. Roach
1986   The productivity puzzle: Peril and hopes. *Economic Perspectives* (April 10):1-15.

Goslar, M., G. Green, and T. Hughes
1986   Decision support tools: An empirical assessment for decision making. *Decision Sciences* 17(1):79-91.

Gould, J.
1980   Productivity of white-collar workers. Pp. 14-33 in P. Mitchell, S.J. Nassau, and S. Struk, eds., *Improving Individual and Organizational Productivity: How Can Human Factors Help?* Washington, D.C.: Human Factors Society.
1981   Composing letters with computer-based text editors. *Human Factors* 23(5):593-606.
1982   Writing and speaking letters and messages. *International Journal of Man-Machine Studies* 16:147-171.

Gould, J., and L. Alfaro
1984   Revising documents with text editors, handwriting-recognition systems, and speech recognition systems. *Human Factors* 26(4):391-406.

Gould, J., and S. Boies
1978   Writing, dictating, and speaking letters. *Science* 201:1145-1147.
1983   Human factors challenges in creating a principal support office system—The speech filing system approach. *ACM Transactions in Office Information Systems* 1(4):273-298.

Gouldner, A.
1954   *Patterns of Industrial Bureaucracy.* New York: Free Press.

Harris, S.E., and J.L. Katz
1988   Profitability and information technology capital intensivity in the insurance industry. Pp. 124-130 in *Proceedings of the Twenty-First Annual International Conference on System Sciences*, Vol. IV. Hollywood, Calif.: Western Periodicals Co.

Harvard Business School
1986   *American Hospital Supply Corporation. (A) The ASAP System.* Harvard Business School Case Services. Cambridge, Mass.: Harvard Business School.

Haynes, R.M.
1990   The ATM at twenty: A productivity paradox. *National Productivity Review* 9(3):273-280.

Kendrick, J.W.
1988   Productivity in services. Pp. 99-117 in B. Guile and J.B. Quinn, eds., *Technology in Services: Policies for Growth, Trade, and Employment.* Washington, D.C.: National Academy Press.

King, J.L., and K. Kraemer
1985   *The Dynamics of Computing.* New York: Columbia University Press.

Klein, D.
1984   Occupational employment statistics for 1972-1982. *Employment and Earnings* (January 1984).

Kling, R., and S. Iacono
1984   The control of information systems: Developments after implementation. *Communications of the ACM* 27:1218-1226.
1988   The mobilization of support for computerization: The role of computerization movements. *Social Problems* 35:226-243.

Kottemann, J., and W. Remus
1987   Evidence and principles of functional and dysfunctional decision support systems. *International Journal of Management Science* 15(2):135-144.

1991   The effects of decision support systems on performance. Pp. 203-214 in H.G. Sol and J. Vecsenyi, eds., *Environments for Supporting Decision Processes.* New York: North-Holland.

Kottemann, J., F.D. Davis, and W. Remus
 In press Computer assisted decision making: Performance, beliefs and the illusion of control. In *Organizational Behavior and Human Decision Processes.* New York: Academic Press.

Kraut, R., S. Dumais, and S. Koch
 1989   Computerization, productivity, and the quality of worklife. *Communications of the ACM* 32:220-238.

Leontief, W., and F. Duchin
 1986   *The Future Impact of Automation on Workers.* New York: Oxford University Press.

Levy, S.
 1989   A spreadsheet way of knowledge. Pp. 318-326 in T. Forester, ed., *Computers in the Human Context.* Cambridge, Mass.: MIT Press.

Loveman, G.
 1988   An Assessment of the Productivity Impact of Information Technologies. Working paper 90S-88-054, Sloan School of Management, Massachusetts Institute of Technology, Cambridge.

Mansfield, E.
 1977   *The Production and Application of New Industrial Technology.* New York: W.W. Norton.

Mark, J.
 1988   Measuring productivity in services. Pp. 139-159 in B. Guile and J. Quinn, eds., *Technology in Services: Policies for Growth, Trade, and Employment.* Washington, D.C.: National Academy Press.

Markus, M.L.
 1984   *Systems in Organizations.* Marshfield, Mass.: Pitman.

Merton, R.K.
 1940   Bureaucratic structure and personality. *Social Forces* 18:89-96.

Mishel, L.
 1988   *Manufacturing Numbers: How Inaccurate Statistics Conceal U.S. Industrial Decline.* Washington, D.C.: Economic Policy Institute.

National Academy of Engineering
 1988   *The Technological Dimensions of International Competitiveness.* Washington, D.C.: National Academy of Engineering.

Office of Technology Assessment
 1988   *Technology and the American Economic Transition.* Washington, D.C.: U.S. Government Printing Office.

Osterman, P.
 1986   The impact of computers on clerks and managers. *Industrial and Labor Relations Review* 39:175-186.

Pascale, R.T., and A.G. Athos
 1982   *The Art of Japanese Management.* New York: Warner Books.

Pentland, B.
 1989   Use and productivity in personal computing. Pp. 211-222 in *Proceedings of the Tenth International Conference on Information Systems.* Boston: International Conference on Information Systems.

Picot, A.
 1989   Assessment of the Current Developments and Trends in Office Automation

and Information Services: Selected Comparative Empirical Data from Germany. Paper presented at workshop on Information Systems: A Strategic Challenge for Corporations, Boston, Mass. (Available from the author c/o Institut fur Organisation, Luswigs-Maximilian Universitat, Ludwigstrasse 22, 8000 Munchen 2, Germany.)

Roach, S.S.

1983   The new capital spending cycle. *Economic Perspectives* (July 13):1-13.

1984   Productivity, investment, and the information economy. *Economic Perspectives* (March 14):1-14.

1986   Macrorealities of the information economy. Pp. 93-104 in R. Landau and N. Rosenberg, eds., *The Positive Sum Strategy.* Washington, D.C.: National Academy Press.

1988a   Stop the dice rolling on technology spending. *Computerworld Extra* (June 20):6.

1988b   Technology and the services sector: America's hidden challenge. Pp. 118-138 in B. Guile and J. Quinn, eds., *Technology in Services: Policies for Growth, Trade, and Employment.* Washington, D.C.: National Academy Press.

1988c   *White-Collar Productivity: A Glimmer of Hope, A Special Economic Study.* New York: Morgan Stanley & Co.

1991   Services under siege: The restructuring imperative. *Harvard Business Review* (September-October):82-91.

Salzman, H.

1989   Computer aided design: Limitations in automating design and drafting. *IEEE Transactions on Engineering Management* 36(4):252-261.

Sharda, R., S. Barr, and J.C. McDonnell

1988   Decision support system effectiveness: A review and empirical test. *Management Science* 34(2):139-159.

Strassmann, P.

1985   *Information Payoff.* New York: Free Press.

1990   *The Business Value of Computers.* New Canaan, Conn.: The Information Economics Press.

Turner, J.

1983   Organizational Performance, Size, and the Use of Data Processing Resources. Working Paper CRIS #58, Center for Research on Information Systems, Stern Graduate School of Business Administration, New York University.

U.S. Department of Commerce

1991   *US Industrial Outlook 1991.* Washington, D.C.: U.S. Department of Commerce.

Warner, T.

1987   Information technology as a competitive burden. *Sloan Management Review* 29(1).

Weill, P.

1988   The Relationship Between Investment in Information Technology and Firm Performance in the Manufacturing Sector. Unpublished Ph.D. dissertation, Stern School of Business Administration, New York University.

3

Individual and Organizational Productivity: Linkages and Processes

Paul S. Goodman, F. Javier Lerch, and Tridas Mukhopadhyay

This chapter addresses the nature of linkages between individual and organizational productivity. If changes are observed in individual productivity, to what extent are those changes observed in organizational productivity? What is the nature of the linkages between individual and organizational levels of productivity that facilitate or inhibit changes at one level being transferred to another level? How do changes in individual productivity contribute to organizational productivity?

Our goal in this chapter is to develop a set of conceptual tools with which to analyze the linkages between individual and organizational productivity. We consider changes at the individual level due to some form of intervention (e.g., new information technology) and trace those changes to changes in organizational productivity. In doing so, we focus on specific work settings and applications designed to increase individual and organizational productivity. We begin the chapter with some basic definitions and then turn to an analysis of factors that inhibit or facilitate the relationship between individual and organizational productivity. In the course of the analysis, we develop a set of propositions about organizational linkages. We conclude with an integration of the concepts and analytic steps developed and a discussion of research opportunities.

BASIC DEFINITIONS

Three terms are central to the discussion in this chapter: productivity, linkages, and processes. Each is defined below.

Productivity

As defined in Chapter 1, *productivity* is the ratio of output to input in a production process. *Total factor productivity* considers all inputs used to produce the outputs. *Partial factor productivity* refers to the ratio of output to a single input (Mahoney, 1988), for example, labor productivity. While measures of partial factor productivity are useful in certain contexts, they provide an incomplete picture for this analysis. Thus, the focus of this chapter is total factor productivity and how changes in individual productivity can contribute to total factor productivity.

Technology-Type Linkages

Many meanings are attached to *link* and *linkage*. In its noun and verb forms, *link* refers to connecting, tying, or joining together. Implicit in the definition are the existence and the joining together of two or more objects. In this chapter, *linkage* is a structural phenomenon referring to the joining together of two or more objects.

In an organizational context, linkage can be described in terms of multiple dimensions. Linkages can vary in terms of *content*. There are technological, organizational, and social linkages. For example, two or more objects (e.g., people, organizational units) can be joined by machines or technological programs or routines. Similarly, objects can be joined by organizational procedures or mechanisms (e.g., a communication channel) or by social norms or customs.

Linkages can also be described in terms of *directionality* or *organizational space*. There are horizontal, vertical, and diagonal linkages. The question is, how do horizontal and vertical linkages help explain the relationship between changes in individual and organizational productivity?

Linkages can also vary in terms of *complexity*, that is, the number of links in any organizational context. The more linkages in an organization, the more complex the environment for tracing changes from individual- to organizational-level productivity. The *degree of interdependence* in a linkage condition also varies. One can conceptualize an organizational system in which all the objects are highly interdependent versus one in which objects are more loosely coupled.

To make this analysis manageable, we focus on a smaller set of linkage dimensions—specifically, technological-type linkages, the complexity of linkages, and the degree of interdependence in the linkage conditions. We selected these dimensions because they should help to explain how changes in individual productivity can contribute to changes in organizational productivity. In the closing section on research opportunities, we speculate about how our analysis of these dimensions may apply to other linkage dimensions (e.g., social linkages).

Our use of technological linkages as a major element in this analysis is consistent with the important role technology plays in defining organizational structure (Scott, 1990) and organizational effectiveness. Below, we illustrate the analytic value of technological linkages by examining three units of analysis: (1) organizational, (2) interrole, and (3) intrarole.

Organizational Linkages

Thompson's (1967) typology of (1) mediating technology with pooled interdependence, (2) long-linked technology with sequential interdependence, and (3) intensive technology with reciprocal interdependence provides a way of thinking about linkages at the organizational level. In mediating technology with pooled interdependence, units (e.g., in a department store) are not linked. Increasing productivity in one unit is independent of productivity in another. Thus, productivity increases in one unit should be observed at the organizational level since the units are relatively uncoupled. In long-linked technology with sequential interdependence, such as in an automobile assembly plant, increasing productivity in one unit has consequences for other units. For example, if the productivity of the body shop in an automobile assembly plant increases, an increase in the productivity of the plant may not occur unless all the sequential operations increase their productivity. In intensive technology with reciprocal interdependence, such as in a bank, increases in productivity in one unit generate reciprocal changes in other units. The net effect of these reciprocal changes may or may not lead to increases in overall bank productivity.

Thompson's typology can be extended to include a relatively pure case of "uncoupled" (Weick, 1982) or "additive" (Steiner, 1972) organizations. In such organizations, there is no interdependence among organizational members. We pose this option because Thompson's typology is about different forms of interdependence. For example, in mediating technology, there is some interdependence. We propose a continuum from no interdependence to complicated forms of interdependence as illustrated by reciprocal interdependence.

This organizational classification of technological linkages has implications for understanding how changes in individual productivity appear at the organizational level. Our first proposition, then, is as follows:

- Forms of interdependence moderate the extent to which changes in individual productivity affect organizational productivity. The connections between changes in individual and organizational productivity are stronger in organizations with uncoupled systems or pooled forms of interdependence.

Interrole Linkages

Both interrole and intrarole linkages have been well documented in the role literature (e.g., Kahn et al., 1964). *Interrole* linkages refer to connections among roles. The connections could be between roles within a group, between groups, between organizational units, or between people and machines. These linkages help one trace why changes at the individual level do or do not appear at the organizational level. They focus on linkages within a firm, whereas organizational linkages, discussed above, identify differences in the types of linkages that characterize firms. Given any organizational-type linkage, such as pooled interdependence, there should be many ways in which interrole linkages can be formed.

Intrarole Linkages

Intrarole linkages are within any role and its subtasks. It is possible that productivity increases in some subtasks may not affect (be linked with) the performance of other subtasks within that role. Attempts to improve individual productivity often focus on certain subtasks. Thus, it is important to understand how subtasks within a role are linked. We elaborate and present propositions on inter- and intrarole linkages later in this chapter.

Complexity and Degree of Interdependence

Complexity refers to the number of linkages. As the number of linkages increases, the connection between individual changes in productivity and organizational changes becomes more difficult to trace. For example, consider a case of sequential interdependence between A and B; B's productivity is a function of A's input plus other factors in B's production operation. As the number of operations (or links) between A and B increases, the number of factors that can change the nature of A's contribution also increases. As the number of links increases, there are more coordination activities and associated costs; more problems—organizational, technological, social—to be solved; and more random events. Therefore, our second proposition is as follows:

- The connection between changes in individual and organizational productivity is stronger when the number of linkages is small. Given a particular form of interdependence (Proposition 1), the smaller the number of linkages, the stronger the connection between individual and organizational productivity.

The last linkage dimension in our set is the level of interdependence. High interdependence implies that changes in object A lead directly to changes in object B. We introduce the concept of level of interdependence because within any type of interdependence (e.g., sequential) there may be different levels of interdependence. The level of interdependence, as is the case with complexity, may help one better understand the connections between changes in individual and organizational productivity. In our analysis below of interrole and intrarole linkages, we expand on the concept of interdependence.

Processes

Understanding the linkages between individual and organizational productivity requires an examination of process, as well as structure. The discussion on linkages provides a way to characterize structure. Given different structural arrangements (e.g., pooled versus reciprocal), it is important to understand how processes facilitate changes in individual and organizational productivity. Because we elaborate the role of processes later in this chapter, we simply list the five processes here: (1) coordination, (2) problem solving, (3) focus of attention, (4) organizational evolution, and (5) motivation.

ANALYSIS

As discussed in Chapter 2, two logical conditions may explain why interventions at the individual level do not contribute to organizational changes. First, interventions may be introduced at the individual level, but no change, a marginal change, or only a temporary change in productivity results. This condition may be explained by the failure to implement the new technological or organizational change successfully. Another reason may be that the intervention was targeted to other organizational goals, such as improvements in employee or customer satisfaction, or to nonorganizational goals, such as increased personal power and prestige. In either case, one would not expect to see changes in individual and organizational productivity. The other logical condition concerns methodologic issues. Productivity changes may occur at the individual level but not be discernible at other levels because of problems in measurement at different levels of analysis or difficulties in identifying the lag structure in the changes.

Because the two logical conditions are discussed in Chapter 2 and elsewhere in this report, we simply acknowledge them here as alternative explanations for the relationship between individual and organizational productivity. We turn now to our analysis of factors that inhibit or facilitate a relationship between individual productivity and organizational productivity.

Inhibitors

Intrarole Linkages and Negative Consequences

Earlier, we introduced the concept of intrarole linkages. Basically, a *role* is a bundle of linked subtasks. Interventions to improve individual productivity can have differential impacts on the subtasks. If an intervention increases individual productivity in some subtasks, it might have a positive impact, no impact, or a negative impact on other subtasks. From this concept of intrarole linkages, our third proposition is as follows:

- If an intervention increases individual productivity[1] in a given subtask but has a negative impact on productivity in other subtasks, the probability is low that the changes will contribute to changes in organizational productivity.

A study by Kraut et al. (1989) can be used to illustrate this proposition. The study examined the impact of a new computerized record system on the work lives and productivity of customer service representatives. The job of the customer service representatives fits the description of a task, or role, composed of a bundle of linked subtasks. The subtasks of these representatives involved providing information over the telephone to customers, making collection calls, handling emer-

---

[1] Increases in productivity can be achieved by increasing output for the same input or reducing input for the same output. In some of the propositions, the emphasis is on increasing output for the same input.

gencies with customer service, setting up credit card applications, and so on. While the new technology increased the productivity of routine tasks (e.g., handling incoming calls about current bills), it made less routine tasks (e.g., handling old bills or bills with missing information) significantly more difficult to perform. Information for these less routine tasks was less accessible under the new system. Although the study does not provide a way to balance the effect of productivity changes in these two types of subtasks or to trace any effects to the organizational level, it shows how interventions might increase productivity in one subtask, but decrease it in other subtasks. The consequence is that net organizational productivity changes are unlikely to occur.

Intrarole Linkages and Slack

The concept of slack is important in understanding the relationship between individual and organizational productivity. In this chapter, *slack* is an excess or unused resource (Scott, 1990). Technology interventions increase the amount of output for a given unit of labor input and thereby create excess time. The key question is, does the excess time remain as slack, or is it reallocated as an input to some other productive activity? Our fourth proposition is as follows:

- If an intervention increases individual productivity in a subtask but that leads to increases in the level of slack[2] in the role or broader production systems, the probability that the changes will contribute to changes in organizational productivity is low.

The slack concept can be illustrated in the context of the U.S. Postal Service. The production system for the Postal Service is a series of connected units organized to sort mail. Within any unit, sorting is performed by automated, mechanized, or manual means. The automation section has two classes of machines. One class reads addresses, sprays on a bar code, and sorts letters. The other class of machines reads bar codes and sorts the mail. Small crews staff each machine. Supervisors manage multiple machines, and a general supervisor manages the entire work area. A simple measure of productivity is the total number of pieces processed by time or by number of workers.

Supervisors in this production system have multiple subtasks to

---

[2]Slack can have positive and negative functions in an organization. In this case, as slack is increased, fewer opportunities exist for the productivity increases to be transferred to other parts of the organization.

perform. They assign people to jobs, do personnel paperwork, coordinate activities with other supervisors, change software programs on the automated equipment, and collect information about mail flows. The slack argument states that increases in the productivity of one subtask may increase the amount of slack within a given role and that increases in slack will not necessarily lead to increases in organizational productivity. If, for example, new information technology reduces the time it takes the supervisor to assign people or do paperwork and the new resource—supervisor time—remains as slack, there should be no increase in organizational productivity.

Intrarole Linkages and Core and Peripheral Activities

The distinction between core and peripheral activities occurs in a number of places in the organizational literature (e.g., Scott, 1990). *Core* activities represent the technological and managerial activities involved in transforming inputs into outputs critical to the organization's survival. *Peripheral* activities are indirectly related to the process of transforming inputs into outputs. This distinction between core and peripheral activities is somewhat arbitrary, however. Activities that may have been considered peripheral in a more traditional setting might be considered core in a new technological environment (Susman, 1990).

To clarify the distinction, we define core activities as those that, if ceased, would stop the other production activities of the organization in the short run. Consider an automotive assembly plant that typically has three major production activities—a body shop, a paint shop, and assembly areas. If one of these operations stops, the whole plant stops. If this was an advanced computer-integrated manufacturing (CIM) auto plant with "just-in-time" (MacDuffie and Krafcik, 1990) features, other activities such as logistics and material handling would be part of the core activities. Cessation of the logistic activities would shut down the plant. On the other hand, there are other activities in the plant, such as medical services, training, or public relations, that are important for the long-run survival of the plant (Parsons, 1951) but are peripheral activities. The cessation of such activities would not stop the core activities of the plant.

One can think about subtasks within a role in terms of the core and peripheral distinction. Core tasks can directly affect other production activities. Peripheral activities in a role may only indirectly affect production activities. Thus, our fifth proposition is as follows:

- If an intervention increases individual productivity in peripheral activities, the probability that the changes will contribute to organizational productivity is low.

Consider the role of the postal supervisor of the bar-code sorting areas. One major subtask in this role is the selection of sorting programs, which has a major impact on total productivity. This supervisor also has to complete a variety of forms for recordkeeping purposes, a peripheral task. Following the core-peripheral argument, if a technology is introduced to increase the productivity of completing forms, it would not have a direct influence on the number of pieces of mail processed. If, however, the technology helped to select sorting programs more effectively, the consequence would be a direct increase in the productivity of the bar-code sorting areas.

Interrole Linkages and Negative Consequences

Interrole linkages refer to connections among roles, whereas the discussion above focused on subtasks within a role. Changes in one role may have positive effects, no effect, or negative effects on other roles with which there is some degree of linkage or interdependence. With interrole linkages, the impacts can be through vertical, horizontal, or diagonal relationships. Our sixth proposition is as follows:

• If an intervention increases productivity in a given role but negatively affects productivity in other roles, the probability that the intervention will contribute to positive changes in organizational productivity is low.

The Kraut et al. (1989) study of the impact of the introduction of a computerized record system on the work of customer service representatives also illustrates this proposition. The introduction of the computer-based system had positive consequences for routine tasks, but it had three negative consequences for the representatives' supervisors. First, supervisors previously evaluated the representatives' work by auditing completed transactions. With the new system, those transactions increased by a factor of 10. Second, the increased number of transactions to review increased the role stress of the supervisors. Third, the intervention shifted the focus of task knowledge away from the supervisors. They were "no longer experts in the operational detail of work" (p. 230). This shift in task knowledge increased the difficulty of problem solving and coordination for the supervisors.

The example above illustrates negative vertical impacts. Similar scenarios could easily be envisaged for environments in which interdependence is more sequential, or horizontal. Increases in productivity in work group A increase the stress in the next work group B, which in turn reduces the productivity of group B.

Interrole Linkages, Constraints, and Slack

In interdependent roles, changes in one role can be mitigated by constraints in another. For example, if the productivity in one role or operation increases, a downstream operation may not have the capacity to absorb the new rate of inputs from the prior operation. In this case, the capacity constraint[3] at the downstream operation would basically create slack and preclude any changes at the organization level. Our seventh proposition follows:

- If an intervention increases productivity in a role or operation, constraints in subsequent interdependent activities may create slack and preclude increases in productivity at the organizational level.

Consider the case of the Postal Service. The automation section is dependent on a material-handling system, which in turn is connected to a delivery system. Sorted mail goes to a dock; from there it is transferred to other post offices, then to a mail carrier, and then finally to the mail destination. Constraints along this flow can reduce the impact of any productivity increases. For example, if the automation section increases productivity by processing mail in less time but the mail-handling or delivery system cannot handle the increased mail processing rate, the increases in the automation section will create excess inventory and slack and should not increase productivity at the facility level. This example illustrates a capacity constraint.

There are many other types of constraints. Consider, for example, the impact of major improvements in optical character reading that made it possible to process more handwritten mail by automation. (Existing automation can read only typed documents.) This would shift more of the incoming mail from the nonautomated to automated sections, which inherently can process more pieces per unit of time. One conclusion from this shift might be that organizational productivity would increase, but this is not necessarily so. If a union-management agreement mandated that the automated and nonautomated sections have the same number of workers, the constraints of the labor agreement

---

[3]There are many types of constraints other than production capacity constraints. For example, limitations in a communication system could limit productivity increases in one area from being processed in another area.

would mitigate any gain in organizational productivity. The shift of mail processing to the automated sections would only create slack in the nonautomated sections.

In these examples, the constraints are embedded in the organizations. External events, random or nonrandom, could also influence how changes at one level of an organization affect another level. For example, severe weather conditions can affect the processing of mail. In some areas, smog alerts can limit the use of trucks and, hence, the delivery process. Such events are temporary shocks that can create constraints and, in turn, mitigate the effects of any increases in individual productivity on organizational productivity.

Interrole Linkages and Core and Peripheral Activities

Our fifth proposition, presented in the discussion of intrarole linkages, states that if an intervention increases individual productivity in peripheral activities, the probability that the changes will contribute to organizational productivity is low.

The core-peripheral distinction is also relevant for interrole linkages. An organization is composed of core and peripheral activities embedded in roles with various linkage arrangements. The decision to target individual productivity changes in core or peripheral activities has consequences for changes in organizational productivity.

In the Postal Service example, there are three core production sorting operations—automated, mechanized, and manual. In addition, a large number of support, or peripheral, activities (e.g., training, community relations) are necessary for the long-run survival of the system. Consider an intervention that increases productivity in any of these peripheral activities. For example, improving the productivity of the community relations staff (intensity of community contact) may not contribute to the productivity of the mail processors. Increases in the productivity of the training department staff may not have an impact on organization-level productivity.

Increases in any of the core production activities, on the other hand, should have a direct impact on organizational productivity. Consider the bar-code sorting operation, which is the last production area in the automation section. There is only one link (material handling) between this production area and contributions to organizational productivity. Increases in the productivity of the bar-code sorting operation, then, directly contribute to increases in productivity if the material-handling function has the capacity to move the increased rate of mail processing.

Facilitators

A set of five organizational processes can facilitate changes in individual productivity having an impact on changes in organizational productivity. The basic hypothesis is that the removal of inhibitors and the activation of these processes strengthen the relationship between individual and organizational productivity.

The inhibitors and facilitators are equivalent in their critical importance. The two concepts are both conceptually independent and interrelated. Inhibitors mitigate or block changes at the individual level from affecting other levels. Facilitators (1) remove inhibitors, (2) create the conditions under which individual productivity will have a positive impact on organizational productivity, or (3) accelerate the effect of individual productivity on organizational productivity.

Inhibitors can be identified by focusing on the individual level and asking what factors at that level prevent productivity increases from increasing productivity at other levels? Facilitators, on the other hand, are derived by focusing on the organizational level and working to the individual level. What are the critical drivers of organizational productivity and how might they contribute to the connection between individual and organizational productivity?

Five Facilitative Processes

In this section we briefly define the five critical facilitative processes. We then present two examples that help to anchor these abstract processes to concrete organizational environments. The examples focus on characteristics of high-productivity organizations. They demonstrate how the linkages between individual and organizational productivity can be identified by "working backward" from the organizational to the individual level. The five processes are defined below:

1. *Coordination* refers to a signaling system for interdependent conditional activities (March and Simon, 1958). Coordination can be characterized in terms of type (e.g., by plan or by feedback), scope (the activity to be coordinated), and temporal requirements.

2. *Problem solving* encompasses monitoring changes in organizational performance, diagnosing causes, and initiating corrective actions to return the organization to some state of equilibrium.

3. *Focus of attention* refers to processes that make certain outcomes (e.g., productivity) and instrumental paths to those outcomes more salient.

4. *Organizational evolution* refers to a process whereby basic struc-

tural changes are introduced as part of a continuous cycle of change and adaptation. In the context of a control chart, the problem-solving process (item 2) identifies performance drifts outside the control chart and returns the organization to a steady state. Organizational evolution, on the other hand, redesigns the basic parameters and processes inherent in the control chart and moves the organization to a new equilibrium.

5. *Motivation* refers to processes that generate energy and the direction of energy in any system.

Combinations of the five processes appear in theoretical and empirical papers as important predictors of organizational productivity (e.g., Goodman et al., 1988; Hackman, 1987; Lawler, 1982). They are also important in understanding the linkage between individual and organizational productivity. Our eighth proposition is as follows:

- Individual productivity contributes to organizational productivity when (1) the five processes of coordination, problem solving, focus of attention, organizational evolution, and motivation are operative and (2) the processes are congruent and reinforcing.

Example 1: Lean Versus Mass Production Systems

Table 3-1 compares the characteristics of lean production and mass production systems. Both systems involve long-linked technology and complex sets of linkages (MacDuffie and Krafcik, 1990). However, the lean production system differs substantially from the mass production system in terms of levels of interdependence. The absence of buffer areas, for example, means that downtime in any point of the system will shut down the total system. The lean production system also differs from the mass production system in its use of multifunctional versus specialized technology, short versus long production runs, lack of repair areas versus designated repair areas, and so on.

The linkage structure in the lean system requires different process configurations than the mass system does in order to enhance individual and organizational productivity. First, because the lean system is a very tightly coupled and fragile system, it requires a special form of coordination. The coordination is by both plan and feedback. To run this system, an elaborate a priori specification of activities, timing, and obligations is needed. At the same time, the ability to respond quickly to environmental change is needed. For example, in an automobile plant we studied, seats for the cars are scheduled to arrive an hour before they are to be used and in the order in which they are to be used. Meet-

TABLE 3-1 Characteristics of Lean and Mass Production Systems

Lean Production Systems	Mass Production Systems
General purpose, multifunctional automated technology	Highly specialized equipment and jobs
Complex, multivendor equipment	Less-complex technology
Short production runs, different products	Long production runs
Highly interdependent system	Moderate interdependence
No buffers	Buffers
Downtime immediately stops system	Downtime effects moderated by buffers
No repair areas	Repair areas

ing this critical path requires elaborate programs specifying obligations, activities, and timing between the vendor and the plant. In addition, real-time information systems are needed to depict the plant's schedule to the vendor so the vendor can immediately react to changes (coordination by feedback) in the plant's schedule.

Second, the coordination must be systemwide. The lean production system is totally integrated so the coordination process must cover all factors of production, both internal and external to the system. Coordination for the lean production system also has to be tightly coupled temporally; there is no room for slack in this system. Changes in interdependent subsystems must be signaled immediately.

Third, since demands for coordination are high in lean production systems, there are constant pressures to simplify organizational activities in order to lower the costs of coordination.

Fourth, the lean production system's use of short production runs also affects coordination requirements. Special coordination switching programs are needed to permit quick and flexible reconfiguration of factors of production to create new products.

Fifth, the fact that downtime in any subsystem of the lean production system shuts down the total system further affects process requirements. When downtime occurs, specific processes are needed, such as a fast and effective problem-solving process. Effective problem solving in this context is affected by the nature of the technology. In the lean production environment the technology is typically complex and computer based, any one piece of equipment is the product of multiple vendors, and so on. Thus, effective diagnosis and problem solving require multiple types of knowledge and skill.

The lean production system example demonstrates that specific process characteristics are required by different linkage arrangements. Coordination is important in any organization, but the coordination process in a lean system differs from that in a mass production system. In the latter, buffers reduce the need for real-time-based coordination or systemwide coordination. Long production runs reduce the need for coordination switching programs. All organizations similarly require problem-solving processes, but the lean production system requires much faster problem-solving processes than does a mass production system.

Facilitative processes do not exist in the abstract; rather, they are embedded in organizational mechanisms and policies. In their analysis of highly productive lean production systems, MacDuffie and Krafcik (1990) noted that such systems have fewer job classifications and more multiskilled workers because both help to simplify coordination in a system demanding a high level of coordination. In a single job skill environment, for example, production activities and maintenance activities are separate and require coordination. In a multiple job skill environment, an individual can perform production and maintenance activities, which reduces coordination costs. Thus, as demands for coordination increase, one response is to simplify the number of objects requiring coordination. More-productive lean production systems adopt such coordination mechanisms, whereas less-productive lean production systems do not.

MacDuffie and Krafcik (1990) also noted that highly productive lean systems provide intensive training in problem solving and have one or more designated problem-solving teams. How do these mechanisms translate into processes? If one combines intensive training, problem-solving teams, and multiskilled work forces, the result is a problem-solving process that is capable of responding quickly and tackling complex problems—a requirement of the lean production system. In other words, the problem-solving process reduces the inhibitors discussed above.

All lean production systems are not highly productive, however. Other critical mechanisms are not as directly driven by the nature of the linkage system. For example, highly productive lean production systems tend to provide employment security and reduced status barriers. Employment security can directly affect motivation and commitment to the organization. Reduced status barriers can also affect motivation and indirectly enhance coordination. In addition, contingent reward systems at the individual, group, and organizational levels focus attention on the links between individual and organizational performance and also affect motivation. These mechanisms induce greater levels of motivation and focus of attention, which should facilitate changes at the individual level having a positive impact on organizational productivity.

In the MacDuffie and Krafcik (1990) analysis, problem-solving teams are used for proactive as well as reactive change. In the proactive context, the teams create new structural alternatives aimed at helping the organization to evolve and become more productive over time. For example, the proactive teams might find new ways to improve equipment or production processes. Such actions would tend to accelerate the transfer of productivity increases at the individual or group level to the organizational level.

We conclude this example by noting that (1) the linkage context in the lean production system requires specific processes of coordination and problem solving; (2) those processes are created by different combinations of organizational structures or mechanisms (e.g., fewer job classifications, a contingent reward system); and (3) other processes, such as motivation, focus of attention, and organizational evolution, are less dependent on the linkage context but contribute to organizational performance. High-productivity lean production exhibits coordination and problem-solving activities that fit the linkage conditions, places a focus of attention on productivity improvement, possesses qualities of high motivation and commitment, and implements evolutionary processes to create structural improvements over time.

Example 2: Gain Sharing

In this section we use gain-sharing programs to illustrate how organizational interventions can affect individual and organizational productivity. Gain-sharing plans are designed at the organizational unit (e.g., a plant) and provide employees additional compensation based on unit-level improvements in costs or productivity. We focus on one type of gain-sharing program—the Scanlon plan. We selected the Scanlon plan because one of the panel members (Goodman and Moore, 1976; Graham-Moore, 1983) studied an installation that has used the plan successfully for over 17 years and because more empirical data are available on the effects of Scanlon plans than on other types of gain-sharing plans (Graham-Moore, 1983; Schuster, 1984). Our interest is not in whether Scanlon plans are successful. Rather, we use one example of a successful installation to illustrate how the five facilitative processes may contribute to the connection between individual and organizational productivity.

In this analysis, we argue that the structure of the Scanlon plan generates processes that facilitate changes between individual and organizational productivity. In particular, we highlight three processes—focus of attention, organizational evolution, and motivation. These processes are important drivers of the relationship between individual and organizational productivity, independent of the specific linkage condition.

Most Scanlon plans have three structural elements—a philosophy, a committee structure, and a bonus system. The Scanlon plan *philosophy* articulates the advantages of labor-management cooperation. It advocates tapping the knowledge base of labor and management—joint problem solving through shared information leads to productivity improvements. The *committee structure* exists to generate and evaluate productivity-related suggestions and to coordinate intra- and interdepartmental activities. The *bonus system* rewards all participants for improvements in productivity.

What are some of the facilitative processes generated by the Scanlon plan, and how do they help one understand the relationship between individual and organizational productivity? As noted, the specific Scanlon installation studied has been successful for more than 17 years (Graham-Moore, 1983). The first major process, the focus of attention, is critical. The committee structure focuses employees' attention on productivity improvement. Committee members solicit ideas from all employees on how to improve productivity. They help employees formulate proposals and then follow up on the status of each proposal. The bonus system is also designed to focus attention on productivity improvements. Employees can make suggestions for improving all aspects of work, but only changes that lead to improvements in organizational productivity are rewarded. Thus, whether changes are introduced at the individual, group, or organizational level, *they must contribute to organizational productivity* for the bonus system to pay off. The key idea is that there are many organizational outcomes (e.g., productivity, satisfaction) and many ways to influence those outcomes. The focus-of-attention process selects one outcome (in this case, productivity) and makes clear that all activities, whether individual, group, or organizational, must contribute to that outcome. Focus of attention, then, is one process that should facilitate the connection between individual and organizational productivity.

The second major process of interest is organizational evolution. This refers to a continuous improvement process whereby the organization evolves over time. As noted above, there is an elaborate committee system to generate productivity-related ideas. An analysis of initial productivity suggestions in a Scanlon installation usually reveals a reactive orientation to solving problems. That is, employees generate ways to solve problems with the existing system. This is similar to the use of problem solving in the lean production system example. However, over time, the problem-solving orientation becomes more proactive in nature. Employees try to find new ways to reconfigure the basic factors of productivity (e.g., technology, organizational arrangements) in order to control and improve the organization's production process. For example, one suggestion by a team in the Scanlon installation led to a change in a labeling process that saved the company a million dollars a year.

The committee system is the mechanism for soliciting, selecting, and implementing suggestions. The key aspects of the organizational evolution process are that it is continuous and it occurs at all levels of analysis—individual, group, and organizational. The assumption is that changes in individual and organizational productivity come about when there are continuous efforts to improve productivity at these levels of analysis. The function of organizational evolution is to accelerate the effect of increases in individual productivity on organizational productivity. One-shot interventions are unlikely to have much effect; mechanisms that generate continuous productivity improvement processes are more likely to sustain organizational productivity.

The Scanlon plan also evokes motivational processes. The most obvious source is the bonus system, which rewards productivity improvements. This type of contingent reward system increases motivation at the individual, group, and organizational levels. However, the committee system provides forms of employee involvement that are also motivators. Evaluation studies of successful Scanlon plans (Schuster, 1984) report positive employee involvement, greater communication opportunities, and organizational identification. The key idea is that the Scanlon plan increases the motivation for productivity improvement.

In this example, we have emphasized the processes of focus of attention, organizational evolution, and motivation because these processes are necessary for continuous changes in productivity at the individual, group, and organizational levels. Changes in individual productivity should contribute to organizational productivity when the three processes are operating together in a complementary fashion (i.e., when the processes are congruent and self-reinforcing). The motivational system in the Scanlon plan energizes the organization and focuses attention on organizational productivity. The focus-of-attention mechanisms also keep the focus on organizational productivity and direct organizational evolution along the lines of organizational productivity improvement.

The Scanlon plan also stimulates the two other processes that enable changes in individual productivity to contribute to organizational productivity—coordination and problem solving. The philosophy of the plan typically represents a set of shared beliefs among organizational participants. The more the philosophy is shared, the more it serves as a coordination mechanism. The committee structure, as noted, also serves as a coordination mechanism. Problem-solving activities also take place within the committee structure.

Implications of Examples

What can be learned from these two examples? First, the processes were key in creating high-productivity systems. Second, in the lean versus mass production example, the configurations of the coordination and problem-solving processes necessary for high productivity are unique to the linkage context; in the Scanlon plan example, the coordination and problem-solving processes are more generic. Third, the processes serve at least three functions: (1) removing inhibitors (problem solving); (2) creating an environment in which individual productivity can increase organizational productivity (good coordination, high motivation, focus on productivity); and (3) accelerating the connection between individual and organizational productivity (organizational evolution). Finally, in both examples, it was the operation of all the processes in a congruent and reinforcing manner that led to high productivity.

AN INTEGRATION

The central question initiating this chapter was, how do changes in individual productivity contribute to organizational productivity? We have analyzed the organizational conditions that enable individual changes in productivity to contribute to organizational productivity.

There is no model, in the formal sense, that identifies those organizational conditions that predict the covariation of individual and organizational productivity. Rather, there is a set of concepts and analytic steps one can use in (1) diagnosing why individual productivity changes do or do not contribute to organizational productivity changes and (2) structuring an organization so that increases in individual productivity will contribute to organizational productivity. These concepts and analytic steps are also tools for explaining and predicting the relationship between individual and organizational productivity.

In this section we integrate the major concepts and analytic steps for creating organizational conditions that enable changes in individual productivity to contribute to organizational productivity.

Antecedent Factors

The most obvious step is to begin with differences in organizational-level technological linkages. At the beginning of this chapter, we introduced a typology of organizational technology and forms of interdependence, which ranged from uncoupled systems to systems with reciprocal interdependence. The basic point is that differences inherent in organizational types provide insight into the covariation between individual and organizational productivity. In organizations with mediated technology, pooled interdependence, and similar output among different levels (e.g., individual, group), one would expect closer relationships between changes in individual and organizational productivity than in organizations with long-linked technology, sequential interdependence, and different output produced by different units.

The inherent complexity of the linkages and the degree of interdependence within organizations are other antecedent factors. When analyzing organizational linkages, describing their complexity and interdependencies would be a useful way to begin to identify inhibitors. For example, as linkage complexity increases, so does the probability of the existence of inhibitors to the relationship between individual and organizational productivity.

Removal of Inhibitors

In an earlier section, we identified a set of inhibitors, including the following:

• negative consequences for some objects that are linked to operations or other objects that have achieved increases in productivity;
• slack—the inability to use excess resources to reduce inputs or increase other outputs;
• constraints—the inability to absorb increases in productivity from a prior linked operation; and
• focusing productivity improvements on peripheral, rather than core, tasks.

Each of the inhibitors was discussed above, and the consequences of their removal should be evident. The key point here is that the removal of these inhibitors creates the conditions necessary for a positive connection between changes in individual and organizational productivity.

Creating Effective Processes

Given a particular linkage system, removing the inhibitors and creating effective processes are key to the connection between individual and organizational productivity. The processes are important because they can remove inhibitors, create the conditions necessary for individual productivity to have an effect on organizational productivity, or accelerate the effect of individual productivity on organizational productivity.

We view the processes (and the identification of inhibitors) as conceptual tools with which to analyze the connection between individual and organizational productivity. The research problem addressed in this report is not one for which there is well-defined theory or a cumulative body of empirical findings. Also, developing a model that would cut across different organizational contexts seems an unmanageable task. There are too many organizational types and combinations within types to permit the development, at least now, of some generalizable theory. The development of contingency-based theories in this complicated context also seems unmanageable. Therefore, our goal in this chapter has been to identify a set of processes; apply those processes to specific settings so as to gain a better understanding of why individual productivity does or does not contribute to organizational productivity; and from those studies, begin to generate a body of empirical findings. This, in turn, will lead to more theory development.

What are the critical processes? How can they strengthen the relationship between individual and organizational productivity?

Effective Coordination

Coordination is a critical process, but the varying technological linkage conditions in organizations demand different levels and types of coordination. In lean production systems, for example, there are high demands for coordination. Such systems place a major premium on systemwide coordination (versus local coordination) and very close temporal coordination. Failure to create these conditions means that any changes in individual productivity will not contribute to organizational productivity. Effective coordination along these dimensions will enhance organizational productivity.

We have also argued that the processes are created by organizational structures and mechanisms. Thus, as demands for coordination increase, multiple, congruent structures and mechanisms for generating the required coordination should emerge. In lean production systems, these multiple structures/mechanisms include multiskilled workers, fewer job classifications, and a contingent reward system.

Effective Problem Solving

The linkage condition in an organization also influences the problem-solving process used to identify inhibitors of organizational performance and initiate corrective action. The linkage condition and the technological environment in lean production systems require very fast response time. In addition, the problems in such systems (versus mass production systems) may be more complex, and the identification of cause and effect relationships may be more difficult because of the tight coupling of components in lean production systems. The challenge, then, in this condition, is to develop a problem-solving process that matches these linkage conditions (i.e., a problem-solving process with fast response time and access to sophisticated knowledge and skills).

An effective problem-solving process creates an environment in which changes in individual productivity should more easily be reflected in organizational productivity. On the other hand, in an organizational system in which performance is allowed to drift outside established parameters and corrective action is slow or ineffective, there will be many conditions that inhibit a positive relationship between individual and organizational productivity.

Focus of Attention on Productivity

Organizations are complex systems with multiple outcomes. Given the turbulence in organizational environments, many conflicting forces affect what outcomes are salient. If the interest is in increasing individual and organizational productivity, the focus of attention must be kept on productivity and the paths to increased organizational productivity. The Scanlon plan's bonus and committee systems are good examples of ways to focus attention on productivity improvements. If the process of focusing attention on productivity causes all organizational participants to work on paths related to organizational productivity, the relationship between individual and organizational productivity will be stronger.

Organizational Evolution

The process of organizational evolution can accelerate the effect of individual productivity on organizational productivity by performing two functions. First, it can focus on learning and change over time.

Some of our examples of individual and organizational productivity have been static in nature. Given a specific change in individual productivity, for example, we have explored the conditions under which the change will contribute to organizational productivity. This point of view focuses on a single change rather than continuous changes over time. We conceive of the process of organizational evolution as creating continuous cycles of change whereby individual change contributes to organizational productivity, which in turn creates more individual productivity changes.

The second function of organizational evolution is that it focuses on structural change. That is, it attempts to change the factors of production, the linkages, the organizational parameters, and other basic elements of the organization as a means of creating greater opportunity for productivity increases at the individual and organizational levels. Our assumption is that the long-term relationship between increases in individual and organizational productivity is dependent on the evolution of the basic structural elements of the technology and the organization.

Motivation

Motivation is a necessary condition for productivity increases in any organization. In the context of organizational linkages, motivation can be thought of as serving two functions. First, the motivational process should be synergistic with the other facilitative processes. Coordination, problem solving, focus of attention, and organizational evolution are the critical processes for enhancing the connection between individual and organizational productivity. Thus, a motivational system must be designed to reinforce those processes. To have a fast-response, problem-solving process with access to complex skills, a motivational system is required that will evoke these skills in a timely manner. In order to focus attention on productivity improvements, the motivational system should also reward such improvements.

Second, the motivational system must also reinforce congruent behaviors across individuals, groups, and the organization as a whole. To increase organizational productivity, then, a reward system is needed that motivates individual and group behaviors that are consistent with organizational productivity.

RESEARCH OPPORTUNITIES

Understanding more about the linkages between individual and organizational productivity has profound theoretical and policy implications. The concepts introduced in this chapter point to a number of exciting research opportunities.

The set of concepts we have proposed about different types of linkages (e.g., organizational, interrole) and mechanisms (e.g., negative consequences, slack) can be used to examine why increases in individual productivity do not contribute to increases in organizational productivity. In our analysis we treated the concepts one at a time, but their interactions have yet to be explained.

Research is needed to examine how different linkage situations generate inhibitors. What types of interventions or productivity changes will more likely evoke slack or negative consequences under different linkage situations? Would slack more likely be generated under forms of serial or reciprocal interdependence? Given the generation of slack, would it have different consequences for the relationship between individual and organizational productivity under different linkage conditions? The answers to these questions are not yet known. Nor is much known about how linkage conditions moderate the effects of different inhibitors on the individual-organizational productivity relationship.

To simplify our analysis, we focused primarily on formal technological linkages. However, the analysis should be extended to other areas, such as social linkages. Social linkages refer to informal arrangements among roles, groups, or organizational units. Consider two organizations whose production processes are characterized by serial interdependence. In one organization a set of norms have developed that encourage competition and noncooperative behavior among units. In the other organization norms that facilitate cooperation and helping behavior dominate. While the technological linkages are the same in both organizations, the relationship between changes in individual and organizational productivity would be explained by the nature of social linkages. Future research should explore the interactions among these different types of linkages.

We have also proposed that processes are key to the individual-organizational linkage. Given certain structural configurations, the processes influence the extent to which changes at the individual level have an impact at the organizational level. In our analysis, we treated the processes as independent although they must be self-reinforcing and congruent. Thus, research is needed to explore interactions among the processes. In the Scanlon plan example we presented, the processes of focus of attention and motivation are highly linked in the structure of the plan. Can the impact of focus of attention be isolated? Do focus of attention and motivation interact, or is their relationship additive? Are the interactive effects among the processes a function of the linkage conditions? Would the interactive effects among focus of attention, motivation, and coordination be greater in long-linked versus mediating technology?

We also treated the problem-solving and organizational evolution processes as independent in our analysis. The role of these processes, however, is probably conditioned by the complexity and uncertainty of the technology and the environment. In organizations with complex and unstable technologies and operating environments, we would expect problem solving and organizational evolution to play a greater role in linking individual and organizational productivity than in organizations operating in more stable environments. The key is that elaboration of the relationships among processes provides opportunities for new theoretical development on the linkage between individual and organizational productivity.

Our analysis, for presentation purposes, has been separated into a discussion of inhibitors and facilitators. An important key to understanding the linkage between individual and organizational productivity is to explore the relationship between the processes and the concepts dealing with the inhibitors. However, we do not want to imply a simple framework that calls for removing the inhibitors and then activating the facilitators. Rather, we see these activities as feeding on each other and enhancing the relationship between individual and organizational productivity. For example, we have argued that slack created through individual productivity increases can inhibit subsequent increases in organizational productivity. We also argued that organizational evolution is a necessary process for enabling changes at the individual level to appear at the organizational level. The concepts of slack and organizational evolution can be self-reinforcing. Slack can create conditions (or resources) for more intensive evolutionary processes of feedback learning and structural change, which in turn could increase the probability that individual productivity increases would contribute to organizational productivity increases. Thus, slack, instead of having inhibitive effects, can have a facilitative effect when coupled with evolutionary processes. The interesting research task is to explore other intersections between inhibitors and facilitators.

In focusing on the individual-organizational link, we have not explored how changes in individual productivity may affect other organizational outcomes. For example, the conditions that enable changes in individual productivity to increase organizational productivity may actually decrease other performance criteria, such as quality, efficiency, or long-run adaptability. Research is needed to determine the functional or dysfunctional consequences of how other criteria change as individual and organizational productivity are more closely linked.

Finally, the focus of this chapter has been solely on productivity as an indicator of organizational performance. Research is needed to expand the analysis to other performance criteria. A central question is how the theoretical framework we applied to productivity applies to other factors, such as quality, cost, adaptability, customer satisfaction. Would the inhibitors we identified explain why changes in quality at the individual level do not have an impact on organizational quality? Would the five facilitative processes influence quality in the same way we have hypothesized productivity changes are transferred from the individual to the organizational level?

REFERENCES

Goodman, P.S., and B. Moore
  1976   Factors affecting the acquisition of beliefs about a new reward system. *Human Relations* 29(6):571-588.
Goodman, P.S., R. Devadas, and T.L. Griffith
  1988   Groups and productivity: Analyzing the effectiveness of self-managing teams. Pp. 295-327 in J.P. Campbell and R.J. Campbell, eds., *Productivity in Organizations*. San Francisco: Jossey-Bass.
Graham-Moore, B., ed.
  1983   *Productivity Gainsharing.* Englewood Cliffs, N.J.: Spectrum Books.
Hackman, J.R.
  1987   The design of work teams. Pp. 315-342 in J.W. Lorsch, ed., *Handbook of Organizational Behavior*. Englewood Cliffs, N.J.: Prentice-Hall.
Kahn, R.L., D.M. Wolfe, R.P. Quinn, J.D. Snoek, and R.A. Rosenthal
  1964   *Organizational Stress: Studies in Role Conflict and Ambiguity.* New York: John Wiley & Sons.
Kraut, R., S. Dumais, and S. Koch
  1989   Computerization, productivity, and quality of work-life. *Communications of the ACM* 32(2):220-238.
Lawler, E.E.
  1982   Increasing worker involvement to enhance organizational effectiveness. Pp. 280-315 in P.S. Goodman, ed., *Change in Organizations*. San Francisco: Jossey-Bass.
MacDuffie, J.P., and J.F. Krafcik
  1990   Integrating Technology and Human Resources for High Performance Manufacturing: Evidence from the International Auto Industry. Paper presented at the Transforming Organizations Conference, Massachusetts Institute of Technology, Cambridge.
Mahoney, T.A.
  1988   Productivity defined: The relativity of efficiency, effectiveness, and change. Pp. 13-39 in J.P. Campbell and R.J. Campbell, eds., *Productivity in Organizations*. San Francisco: Jossey-Bass.
March, J.G., and H.A. Simon
  1958   *Organizations.* New York: John Wiley & Sons.
Parsons, T.
  1951   *The Social System.* New York: Free Press.
Schuster, M.
  1984   The Scanlon plan: A longitudinal analysis. *The Journal of Applied Behavioral Science* 20(1):23-38.

Scott, W.R.
   1990   Technology and structure: An organizational-level perspective. Pp. 109-143 in P.S. Goodman and L.S. Sproull, eds., *Technology and Organizations*. San Francisco: Jossey-Bass.

Steiner, I.D.
   1972   *Group Process and Productivity*. Orlando, Fla.: Academic Press.

Susman, G.I.
   1990   Work groups: Autonomy, technology, and choice. Pp. 87-108 in P.S. Goodman and L.S. Sproull, eds., *Technology and Organizations*. San Francisco: Jossey-Bass.

Thompson, J.D.
   1967   *Organizations in Action*. New York: McGraw-Hill.

Weick, K.E.
   1982   Management of organizational change among loosely coupled elements. Pp. 375-408 in P.S. Goodman, ed., *Change in Organizations*. San Francisco: Jossey-Bass.

4

What Is Enough? A Systems Perspective on Individual-Organizational Performance Linkages

Benjamin Schneider and Katherine J. Klein

Changing a single aspect of an organization almost never results in a substantial change in organizational performance. Organizations are too complex, their performance too multidetermined, and their inertia too great for a single intervention at the individual level to have a substantial impact on organizational performance. Thus, when it comes to improving organizational productivity, it is not enough simply to put in a new personnel selection system, a job enrichment program, a new computer-aided design system, or new office automation equipment. First, the new system, regardless of what it is, may not be successfully implemented. Second, the new system is unlikely to be used by employees as it was designed to be used. Third, even if it is successfully implemented and even if employees use it as designed, the new system may be insufficient by itself to change individual productivity. Fourth, even if the system has a substantial impact on individual productivity, a change in individual productivity, even in the productivity of many individuals, it may not engender change in organizational productivity. For the latter to improve, the activities and productivity of numerous organizational subsystems must also change. In sum, to change organizational productivity, it is not enough to change one aspect of the organization at one level of performance.

THE NATURE OF ORGANIZATIONAL PERFORMANCE

As noted in earlier chapters, the organizational psychology and organizational behavior literatures often refer to individual, group, and organizational performance as if they were somehow separable. In the real world of organizations, however, performance cannot meaningfully be disaggregated. For example, individual performance is clearly not only a function of individual attributes but also of group norms (Roethlisberger and Dickson, 1939) and organizational climate (Pelz and Andrews, 1966). There is evidence, for example, that one can predict the absenteeism of an individual based on that individual's previous absenteeism and his or her job satisfaction and then improve on that prediction by knowing the absenteeism "norm" of the individual's work group (Mathieu and Kohler, 1990). Similarly, group performance is a function not only of the nature of the group and its task but also of the diversity of the individuals in the group (Bass, 1982), especially the leader (George, 1991), as well as the nature of the larger organizational environment in which the group functions (Lawrence and Lorsch, 1969). Finally, organizational performance is a function not only of characteristics of the organization itself, but also of the strategic decisions made by top management (an individual-level variable) and the turbulence of the larger environment in which the organization competes (Joyce and Slocum, 1990). For example, a seemingly excellent strategic decision by a typewriter manufacturer to redesign an electric typewriter was for naught in terms of organizational performance with the introduction of the personal computer by competitors in the environment.

Thus, if one is to improve organizational performance, one should not target a single level or facet of an organization. Rather, as we attempt to show throughout this chapter, one must consider, evaluate, and change the multiple levels and subsystems of an organization, influencing not just individual behaviors and attitudes, not just group norms and interactions, not just organizational structures and strategies—but all of these. All of these must be simultaneously addressed because they are simultaneously linked. We hypothesize that attention to these multiple linkages augments the potential effectiveness of organizational interventions; inattention to these linkages is likely to yield little in the way of improvement in organizational performance (Schneider et al., 1992). Consider three examples. Hackman and Oldham (1980) described a series of studies in which individuals' jobs were changed to be more enriched and, therefore, more motivating, in the hope of improving individual and organizational performance. They showed that an intervention can fail to yield changes even in individual performance unless a network of larger system attributes is in place to facilitate the primary intervention. This network of attributes includes the *way* in which the intervention is introduced (e.g., with the participation of the workers affected or with no participation), the degree of management and supervisory support for the intervention, the extent to which the resources needed to make the intervention work are provided, and so forth.

A similar effect has been documented with regard to training interventions in organizations. For example, Fleishman (1953) evaluated the effectiveness of a management training program in improving the interpersonal competencies of first-line supervisors. He found a significant effect for the training. At the end of training, those trained were more interpersonally sensitive than those not trained. A follow-up study to test for the transfer of the training to the job did not show the same differences, however. Those trained were equally unlikely as those untrained to be sensitive back on the job. Fleishman explored why this might be true and discovered that trainees were sensitive back on the job to the degree that their supervisor rewarded and supported the sensitivities learned in the training. Fleishman called this the "leadership climate" effect. One behaves the way one's leader rewards one for behaving. Rouiller and Goldstein (1993) recently reported a similar finding.

Finally, research by the U.S. General Accounting Office (1987) suggests that employee ownership is unlikely to have a significant effect on organizational performance unless it is coupled with worker participation in decision making. Worker participation alone may also be insufficient to enhance organizational performance (Locke and Schweiger, 1979; Miller and Monge, 1986). But together, employee ownership and worker participation in decision making may improve organizational performance.

Interventions, be they technological or human resources management in nature, are often implemented in ways that limit their effectiveness—at both the individual level at which they are initially targeted and the organizational level. Our hypothesis, which builds on the discussion of organizational linkages in Chapter 3, is that this failure to produce the intended effect is associated with a failure to conceptualize performance in organizations as a consequence of multiple levels of reciprocal linkages. In this chapter we present an organizational systems framework to clarify the multiple reciprocal linkages that can determine organizational performance. The framework emphasizes the intraorganizational linkages that must be understood and managed if interventions designed to enhance individual performance are to yield increases in organizational performance. We chose office automation as the intervention of interest, but the principles we present are applicable to a wide variety of attempts to improve individual and organizational performance.

Below, after a brief introduction to office automation, we explore a number of reasons why interventions, such as office automation, can fail to yield improvements in organizational performance. We conclude by presenting summary propositions that address the conditions under which individual and organizational performance will be more closely linked.

THE NATURE OF OFFICE AUTOMATION

Office automation refers to the application of information technology (IT) and communication technology to the processing and use of information for tracking, monitoring, recording, directing, and supporting activity in the workplace. Office automation is designed to improve performance in offices, but as the review of the literature in Chapter 2 made clear, too often improvements in office performance have not followed the implementation of office automation. In 1985, the U.S. Congress ordered a study to determine why office automation had not yielded the improvements predicted. The report of that study, *Automation of America's Offices* (U.S. Office of Technology Assessment, 1985), provides a basis for our discussion.

The 1985 Office of Technology Assessment review of office automation stated: "It is possible to see the latent enhancing effects of office automation as water building behind a dam. The dam is made up of institutional inertia and the unavoidable transition problem" (p. 33). Our goal in this chapter is to elucidate the nature of institutional inertia and the transition problem and to suggest ways to overcome both. As suggested above, these issues plague most, if not all, organizational interventions. Thus, the principles and hypotheses we present apply equally to all forms of interventions, not only to office automation.

A SYSTEM PURCHASED IS NOT A SYSTEM IMPLEMENTED

Having purchased, or designed, a new office automation system or any other system, an organization faces the challenge of implementing the system, of ensuring that it is accepted and used optimally by target employees. A growing body of literature (e.g., Klein and Ralls, in press; Tornatzky and Fleischer, 1990) indicates that implementing computerized technology is indeed a challenge. For a variety of technical and organizational reasons, employees may not use the new system at all or may use only a limited number of its features. Thus, a substantial proportion of organizations fail to implement new computerized systems successfully (Ettlie, 1986; Tornatzky and Fleischer, 1990).

Employees are likely to resist or reject systems whose benefits they question. As Leonard-Barton and Krauss (1985:108) noted, "An innovation must offer an obvious advantage over whatever it replaces, or potential users will have little incentive to use it." But even if employees believe that a system will enhance their performance in some way, they may still resist or reject it if it is (1) difficult to learn and use (i.e., not user friendly), (2) unreliable, (3) slow to respond, or (4) awkward or difficult to access (e.g., Ettlie, 1986; Klein et al., 1990; Rivard, 1987; Rousseau, 1989).

Even if the hardware and software meet the rudimentary requirements suggested above, implementation may nevertheless stall or fail altogether as a result of a variety of social and organizational factors. Indeed, the literature on the implementation of computerized systems suggests a veritable laundry list of organizational factors that may determine the success of implementation. They include (1) the quality of the computer training provided to users (e.g., Beatty and Gordon, 1988; Graham and Rosenthal, 1986; Klein et al., 1990); (2) the availability of ongoing user support (e.g., Graham and Rosenthal, 1986; Klein et al., 1990; Rivard, 1987); (3) the availability of time for users to experiment with the new system (e.g., Fleischer et al., 1988; Klein et al., 1990); (4) the extent of user involvement in decision making regarding the purchase and implementation of the new system (e.g., Foulkes and Hirsch, 1984; Leonard-Barton, 1988; Parsons et al., 1989); (5) the availability of rewards for use of the new system (e.g., Leonard-Barton and Krauss, 1985; Rousseau, 1989); (6) the extent of employee job security (e.g., Argote et al., 1983; Roitman et al., 1988); (7) the extent of coordination among employee groups affected by the new system (e.g., Abdel-Hamid and Madnick, 1989; Beatty and Gordon, 1988); and (8) the extent of political conflict within the organization regarding the new system (e.g., Markus, 1987; Pearce and Page, 1990).

In sum, money invested in office automation may not yield a subsequent productivity payoff because employees do not use the system at all or do not use its most complex and potentially advantageous features. Indeed, the mere decision to adopt almost any innovation—a new management approach, a new performance appraisal system, a new quality improvement program—does not ensure that the new system or approach will, in fact, be used.

Program evaluators (e.g., Posavac and Carey, 1985) advocate that one not only determines the outcomes of an intervention, but also establishes that the intervention occurred as planned. This is an important point for the study and implementation of new computer systems and of other new systems, be they human resource or technological interventions.

A SYSTEM IMPLEMENTED AND USED
MAY NOT INCREASE PRODUCTIVITY

Even when a system is implemented successfully (i.e., when employees do in fact use the new system), it may not yield improved organizational performance for at least two important reasons. The first reason, which is well documented in the literature on computer automation and indeed may be unique to computer automation, was discussed in Chapter 2. That is, when automated office systems render a given task easier and faster to accomplish, people often respond by performing the task (e.g., editing a document) more often, with no greater output, precisely because it is now easier and faster to do so. For this reason alone—more frequent use rather than higher levels of relative performance—the successful implementation of office automation is no guarantee of an increase in the performance of the office in which the new system was successfully implemented.

But even if people did not perform the same tasks more often after automation than before, the relative performance of the worker and office may still not increase. That is, it still might not be enough because, with some exceptions, office automation affects only a limited portion of users' work tasks.

Consider college professors. Access to a computer and word processing package speeds writing, but only in the most limited sense. It does not shorten the time it takes to conduct library, field, or laboratory research; to read background materials; to organize one's thoughts; or to compose a sentence. These are the tasks that consume a professor's writing time, not the physical task of putting letters on a sheet of paper or computer screen.

Professors are perhaps an extreme example, but consider secretaries. Secretaries who are asked to carry out edit, after edit, after edit, may well suffer the brunt of the "now it is faster and easier" problem described above. But, for secretaries, much as for professors, office automation affects only a limited portion of their work. Aided by new office systems, secretaries nevertheless still answer telephones; still copy, distribute, and file papers; still look up information; and still meet with their supervisors—all much as they have for decades. In fact, as also pointed out in Chapter 2, office automation may make some portion of an individual's work more efficient while making other portions more difficult.

The same principle applies to many other types of organizational interventions. That is, many interventions may influence only a limited part of the targeted employees' jobs. For example, when an organization implements an incentive pay system that rewards specific employee behaviors, employees are likely to increase their performance of those behaviors. Their performance of other important aspects of their jobs that are not rewarded by the new pay plan may be unchanged or even impaired. This is the dilemma faced by organizations when they implement incentive systems to increase raw productivity. Productivity may go up while quality goes down (Kerr, 1988).

Similar problems may arise with the purchase of automated manufacturing systems. If a company purchases a new computerized manufacturing resource planning system in the hope of improving company performance, production planning and scheduling may well improve. But improvements in planning and scheduling will yield overall performance improvements only if the company product is well made, marketed well, and suitable for the intended market segment. The point is that improving only one aspect of employee performance is unlikely to be linked to total organizational performance unless attention is also paid to the larger organizational system in which the employee performs.

ORGANIZATIONS AS OPEN SYSTEMS: THE OTHER SYSTEMS THAT MATTER

Even if office automation did increase individual performance, would that be enough to augment organizational performance? The answer is probably not. This answer rests on the assumption that organizations are "open systems" (Katz and Kahn, 1978), that is, "living systems, existing in a wider environment on which they depend for the satisfaction of various needs" (Morgan, 1986:39). This conceptualization provides, as Morgan notes, "the crux of many of the most important developments in organization theory over the last fifty years" (p. 39). Within organizational theory, the open systems metaphor has supplanted the "machine metaphor," the notion that organizations, like machines, can and should perform highly repetitive, predictable tasks as efficiently as possible (Morgan, 1986). Instead, the open systems metaphor directs attention to the organization's adaptation to its environment, issues of organizational survival and effectiveness, and the complex interplay of the organizational subsystems that make up the larger organizational system (Katz and Kahn, 1978; Morgan, 1986).

Katz and Kahn (1966, 1978) popularized the open systems concept in studying organizational performance. Based on von Bertalanffy's (1950, 1956) work in physics and biology, they proposed a view of organizations as systems of interacting individuals and groups in continuous dynamic relationship to the larger environment in which the organization functions. The inclusion of the larger environment in their model makes it an *open* systems model, open to the vagaries of the larger world.

Building on von Bertalanffy's work, Katz and Kahn identified four major principles that characterize all open systems, be they plant cells, animal organs, individuals, dyads, groups, or organizations. Below, we use their four principles to hypothesize further why single-level, targeted interventions, such as office automation, may fail to yield improvements in organizational performance.

One key principle is that of *differentiation, integration, and coordination.* "Open systems move in the direction of differentiation and elaboration. Diffuse global patterns are replaced by more specialized functions. . . . Social organizations move toward the multiplication and elaboration of roles with greater specialization" (Katz and Kahn, 1978:29). To manage and counterbalance this differentiation, this complexity, all open systems develop integrating and coordinating mechanisms "that bring the system together for unified functioning" (p. 29).

Describing the differentiation of organizational systems further, Katz and Kahn suggested that five organizational roles, or subsystems, characterize all organizations: (1) the managerial subsystem (responsible for controlling and coordinating the other subsystems), (2) the adaptive subsystem (responsible for environmental sensing), (3) the maintenance subsystem (responsible for supporting the people and equipment required to do the work), (4) the production subsystem (responsible for transforming organizational inputs into organizational outputs), and (5) the support subsystem (responsible for procurement and disposition as well as facilitating production). The managerial subsystem, as suggested above, coordinates and integrates the subsystems. The greater the effectiveness of the subsystems themselves and their coordination, the greater the effectiveness of the organization.

A second open systems principle is that *changes in one part of the larger system will have reverberating effects on other parts of the system.* The intensity of the reverberations depends on the closeness or tightness of the linkage between the changed element and other elements in the system. Thus, in loosely coupled systems (Weick, 1976), changes in one subsystem can be relatively isolated from the larger system. In tightly coupled systems, however, a small change in any subsystem will yield changes elsewhere in the system through reciprocating linkages. Landing a jet on the deck of an aircraft carrier is an example of a tightly coupled system (Roberts and Sloane, 1988). In this system the smallest deviations in speed of the ship, list of the ship, wind direction, speed of the jet, altitude of the approach, and so forth have great consequences for performance—the safe landing of the jet. Conversely, providing a professor in a university with a personal computer and word processing software may be very loosely linked to university performance, even if the professor is more "productive."

While change in one part of an open system may reverberate throughout the system, change in one part of the system may or may not cause a permanent change in other parts of the system. Indeed, sensing a change in one part of the system, the organization may seek to quell the change, that is, to ensure that the changed element of the system returns to its former state. This is a third key principle of open systems, *dynamic homeostasis*. As Katz and Kahn (1978:27) explained, "Any internal or external factor that threatens to disrupt the system is countered by forces which restore the system as closely as possible to its previous state. . . . *The basic principle is the preservation of the character of the system*" (emphasis in original).

The fourth principle of open systems is that of *equifinality*, that is, "a system can reach the same final state from differing initial conditions and by a variety of paths" (p. 30). Equifinality for organizations as systems is equivalent to the compensatory model for predicting individual performance. The compensatory model indicates that numerous strengths correlate with performance, but they can exist in different configurations and still yield equivalent levels of performance. In the study of organizations as systems, a similar compensatory flavor exists.

Below, we present some hypotheses derived from these open systems principles that are useful for understanding individual-organizational performance linkages. Again, we focus on office automation as a continuing foil for the explication of our perspective, but the principles apply equally well to other performance-enhancing interventions.

Differentiation, Integration, and Coordination

The open systems principle of differentiation, integration, and coordination suggests that automating office systems may differentially affect the subsystems of an organization. Just as office automation may speed and ease only a subset of an individual office worker's tasks, so the system may speed and ease only a subset of an organization's tasks. In fact, automating one set of tasks in an organization may make other tasks even more difficult, and not only for the job that is automated. Often, then, automating a job is most likely to enhance only the production subsystem of the job that is automated. Word processing, for example, speeds the production of documents, but it fails to speed the production of research, of thoughts, or even of sentences.

Automated office systems, hypothetically, should augment the support subsystem of the organization. Automated teller machines (ATMs), for example, ease the receipt of deposits from customers and the distribution of cash to customers, a support function in banks. But, as noted in Chapter 2, because ATMs make these functions easier, customers make deposits and withdrawals at more frequent intervals than prior to this automation.

Automated office systems are even less likely to ease or enhance managerial and adaptive tasks. Indeed, Schrage (1991:C-3) suggested that at least some office automated systems are inimical to effective managerial and adaptive performance:

The most dangerous, hideously misused and thought-annihilating piece of technology invented in the last 15 years has to be the electronic spreadsheet. Every day, millions of managers boot up their Lotus 1-2-3s and Microsoft Excels, twiddle a few numbers and diligently sucker themselves into thinking they're forecasting the future. . . . It's an intellectual exercise that stretches the fingers more than the mind. . . . You can't understand risk—let alone manage or reduce it— by cramming it into a spreadsheet or the quantitative "flavor of the month."

In sum, office automation may in some ways enhance the performance of some organizational subsystems (production of office work, support); may impair the performance of other subsystems (managerial, adaptive); and may, as we discuss below, tax other organizational subsystems, particularly the maintenance subsystem.

The analysis thus far points to one reason office automation may not engender improvements in organizational performance: Even if the automation is successfully implemented, the positive effects may be limited and the unintended negative consequences may cancel the positive effects. Organizational performance, in our view, is the culmination of the coordinated integration of all organizational subsystems. Improving the performance of one small part of the work that must be accomplished in an organization is unlikely to enhance organizational performance, we hypothesize, especially if the performance of some organizational subsystems is reduced in the process.

Reverberations Throughout the System

When office automation alters an organization's production, support, managerial, or adaptive subsystems, the changes will reverberate throughout the organization and may necessitate ancillary and often unintended changes in other subsystems. Thus, for example, the installation of new equipment in the production subsystem may necessitate changes in the lighting, temperature, cleanliness, and technical maintenance of the production area. It may also require installation of privacy, confidentiality, and security safeguards to protect the data contained within the new office system (U.S. Office of Technology Assessment, 1985). And it may require new procedures to coordinate work tasks within the production function.

The reverberations from the installation of new office automation surely will be felt beyond the subsystem in which the new office system is installed (Loveman, 1988; Majchrzak and Klein, 1987; Trist, 1981). Thus, for example, the installation of new office automation necessitates changes in the maintenance subsystem, the people and equipment required to do the work. While the installation of office automation is often expected to reduce direct labor costs (Ayres and Miller, 1983), the available evidence (e.g., Gutek et al., 1984) suggests that reductions in labor cost are in fact rare. Moreover, the installation of office automation may require changes in the skills employees need to perform their jobs (Majchrzak and Klein, 1987; U.S. Office of Technology Assessment, 1985). This can require the hiring of more highly skilled persons who require higher salaries. Further, current employees may need retraining, jobs may have to be redesigned, reward systems may have to be changed, and supervisory relations may change (Barley, 1986; Helfgott, 1988; Klein et al., 1990; Majchrzak and Klein, 1987; Schneider, 1990b). Even the employees of the vendors from whom the equipment was purchased may have to be integrated into the work force as they try to maintain, literally, the office automation (Hines, 1985).

The changes described above are expensive and disruptive. It takes time, money, and extensive planning and coordination for them to work smoothly and effectively. Selection and training for the new system apply not only to people who will use the new system, but to the recipients of the materials that the new system produces. Especially in tightly coupled systems, change is like a ricocheting bullet introduced into a room with steel walls; it is difficult to predict exactly where it will hit next, but it will hit.

Thus, from the principle of reverberation, we derive additional reasons why the implementation of office automation may fail to yield the anticipated improvements in organizational performance: Gains in the outputs of some subsystems (e.g., production) may be offset, at least for some period of time, by increases in the costs of other subsystems (e.g., maintenance). Nothing presented here about the implications of the principle of reverberation should be read as unique to the problems associated with office automation. We make the point again, then, that these principles apply to diagnosing and understanding the possibilities for enhancing the potential of all kinds of interventions that might improve the linkage between individual and organizational performance.

Dynamic Homeostasis

The analysis above implies that organizations should change their maintenance subsystems in response to changes in performance-enhancing interventions. The principle of dynamic homeostasis suggests the hypothesis that, in many cases, organizations may not change their maintenance or any other subsystems to maximize the benefits of innovation. Rather, according to this principle, organizations may attempt to preserve the status quo, changing the innovation to fit the maintenance subsystem rather than vice versa. Unfortunately, this, too, may minimize the benefits of office automation for organizational performance.

Thus, for example the Manufacturing Studies Board (National Research Council, 1986) advised organizations to alter dramatically their human resource practices (plant culture, job design, career advancement, reward and compensation systems, and personnel selection—the human element of what we are calling the maintenance subsystem) in order to realize the benefits of advanced manufacturing technologies. The clear implication is that many manufacturing companies have not done so and may thus fail to reap the potential benefits of automation.

Child et al. (1987:91) made much the same argument in their persuasive analysis of "organizational conservatism" in response to the implementation of computer-automated technologies in hospital laboratories, retail settings, and banks. These technologies, the authors argued, allow organizations to undertake major innovations in their organizational and management practices. Thus, for example, the installation of electronic-point-of-sales terminals

could be used to decentralize buying decisions. With the detailed sales and stock information provided, local store managers could be in a position to respond independently to the needs of their local markets and take decisions on the selection of items for sale, on the quantities to stock, on pricing, and on staffing. . . . The new technology could also be used to increase the discretion of sales staff, particularly in department stores. . . . In short, new retailing technology can be used to facilitate organizational innovation in the direction of decentralization (p. 91).

Based on their case study research, however, Child et al. reported that these kinds of innovations have not occurred in hospital laboratories, retail stores, or banks. They (1987:111) attributed this failure of innovation to organizational conservatism, an organizational syndrome that may be the result of several factors. They suggested, for example, that "radical organizational changes are more expensive; they require more analytical work; a larger number of jobs and departments are affected." Further, "principles of organization that have a long history influence the way in which experts perceive organizational problems and design solutions for these problems." In addition, "rules of good practice are embedded within the culture of a society; organizations that violate these rules by being innovative run the risk of losing legitimacy" (p. 111).

The principle of dynamic homeostasis is by no means limited to office automation. For example, we described above job-enrichment and supervisory training efforts that had little impact because the larger organization within which they were attempted failed to support the innovations. A growing body of literature on organizational climate and culture (e.g., Schneider, 1990b) predicts that changes that do not fit the culture will be ignored or absorbed as the various subsystems strive for homeostasis. The literature clearly suggests that a change can have an effect only when the subsystems of the organization collectively facilitate the change (see Schoorman and Schneider, 1988).

Equifinality

The principle of equifinality suggests that there may be alternative routes to the same outcome. This principle, then, suggests that while one organization may achieve performance improvements through a focus on office automation, another organization may achieve the same improvements in other ways. For example, an organization might achieve performance improvements by focusing on its reward systems (Kerr, 1988), increasing the use of management by objectives (Rodgers and Hunter, 1991), or implementing a total quality management (TQM) program (Juran, 1987; Schneider et al., 1992).

The principle of equifinality suggests that innovations to improve organizational performance must be strategically and culturally appropriate. By *strategically appropriate* we mean the innovation must be chosen to achieve goals that fit the long-term marketing objectives of the organization. It should not be chosen simply because others are using it. For example, many organizations have adopted TQM as the "magic bullet" for achieving competitive advantage. But TQM must be adapted by each organization to fit the demands of its customers; the quality standards will vary as a function of the strategic imperatives of a particular organization.

By *culturally appropriate* we mean that the adoption of some innovations may be antithetical to the norms, values, and principles of an organization. Such innovations are unlikely to yield outcomes that improve organizational performance. Consider, for example, an organization that has functioned on the basis of close teamwork yet adopts an innovation that separates workers from each other because the innovation is said to yield improved individual productivity. Since the early 1950s it has been known that separating individuals who are accustomed to working in teams can destroy morale, increase accidents, and decrease productivity (Trist, 1981). Recent case studies reveal similarly inappropriate choices of technology when seeking productivity improvements (e.g., Klein et al., 1990).

Organizations may err in thinking that there is only one way to achieve productivity—be that one way office automation or TQM. Indeed, the open systems framework suggests that each organizational system is unique and is embedded in its own unique environment. Thus, each system must find its own way to maximize performance. What works for one organization may not work for another. Indeed, it probably will not.

Implications of Open Systems Theory

Although our focus has been on explaining why interventions designed to improve individual performance fail to enhance organizational performance, open systems theory suggests a number of strategies by which organizations can maximize the potential performance benefits of an intervention. First, organizations should devote ample resources (including time and money) to effective implementation of the intervention. Unless implementation is effective, unless employees accept and use the most advantageous procedures of the new system, the intervention is doomed to have a minimal, or even harmful, effect on organizational performance (Tornatzky and Fleischer, 1990). The "laundry list" of suggestions for enhancing implementation presented above—including providing extensive training, user support, time to experiment with the new system, rewards, user involvement, and so on—may lack theoretical parsimony; but at the least it provides a useful checklist for organizations in the process of implementing new systems. Tornatzky and Fleischer (1990) and Klein and Ralls (in press) present an extended treatment of these suggestions for enhancing the usefulness of interventions in organizations.

Second, organizations should analyze carefully the potential impact of an intervention, even under ideal circumstances, on the *facets* of individual performance. Even successfully implemented interventions may fail to enhance total individual performance, let alone organizational performance, because the system is targeted at only one or several facets of a more complex job. Office automation is a good case in point. It is a mistake, as we discuss in greater detail below, to assume that a new software program for word processing will turn total individual performance around. It is also, we believe, a mistake to focus on the production of software programs as the culprit keeping down the expected increments in organizational performance from implementing office automation (Abdel-Hamid and Madnick, 1989).

Third, organizations should attend to the multiple subsystems of the organization that might be affected by the intervention. Installing new automated systems for the production subsystem of the organization alone may well fail to enhance organizational performance. Installing new automated systems for the production subsystem *and* making coordinated changes to the other subsystems of the organization may enhance organizational performance.

There is some evidence that attention to other subsystems can yield positive outcomes from an intervention. For example, Schneider (1990a) described a personnel selection intervention that, when combined with changes in training for the new incumbents and the old supervisors, new reward systems for incumbents, and new career plans, resulted in a 30 percent reduction in turnover; the estimated decrease in turnover given the selection program alone was 10 percent. Other examples of how a multisubsystems approach to understanding the potential in an intervention can yield positive consequences for organizational performance exist. For example, Banas (1988) described such an approach for a program designed to enhance participation in decision making at the Ford Motor Company, and Shea and Guzzo (1986) described a similar perspective for the successful use of quality circles.

Fourth, the open systems model suggests that organizations should undertake multiple kinds of interventions in multiple subsystems of the organization when the goal is to enhance total organizational performance. In combination, suggestions three and four hypothesize that when a multifaceted intervention is placed into the organization the consequence can be enhanced organizational performance. The principle here, derived from an open systems framework, is that simultaneous implementation of a variety of changes across a variety of organizational subsystems can yield the intended effect. Thus, for example, an organization might implement new office automation systems to speed production tasks (e.g., new computer graphics and word processing systems to speed the production of advertising copy) and at the same time target the following:

1. the maintenance subsystem (e.g., by implementing goal setting, training, new selection systems, team-building exercises, or group incentives);

2. the support system (e.g., by implementing new customer ser-

vice procedures and customer feedback mechanisms and new information strategies for keeping employees informed);

3. the adaptive subsystem (e.g., by undertaking new market research and R&D, and developing alternative scenarios of the future organizational environment); and

4. the managerial subsystem (e.g., by increasing efforts to provide organizational members with a vision of the organization of the future and increasing coordination among all subsystems to ensure a sharing of the new vision).

Surely, such a multifaceted, large-scale effort at organizational change cannot be undertaken all at once (Mohrman et al., 1989; Roitman et al., 1988). Yet this description provides, we think, a realistic assessment of the magnitude of the effort necessary for an intervention targeted on individuals to improve the performance of an organization.

Beyond Open Systems Theory: The Symbolism and Politics of Office Automation

The open systems model is a powerful heuristic for understanding organizational functioning and performance. It suggests several provocative and convincing hypotheses about why the implementation of any one intervention in an organization may fail to augment organizational performance. Nevertheless, the open systems framework may be limiting in some respects. That is, it directs attention primarily to the rational structure and functioning of organizations and to the human resources consequences of organizational structure and functioning. Although adopting an open systems perspective broadens the range of issues requiring attention, it still excludes some psychologically important issues. That is, the open systems perspective may be a bit too neat to capture the feelings, meanings, and emotions attached to working and living in organizations, especially the feelings, meanings, and emotions attached to innovations in how people work.

Bolman and Deal (1984, 1991) offered such an alternative systems view of organizations. They proposed four frames, or lenses, through which to view organizational phenomena. Each frame has considerable theoretical and empirical support. The four frames are (1) the structural or rational frame, (2) the human resources frame, (3) the political frame, and (4) the symbolic frame.

The structural or rational frame emphasizes the intentionality and goal directedness of organizations and how decision making is influenced by intentions and the larger context of the organization. The open systems framework fits this lens. The human resources frame emphasizes the idea that people occupy organizations and behave like people (with all their complex abilities, personalities, defenses, and so forth) and that organizations should be organized in ways that acknowledge the humanness of people. In our description of the open systems model, we emphasized the human assets of organizations, especially in our discussion of the implications of office automation for the maintenance subsystem.

Bolman and Deal's third frame, the political frame, acknowledges the fact that organizations do not have an unlimited supply of resources to meet all individual, group, and functional desires. Limited resources create conflict in all systems. An understanding that this conflict is invariably traceable to the scarcity of resources helps to explain the existence of conflict in organizations, the formation of coalitions, and the negotiation over organizational goals and decisions. Within the political frame, power is the critical resource—the resource that controls the distribution of other scarce resources. Finally, the symbolic frame focuses on the issue of "meaning," the processes by which events are given meaning, and the different meanings the same events may have as a result of the relative ambiguity of the context of the event. Humans *must*, by their very nature, make casual attributions about *why* events occur and *what* they mean. By making these attributions, people derive meaning. Some call this meaning climate, others call it culture (Schneider, 1990b). Regardless, it is not what *actually* happens that is important, but the meaning ascribed to it.

The four frames allow one "to try on a variety of spectacles and spend more time dealing with the complexity of human organizations before we can safely conclude that they are *actually* as simple as existing models make them out to be" (Bolman and Deal, 1984:239; emphasis in original). The symbolic and political frames provide valuable and relatively new perspectives on the organizational consequences of the implementation of office automation and other interventions.

The symbolic frame offers a way of understanding some psychological consequences of organizational interventions. Using this frame, one asks, from an employee's vantage what is the symbolic meaning of a given organizational intervention? That is, what message is sent to employees when they know the intervention is being put in place? For office automation, the message may be, you are not valued as a person with hopes, feelings, desires, and needs; you are a machine and we are buying a more reliable, less costly one and you are gone. Thus, for those affected, office automation may be a disheartening and even a deeply insulting symbol to office workers. Indeed, in their study of the implementation of computer-integrated manufacturing at a 150-employee manufacturing company, Roitman et al. (1988) found that employee reactions to the new technology were shaped by the extent to which each employee's job was likely to be eliminated, or their power and status diminished, because of the planned changes.

On the other hand, office automation may have a positive symbolic value for employees. It may indicate that they are valued ("management cares enough to give us new and better tools to work with") and that the organization is moving ahead ("we really are an organization of the 1990s"). Office automation may also have a symbolic value for customers, symbolizing (managers hope) the success, efficiency, and modernity of the organization (Schneider and Bowen, 1985).

The political frame encourages one to analyze the political issues surrounding an organizational intervention. Pettigrew's (1973) classic study of a large British retail chain's decision to purchase a computer for automated recordkeeping documented the politics of decision making regarding this innovation. In a large-scale qualitative effort, Pettigrew gained access to letters exchanged between members of the retail chain and potential suppliers of the new computer system. He showed that members of one coalition within the retail chain, who favored one vendor over all others, were able to dominate negotiations, to solicit favors from the preferred vendor, and to dictate the eventual choice. More recently, Dean (1987) recorded the politics of the decision-making process for the purchase of automated manufacturing equipment (e.g., computer-aided design, manufacturing resource planning, robotics, computer-integrated manufacturing). Dean (1987:56-57) wrote,

It turns out that it is a "bottom-up" decision process, with technology proponents attempting to build a strategic/financial, social, and political structure to support approval. Numerous subtle tactics are used by proponents in constructing this support.

Focusing not on the adoption process but on the reactions of users to a new computer-automated technology (specifically to a computer-automated financial information system), Markus (1987:80) provided a similar analysis of the politics of computerization:

When the introduction of a computerized information system specifies a distribution of power which represents a loss to certain participants, these participants are likely to resist the system. Conversely, when the distribution of power implied in the design of an information system represents a gain in power to participants, these participants are likely to engage in behaviors that might signify acceptance of it. . . . In general, one would not expect people who are disadvantaged in their power position by a system to accept it (gracefully), nor would one expect people who gain power to resist.

Finally, Klein et al. (1990:27) described the organizational consequences of such a shift of power in their case study of the implementation of computer-aided design and drafting:

Because Buildco drafters and designers received training and their managers and supervisors did not, drafters and designers gained technical expertise that both supervisors and managers lacked. As a result, supervisors guided their employees with shaken confidence and diminished power.

The implication of the application of Bolman and Deal's four frames to the individual-organizational linkage problem is that it may not be enough for an organization to consider the structural and rational benefits and consequences of an intervention. Nor may it be enough for an organization to consider an intervention's structural/rational and human resources consequences, although that is a substantial improvement over the first tactic. We hypothesize that organizations that consider the implications and consequences of interventions for each frame are likely to experience improved organizational performance. Thus, organizations must ask the following questions: (1) To what extent does the intervention improve the structure and heighten the rationality of key organizational subsystems? (2) To what extent does it require or invite changes in the human resources practices of the organization? (3) What does it symbolize to organizational members (and perhaps to customers, too; Zeithaml et al., 1990)? (4) How will its implementation alter the existing balance of power within the organization?

SUMMARY AND CONCLUSION

In this chapter we have outlined a number of reasons why a single, individual-level intervention, such as office automation, may fail to improve organizational performance. To summarize, we offer the following propositions regarding the relationships one may expect to find between interventions targeted on improving individual performance and increments in organizational performance:

1. The decision to adopt an organizational intervention does not ensure its successful implementation or use. Many interventions are adopted but unused or underused, so links between the intervention and organizational performance will be nonexistent.
2. Even organizational interventions that are successfully implemented and used may do little to improve individual—much less, organizational—performance. This is because such interventions may have an effect on only a few dimensions of individual performance.

3. An intervention put in place in one subsystem of an organization (e.g., the production subsystem) can improve organizational performance to the degree that the intervention is integrated with the imperatives of the other subsystems of the organization (e.g., the maintenance subsystem). The managerial subsystem in organizations is responsible for ensuring the coordination and integration of interventions across the subsystems of the organization.

4. Particular interventions may fail to enhance organizational performance because they are not the most appropriate intervention for an organization. Interventions that will enhance organizational performance are likely to have been carefully chosen to fit the requirements and culture of the setting, to focus ideally on reducing costs and on improving output, and to not be based on a quick-fix mentality or keeping up with the Joneses.

5. Interventions in organizations are likely to enhance organizational performance to the degree that they are symbolically positive with respect to the employees' productivity motivation, individual desires, and perceptions of organizational needs.

6. The decision to adopt an intervention, the procedures by which an intervention is implemented, and the organizational reaction to the intervention all have political overtones. The effects of an intervention on organizational performance will be determined by the degree to which political issues are dealt with in a way that yields a sense of trust throughout the organization.

It is our hypothesis that *all* of the issues illuminated in these propositions require simultaneous attention if an intervention targeted on improving individual performance is to improve organizational performance. The research literature and our conceptualization of organizations as open systems with important symbolic and political overtones coalesce to yield the conclusion that quick fixes and fads do not work. Interventions that are carefully adopted, implemented in ways that take into account their symbolic and political realities, and integrated throughout the multiple subsystems of organizations may yield improved organizational performance.

REFERENCES

Abdel-Hamid, T.K., and S.E. Madnick
  1989   Lessons learned from modeling the dynamics of software development. *Communications of the ACM* 32:1426-1438.
Argote, L., P.S. Goodman, and D. Schkade
  1983   *The Human Side of Robotics: Results from a Prototype Study on How Workers React to a Robot.* Report No. 83-11, The Robotics Institute. Pittsburgh: Carnegie Mellon University.

Ayres, R.U., and S.M. Miller
  1983   *Robotics: Application and Social Implications.* Cambridge, Mass.: Harper & Row.
Banas, P.A.
  1988   Employee involvement: A sustained labor/management initiative at Ford Motor Company. Pp. 388-416 in J.P. Campbell and R.J. Campbell, eds., *Productivity in Organizations.* San Francisco: Jossey-Bass.
Barley, S.R.
  1986   Technology as an occasion for structuring: Evidence from observations of CT scanners and the social order of radiology departments. *Administrative Science Quarterly* 31:78-108.
Bass, B.M.
  1982   Individual capability, team performance and team productivity. In M.D. Dunnette and E.A. Fleishman, eds., *Human Performance and Productivity: Human Capability Assessment.* Hillsdale, N.J.: Erlbaum.
Beatty, C.A., and J.R.M. Gordon
  1988   Barriers to the implementation of CAD/CAM systems. *Sloan Management Review* Summer:25-33.
Bolman, L.G., and T.E. Deal
  1984   *Modern Approaches to Understanding and Managing Organizations.* San Francisco: Jossey-Bass.
  1991   *Reframing Organizations: Artistry, Choice, and Leadership.* San Francisco: Jossey-Bass.
Child, J., H. Ganter, and A. Kieser
  1987   Technological innovation and organizational conservatism. Pp. 87-116 in J.M. Pennings and A. Buitendam, eds., *New Technology as Organizational Innovation.* Cambridge, Mass.: Ballinger.
Dean, J.W., Jr.
  1987   Building the future: The justification process for new technology. Pp. 35-87 in J.M. Pennings and A. Buitendam, eds., *New Technology as Organizational Innovation.* Cambridge, Mass.: Ballinger.
Ettlie, J.E.
  1986   Implementing manufacturing technologies: Lessons from experience. Pp. 72-104 in D. Davis and Associates, eds., *Managing Technological Innovation.* San Francisco: Jossey-Bass.
Fleischer, M., J. Liker, and D. Arnsdorf
  1988   *Effective Use of Computer-Aided Design and Computer Aided Engineering in Manufacturing.* Ann Arbor, Mich.: Industrial Technology Institute.
Fleishman, E.A.
  1953   Leadership climate, human relations training, and supervisory behavior. *Personnel Psychology* 6:205-222.
Foulkes, F.K., and J.L. Hirsch
  1984   People make robots work. *Harvard Business Review* 62(1):94-102.
George, J.M.
  1991   State or trait: Effects of positive mood on prosocial behaviors at work. *Journal of Applied Psychology* 76:299-307.
Graham, M.B.W., and S.R. Rosenthal
  1986   Flexible manufacturing systems require flexible people. *Human Systems Management* 6:211-222.
Gutek, B.A., T.K. Bikson, and D. Mankin
  1984   Individual and organizational consequences of computer-based office informa-

tion techniques. Pp. 231-254 in S. Oskamp, ed., *Applied Social Psychology Annual*, Vol. 5. Beverly Hills, Calif.: Sage Publications.

Hackman, J.R., and G.R. Oldham
1980   *Work Redesign.* Reading, Mass.: Addison-Wesley.

Helfgott, R.B.
1988   *Computerized Manufacturing and Human Resources.* Lexington, Mass.: Lexington Books.

Hines, V.D.
1985   *Office Automation: Tools and Methods for System Building.* New York: John Wiley & Sons.

Joyce, W.F., and J.W. Slocum, Jr.
1990   Strategic context and organizational climate. Pp. 130-150 in B. Schneider, ed., *Organizational Climate and Culture.* San Francisco: Jossey-Bass.

Juran, J.M.
1987   *On Quality Leadership.* Wilton, Conn.: Juran Institute.

Katz, D., and R.L. Kahn
1966   *The Social Psychology of Organizations.* New York: John Wiley & Sons.
1978   *The Social Psychology of Organizations*, 2d ed. New York: John Wiley & Sons.

Kerr, S.
1988   Some characteristics and consequences of organizational reward. Pp. 43-76 in F.D. Schoorman and B. Schneider, eds., *Facilitating Work Effectiveness.* Lexington, Mass.: Lexington Books.

Klein, K.J., and S. Ralls
In   The organizational dynamics of computerized technology implementation: A
press   review of the empirical literature. In L.R. Gomez-Mejia and M.W. Lawless, eds., *Implementation Management in High Technology.* Greenwich, Conn.: JAI Press.

Klein, K.J., R.J. Hall, and M. Laliberte
1990   Training and the organizational consequences of technological change: A case study of computer-aided design and drafting. Pp. 7-36 in U.E. Gattiker and L. Larwood, eds., *Technology and End-User Training.* New York: Walter de Gruyter.

Lawrence, P.R., and J.W. Lorsch
1969   *Organization and Environment: Managing Differentiation and Integration.* Homewood, Ill.: Irwin.

Leonard-Barton, D.
1988   Implementation as mutual adaptation of technology and organization. *Research Policy* 17:251-267.

Leonard-Barton, D., and W.A. Krauss
1985   Implementing new technology. *Harvard Business Review* 63(6):102-110.

Locke, E.A., and D.M. Schweiger
1979   Participation in decision making: One more look. Pp. 265-340 in B.M. Staw and L.L. Cummings, eds., *Research in Organizational Behavior*, Vol. 1. Greenwich, Conn.: JAI Press.

Loveman, G.W.
1988   An Assessment of the Productivity Impact of Information Technologies. Working Paper 90s-88-054. Sloan School of Management, Massachusetts Institute of Technology, Cambridge.

Majchrzak, A., and K. Klein
1987   Things are always more complicated than you think: An open systems approach to the organizational effects of computer-automated technology. *Journal of Business and Psychology* 2(1):27-49.

Markus, M.L.
  1987   Power, politics, and MIS implementation. Pp. 68-82 in R.M. Baecker and W.A.S. Buxton, eds., *Readings in Human-Computer Interaction: A Multidisciplinary Approach*. Los Altos, Calif.: Morgan Kaufmann.
Mathieu, J.E., and S.S. Kohler
  1990   A cross-level examination of group absence. *Journal of Applied Psychology* 75:217-220.
Miller, K.I., and P.R. Monge
  1986   Participation, satisfaction and productivity: A meta-analytic review. *Academy of Management Journal* 29:727-753.
Mohrman, A.M., Jr., S.A. Mohrman, G.E. Ledford, Jr., T.G. Cummings, and E.E. Lawler III, eds.
  1989   *Large-Scale Organizational Change*. San Francisco: Jossey-Bass.
Morgan, G.
  1986   *Images of Organization*. Beverly Hills, Calif.: Sage.
National Research Council
  1986   *Human Resource Practices for Implementing Advanced Manufacturing Technology*. Manufacturing Studies Board. Washington, D.C.: National Academy Press.
Parsons, C.K., R.C. Liden, E.J. O'Connor, and D.H. Nagao
  1989   Employee Responses to Technologically Driven Change: The Implementation of Office Automation in a Service Organization. Unpublished manuscript, Georgia Institute of Technology, Atlanta.
Pearce, J.L., and R.A. Page, Jr.
  1990   Palace politics: Resource allocation in radically innovative firms. *High Technology Management Research* 1:193-206.
Pelz, D.C., and F.M. Andrews
  1966   *Scientists in Organizations*. New York: John Wiley & Sons.
Pettigrew, A.M.
  1973   *The Politics of Organizational Decision-Making*. London: Tavistock.
Posavac, E.J., and R.G. Carey
  1985   *Program Evaluation: Methods and Case Studies*, 2d ed. Englewood Cliffs, N.J.: Prentice-Hall.
Rivard, S.
  1987   Successful implementation of end-user computing. *Interfaces* 17(3):25-33.
Roberts, K.E., and S.R. Sloane
  1988   An aggregation problem and organizational effectiveness. Pp. 125-144 in F.D. Schoorman and B. Schneider, eds., *Facilitating Work Effectiveness*. Lexington, Mass.: Lexington Books.
Rodgers, R., and J.E. Hunter
  1991   Impact of management by objectives on organizational productivity. *Journal of Applied Psychology* 76:322-336.
Roethlisberger, F.T., and W.J. Dickson
  1939   *Management and the Worker*. Cambridge, Mass.: Harvard University Press.
Roitman, D.B., J.K. Liker, and E. Roskies
  1988   Birthing a factory of the future: When is "all at once" too much? In R.H. Kilmann and T.J. Covin, eds., *Corporate Transformation*. San Francisco: Jossey-Bass.
Rouiller, J.Z., and I.L. Goldstein
  1993   The relationship between organizational transfer climate and positive transfer. *Human Resource Development Quarterly* 4:377-390.

Rousseau, D.M.
  1989   Managing the change to an automated office: Lessons from five case studies. *Office: Technology and People* 4:31-52.
Schneider, B.
  1990a   Alternative models for creating service-oriented organizations. In D.E. Bowen, R.B. Chase, and T.G. Cummings, eds., *Service Management Effectiveness*. San Francisco: Jossey-Bass.
  1990b   *Organizational Climate and Culture*. San Francisco: Jossey-Bass.
Schneider, B., and D.F. Bowen
  1985   Employee and customer perceptions of service in banks: Replication and extension. *Journal of Applied Psychology* 70:423-433.
Schneider, B., R.A. Guzzo, and A.P. Brief
  1992   Establishing a climate for productivity improvement. In W.K. Hodson, ed., *Maynard's Industrial Engineering Handbook*. New York: McGraw-Hill.
Schoorman, F.D., and B. Schneider, eds.
  1988   *Facilitating Work Effectiveness*. Lexington, Mass.: Lexington Books.
Schrage, M.
  1991   Rather than spreadsheets, companies need scenario software. *The Washington Post*, April 12:C-3.
Shea, G.P., and R.A. Guzzo
  1986   Quality circles: The danger of bottled change. *Sloan Management Review* 33-46.
Tornatzky, L.G., and M. Fleischer
  1990   *The Process of Technological Innovation: Reviewing the Literature*. Lexington, Mass.: Lexington Books.
Trist, E.L.
  1981   The sociotechnical perspective. Pp. 19-75 in A.H. Van de Ven and W.F. Joyce, eds., *Perspectives on Organization Design*. New York: John Wiley & Sons.
U.S. General Accounting Office
  1987   *Employee Stock Ownership Plans: Little Evidence of Effects on Corporate Performance*. Washington, D.C.: U.S. General Accounting Office.
U.S. Office of Technology Assessment
  1985   *Automation of America's Offices*. Washington, D.C.: U.S. Government Printing Office.
von Bertalanffy, L.
  1950   The theory of open systems in physics and biology. *Science* 3:23-28.
  1956   General systems theory. *General Systems* 1:1-10.
Weick, K.E.
  1976   Educational organizations as loosely coupled systems. *Administrative Science Quarterly* 21:1-19.
Zeithaml, V.A., A. Parasuraman, and L.L. Berry
  1990   *Delivering Quality Service: Balancing Customer Expectations and Perceptions*. New York: Free Press.

5

Measuring and Managing Individual Productivity

William A. Ruch

As important as productivity is to the continued economic development of the world, it is surprising that so little is known about measuring and managing it. Part of the problem may lie in the unit of analysis industry uses to measure productivity and in a failure to recognize the complexity of the relationships between the productivity of the individual worker and the total performance of the organization. The body of research knowledge provides little help. A multitude of micro studies of individual work behavior exist, but the measure of productivity used is seldom comparable to those developed in industry. Organizational studies generally focus on the total performance of the organization, but even those that are centered on organizational productivity rarely attempt to disaggregate findings to the business unit, work group, or individual level in any systematic way.

In a general sense, the productivity of the world is a function of the productivity of each of the world's economies; the economies, in turn, are as productive as the organizations within them. Within the organization, individual workers performing specific jobs form the base level for all productive endeavor. In modern, complex organizations, however, the linkage between individual productivity and the productivity of organizational systems becomes blurred. For a variety of reasons, the linkages are seldom one to one. Only by understanding the individual level of productivity, however, can practitioners and researchers begin to build the theories and models that deal with the dysfunctions and synergies that occur when individuals are grouped into work teams, departments, organizational systems, and economies.

It is important to note at the outset that focusing on individual productivity measures provides a myopic view of the organizational world. Organizations are set in the context of a changing, competitive environment in which strategies are developed to guide the efforts of management and workers toward a common vision and set of objectives. Even the best-designed processes will fail without a supportive culture within the organization that values change, continuous improvement, goal commitment, group cohesion, and respect for people. Every concept in this chapter assumes that the individual worker and the work group are set in an organizational context that is internally consistent and environmentally consonant.

It is also important to note that productivity, although a major concern, is not the only indicator of individual or organizational performance. Productivity interacts with other aspects of employee performance, financial controls, innovation, and competitive effectiveness—any one of which can lead to organizational failure. In Chapter 6 Sink and Smith identify seven related but separable performance criteria for an organizational system: (1) effectiveness, (2) efficiency, (3) productivity, (4) quality, (5) quality of working life, (6) innovation, and (7) profitability (profit center) or budgetability (cost center). Other authors, such as Pritchard (Chapter 7) and Campbell (Chapter 8), have slightly different ways of relating or combining these performance dimensions. For the purposes of this chapter, my definition of productivity includes effectiveness (producing the right products or services), efficiency (prudent utilization of resources), and quality (meeting technical and customer specifications).

My purpose in this chapter is to assimilate knowledge about the measurement and management of individual productivity in order to provide a link in the chain of understanding regarding how individual productivity contributes to group productivity, which in turn contributes to organizational productivity. My intent is to aggregate existing knowledge and propose some theoretical foundations in order to reveal areas in which theory development and empirical research are needed. Throughout, I make an effort to bridge the gap between the concerns of researchers and the needs of practitioners in industry.

PRODUCTIVITY MEASUREMENT AND GOAL ALIGNMENT

In industry, the measurement and analysis of individual-level productivity serves the following five major functions:

1. Define productivity and direct behavior: The measurement system provides an implicit definition of productivity for the operation. It communicates to the worker, the supervisor, and others the common expectation from the task. The productivity measurement provides specific direction and guides the worker toward productive activities.

2. Monitor performance and provide feedback: The measurement system provides a means to check progress toward an objective. In addition, it can be a major part of the employee's performance evaluation leading to rewards or disciplinary action.

3. Diagnose problems: Productivity analysis, particularly the examination of trends, helps identify problems before they become crises and permits early adjustment and corrective action. Like any other indicator, productivity measurements do not necessarily identify the source of the problem, only that one exists.

4. Facilitate planning and control: Productivity measurement provides information on costs, time, output rate, and resource usage to allow decision making with respect to pricing, production scheduling, purchasing, contracting, delivery scheduling, and many other activities in the industrial cycle. Productivity analysis, together with other elements of a competitive strategy, may determine which products or processes should be expanded and which should be phased out.

5. Support innovation: Productivity analysis, combined with cost data, aids in the evaluation of proposed changes to existing products or processes and the introduction of new ones. It is one of the primary foundations for the continuous improvement efforts that are both popular and necessary for survival in business firms today.

The purpose of the measurement system is critically important in determining the specific measures to be used. For example, if the measures are to be used only for planning and control purposes, the inputs into the measures and the outputs may be imprecise aggregate figures that provide guidance for setting schedules and future capacity requirements. If, however, the measures will be used as a basis for an employee evaluation system leading to bonuses, pay raises, layoffs, and disciplinary actions, inputs and outputs of the measures must be more precise and accurate for shorter time periods, and they must exclude factors outside the control of the worker. Questions of equity and interaction among individual jobs become evident.

The functions of monitoring performance and providing feedback, diagnosing problems, facilitating planning and control, and supporting innovation are common to many types of measures, and productivity is no exception. The function of defining productivity and directing behavior, however, warrants more explanation because it is important to managers in the successful operation of their business units, and because it is important to researchers in the design of studies that shed light on human behavior at work.

A simple example of a waiter in a restaurant can be used to explain how measures of productivity can direct behavior. If the measure of productivity is customers served per hour, the emphasis is on speed and throughput, and the waiter will try to complete each transaction as quickly as possible. On the other hand, a measure of dollars of food served per customer would lead to totally different behaviors; the waiter would suggest more expensive items and would encourage the customer to have appetizers, wine, and dessert, regardless of the time taken. In this case, time is not a factor; the quick turnover of customers would be a disadvantage. Other possible measures could each lead to a different set of behaviors.

One way to view individual productivity is to consider how the efforts of an individual contribute to the productivity or success of the organization. Whether the actions of the waiter in each of the examples above would be productive or counterproductive depends on the type of restaurant and, specifically, its goals and objectives. A downtown delicatessen would have one set of goals and circumstances; speed in serving customers would be a distinct advantage. A fine restaurant in the suburbs would operate in a different milieu; speed in this case could be a detriment.

The fundamental question is not, what productivity measures should be used? The fundamental question is, what are the organizational objectives? The secondary question is, what set of individual productivity measures will direct the behavior of employees to meet those objectives as they work toward their own personal goals? The aim of the organization is to align work behavior with organizational goals. It is the responsibility of management, therefore, to develop measures that will elicit organizationally desirable behaviors. These relationships are illustrated in the model shown as Figure 5-1 (Werther et al., 1986).

The law of effect, the cornerstone of operant psychology, says that behavior is a function of its consequences; positive outcomes reinforce behaviors, which leads to their being repeated and expanded. Simply establishing a measure and feeding back the results to the employee can be regarded as a form of reinforcement; employees tend to work on the basis of the measure in any circumstances. If there is a net incentive for high performance, the link between behavior and the measure will be stronger. The greater the incentive, the stronger the relationship between the two.

The term *net incentive* indicates that many incentives and disincentives may operate in a given set of circumstances. For example,

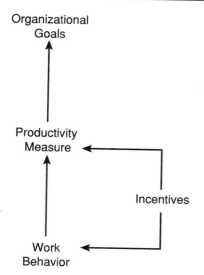

FIGURE 5-1 Goals, measurement, and behavior model. SOURCE: Werther et al. (1986:230).

peer pressure not to exceed production standards, the desire by some for an easy job, and the tendency to socialize at work interact with such positive incentives as financial rewards for high performance, opportunity for promotion, satisfaction from a job well done, and many others. Worker motivation is a complex issue; in taking all of that complexity into consideration, the model suggests that the net incentive should be positive and tied to performance.

Unfortunately, many organizational incentive systems are based on productivity or other performance measures that are not in line with organizational goals. Programmers, for example, may be measured and rewarded for lines of code written per hour. Accountants may be evaluated on the number of reports produced, and maintenance personnel on the number of routine equipment overhauls performed. In each instance (and many more), maximization of the measured criterion would likely be counterproductive to the organization.

Following the same logic, the productivity measurement system at each level of analysis should be developed to direct behaviors and performance at one level of the organization to the goals at the next higher level. These relationships are depicted in their ideal state in my Goal Alignment model, Figure 5-2. Across the top of the model, the organization attempts to make business unit goals (at all intermediate levels) congruent with organizational goals. Since the organization has no control over the individual's goals or the non-work-related goals of the group, it must accept them as given and design the organization to be compatible with them. For the sake of simplicity, this model does not consider

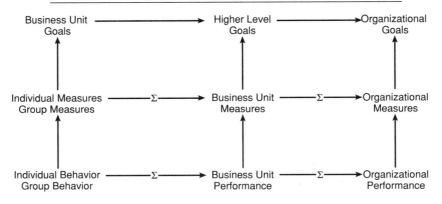

FIGURE 5-2 Goal Alignment model.

the compatibility of individual goals with group goals, or the resultant effects on performance, but it assumes that the behavior of one or the other, individual or group, is the basic unit of analysis determined by the process.

Productivity measures at the individual or group level direct behaviors to the business unit goals, if properly aligned. That is, the individuals or groups will work to the measures; it is the responsibility of the organization to ensure that the measures are in line with the goals.

Reading horizontally across the bottom of Figure 5-2, the model indicates that the productivity (performance) of a business unit is a direct function of the productive behavior of each of the individuals and groups within the unit. In turn, organizational productivity is a function of the productivity of each of the units. The degree to which this is true depends on the definition of productivity at each level and the interactions among the elements. Also, in this ideal model, the individual or group productivity results would sum to the productivity of the next higher business unit and ultimately to the productivity of the organization.

At the business unit level, managers will direct activities, allocate resources, and make other decisions to maximize performance as specified in the measurement system (especially if rewards are tied to performance). At each intermediate level of analysis, therefore, productivity measures should be selected and positioned such that the performance of the unit directly contributes to the goals at the next higher level.

The Goal Alignment model suggests that individuals, groups, and business units are not goal driven, but *measurement driven.* The old saying that "you get what is inspected, not what is expected" is relevant here. It is one thing for a firm to establish and communicate goals. It is quite another to devise and implement measurement systems that can be maximized only by behavior and performance that lead directly to goal accomplishment.

Organizations are real, not ideal. The Goal Alignment model, as well as many of the other models and concepts in this chapter, represent targets toward which organizations should strive. The degree to which they can achieve these targets, resolve the related issues, and design perfect productivity measurement systems determines their probability of survival and success. Researchers can help in this effort by empirically testing the relationships suggested in the Goal Alignment model.

TWO MODELS OF INDIVIDUAL PRODUCTIVITY

From one perspective, virtually everything that is known about technology and the behavior of people at work is a factor affecting individual productivity. Attempts to amalgamate all of that knowledge into a comprehensive, unified theory of individual productivity would likely prove fruitless. What is needed is a framework that will provide guidance for theory development, model building, empirical studies, and other forms of research. One such framework is the separation of the factors affecting individual productivity into five distinct, but interacting, sets of variables: (1) individual characteristics (e.g., size, strength, stamina); (2) psychological variables (e.g., individual attitudes and beliefs); (3) sociological variables (i.e., factors that come into play when individuals interact in groups of various sizes); (4) technological variables (e.g., tools, equipment, materials); and (5) system variables (e.g., policies, management style, communication systems).

Each of these sets of variables involves one or more disciplines; together they approach the boundaries of the body of knowledge of work. Obviously, they overlap and interact. But somewhere within the complex interactions of all of these variables lie the determinants of individual productivity. Development of a comprehensive theory of individual productivity is too much to ask, but perhaps it can be approached as would building a cathedral—one stone at a time. To develop a theory or build a cathedral, one needs plans and models. In this section, I discuss two models of individual productivity that encompass a wide range of variables.

A Conceptual Productivity Model

Ruch and Hershauer (1974) developed the Conceptual Schematic Productivity model to diagram the major influential relationships of a

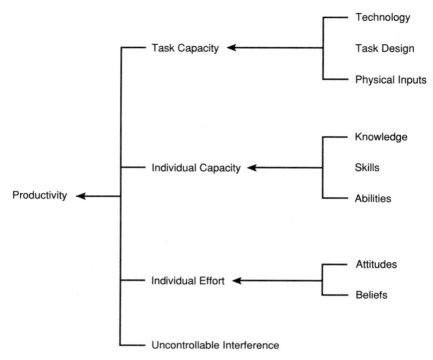

FIGURE 5-3 A conceptual model of individual productivity. SOURCE: Adapted from Ruch and Hershauer (1974).

number of variables that affect individual productivity. They categorized the variables as primary factors, secondary factors, individual factors, organizational controllables, individual and organizational demographics, and bodies of knowledge or files of information. In this section, I use a revised and greatly simplified version of their model (see Figure 5-3) as a basis for explaining the principal influences on the productivity of the individual worker.

In this Conceptual Productivity model, productivity is a function of four major factors: task capacity, individual capacity, individual effort, and uncontrollable interferences. Taken together, the first two factors establish the potential productivity of the task. When this potential meets the individual effort, moderated by possible interferences, the actual productivity of the task for a given time period results. Interference cannot be controlled by the individual worker, and it may or may not be controllable by the organization. For example, material shortages and machine breakdowns might have been prevented by better scheduling or maintenance, but a general power outage caused by a storm cannot be avoided except through backup procedures that are not cost justified.

The basic components of each of the first three factors in the model are identified in highly simplified form in Figure 5-3. *Task capacity* is a function of the level of technology employed (the technological variables referred to earlier); the design of the task (one of many system variables); and physical inputs (which span technological and systems variables). *Individual capacity* is a function of the individual characteristics that constitute the knowledge, skills, and abilities an individual brings to a task. Finally, *individual effort* is a function of attitudes and beliefs covering all of the cognitive characteristics of the individual that motivate a person to productive behavior on the job.

In the original model from which this version is derived, Ruch and Hershauer (1974) discussed direct and indirect causal relationships, interactions among factors, feedback loops, possible trade-offs, and a number of other refinements. One can easily see, even in the reduced version of the model used here, that a change in the workplace, such as the introduction of a more sophisticated data management system (technology), can have resounding effects for almost every element of the model. Individual knowledge is suddenly obsolete, which leads to the need for training by the organization. Attitudes and beliefs of the worker (e.g., resistance to change, fear of job loss, the challenge of a new job) will almost certainly be affected by the way the change is introduced and implemented, the training provided, and the way postimplementation activities are handled by management. But the degree and direction, positive or negative, of these rippling effects are difficult to predict. The resulting effect on individual productivity, given incomplete knowledge of the interactions of these many variables, is far from certain.

The primary purpose of this model is to organize and enhance understanding of the complex interactions of many variables operating in the workplace. It keeps the larger picture in view and thereby helps to avoid the myopia of focusing on one variable and assuming that everything else remains unchanged.

One important aspect of this model is that it separates potential productivity (determined by the first two factors) from the achievement of that potential (a function of the second two factors). It is one thing to increase the potential productivity of a task through higher levels of technology, better equipment and materials, more training, and the selection of employees with excellent skills. It is quite another matter to realize that potential in the form of sustained productivity increases by all employees. From a problem-solving point of view, cases of "poor" productivity should first be diagnosed as lack of potential, then a failure to meet potential, or some combination of the two. The optimal corrective action for one condition may fail if the other condition ensues.

Similarly, if the capacity of the task is increased and productivity remains constant or declines, one should look to the antecedents of individual effort or to instances of interference that could be corrected through changes in system variables. If an incentive system has little or no effect on productivity, one should explore the determinants of the capacity of the task and the individual to see if they are at their technological limits.

This Conceptual Productivity model is a simplistic representation of a highly complex system of interrelated variables that influence the productivity of individual workers and, in turn, the productivity of higher levels of the organization. It is intended as a framework within which existing and future research can be organized with the aim of making research results more meaningful and relevant to the needs of industry. To some extent, this type of analysis, using even a simple framework such as this one, may help explain the paradox of the lack of productivity improvement from investments in information technology noted in Chapter 2.

The Productivity Servosystem Model

Whereas the Conceptual Productivity model attempts to relate a few major antecedents of productivity but with little emphasis on the nature of their relationships, the Productivity Servosystem model developed by Hershauer and Ruch (1978) attempts to present a normative model that illustrates the interaction of factors influencing worker performance (see Figure 5-4). As with the previous model, I use a simplified version of the Servosystem in this discussion. Thus, many of the factors shown in Figure 5-4 could be disaggregated into several levels of analysis. The term *performance* is used in this model to indicate productivity as well as other work-related behaviors.

Individual worker performance is shown as the focal point of the model; organizational and individual factors either directly or indirectly affect this performance. Any factor shown can be traced through the model as an input to worker performance. In fact, many factors can also be traced to performance as an output. Because of this feedback effect and the time delay mechanism in the model, the model is called a Servosystem.

The factors influencing worker performance are indicated in the model in several ways. First, individually controlled factors are distinguished from organizationally controlled factors. Second, factors that

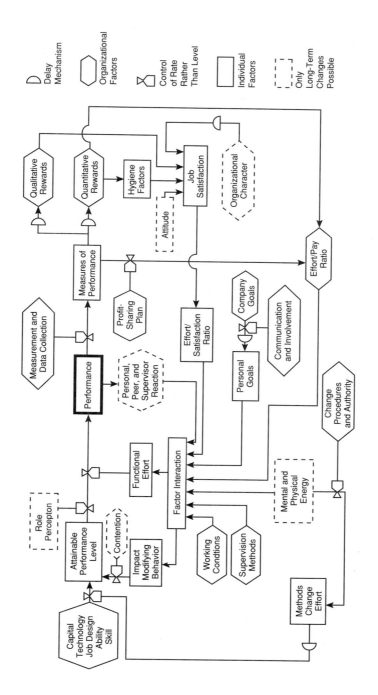

FIGURE 5-4 Productivity Servosystem model. SOURCE: Hershauer and Ruch (1978).

115

may be changed significantly only in the long run are identified separately. Third, some factors that control the rate of transfer of one or more of the other variables are identified. Fourth, the model includes time as an implicit factor since the feedback would take place over time. The time factor is also explicitly included by the time delays shown at a number of places in the model. These delays indicate that changes in the factors to which they relate will affect performance rather gradually over time.

My colleague and I developed the Productivity Servosystem model based on inputs derived from a review of the literature and information we gathered during visits with several productivity-conscious organizations. The models by Lawler (1971) and Sutermeister (1969) were particularly useful in forming the version of the model presented here. In addition, the modeling procedures of industrial dynamics as developed by Forrester (1961) have guided the form we used.

Elements of the Model

A brief walk-through will help explain the elements of the model and their relationships. Worker performance leads to reported measures of performance, buffered by the measurement system and methods of data collection. Performance data lead to various positive or negative rewards, which along with other factors, influence job satisfaction. Within each individual there exists an effort/satisfaction ratio that reflects the equitable balance of effort expended and rewards received. Correspondingly, the organization has an implicit effort/pay ratio (a fair day's work for a fair day's pay). These two ratios combine with other factors to determine the functional effort the worker brings to the job.

The factor interaction block in Figure 5-4 indicates that the functional effort of individuals is a complex phenomenon representing more than a simple addition of the levels of factors that are direct inputs to the individual. It is some function of the effort/satisfaction and effort/pay ratios, the individual's personal goals and general level of energy, and work-related elements (e.g., working conditions and supervisory methods). Also, different levels of performance elicit reactions within the individual and among coworkers that may encourage or retard future efforts, and that becomes part of the factor interaction.

The mental and physical energy of the worker can be directed to making suggestions for improving the process (methods change effort), moderated by organizational systems (e.g., suggestion programs), or it can be directed toward functional effort. In routine, repetitive jobs, some worker effort may be directed to impact-modifying behavior to relieve boredom. These actions may be nonproductive (e.g., taking unauthorized breaks), or antiproductive, (e.g., stopping an assembly line or damaging equipment). Impact-modifying behavior is moderated by the degree of contention in management-labor relations.

The organization's selection of capital, level of technology, and job design combines with the worker's abilities and skills to establish the attainable performance level or potential productivity of the job. The functional effort of the worker, in simplest terms, determines the degree to which the potential is realized in actual performance.

Summary

The Servosystem model is intended to provide a theoretical foundation for understanding and analyzing worker performance. Because of the complex interactions represented by the variables and relationships in the model, it may never be totally validated, nor is it likely that "the formula" for the factor interaction block will ever be expressed as an equation. The model does provide, however, a conceptual framework for organizing current knowledge and directing research efforts toward understanding individual productivity.

WHEN INDIVIDUALS BECOME GROUPS

Four considerations are key when combining measures of individual productivity into evaluations of group or team performance and, ultimately, organizational performance. The considerations are (1) the complexity of group analysis, (2) differing inputs included at the individual and group levels, (3) problems of aggregation, and (4) the need to align measures with goals.

Complexity

As workers are formed into groups (independent members) or teams (interdependent members), the factors affecting productivity become more complex. Even in groups of workers who are loosely connected, group dynamics begin to affect performance both negatively and positively; in interdependent teams those forces are intensified. Bottlenecks, unbalanced work loads, inability to cooperate, feelings of inequity, and the "committee phenomenon" (in which all members gravitate to the average) are just a few of the detrimental effects that can emerge.

Conversely, teamwork can have positive, synergistic effects through cooperation, mutual stimulation, combined skill and capability, support, and mentoring. Some tasks can be performed only by a cooperating team, in which case individual contributions are obscured. For other tasks, work is divided and assigned to team or group members by matching the difficulty of the work with the seniority of the member. Under any circumstances, the group level of analysis involves all of the influencing variables of the individual level of analysis plus the variables associated with group dynamics. Much research has been done on the behavior of individuals within work groups, but often the dependent variables include effectiveness, performance, goal achievement, satisfaction, output, or other measures that may or may not be clearly defined. It is difficult to review these studies to determine if the findings relate to the productivity of the group as it would be measured in an output to input ratio.

Input Factors

At the individual level of work, the primary focus is on labor input; it is difficult, sometimes impossible, to identify all the other inputs (material, capital, and energy) associated with a specific job. At the organizational level, total productivity measurement systems demand that all inputs be considered. In between (in work groups, departments, divisions, and so on), the other factors of production may or may not be considered in the measurements as circumstances dictate. The fundamental differences between total and partial measures of productivity reduce the ability of decision makers to plan and control operations across levels. Researchers experience similar barriers in attempting to design studies in which individual productivity rates can be aggregated to form measures of the productivity of work groups or business units.

At higher levels of analysis, such as departments within an organization, interactions among business units become relevant and the very concept of productivity becomes more complex. For example, the purchasing department may be very productive in its use of resources to buy raw materials, according to the measures applied. However, if the materials purchased do not meet specifications or arrive late, the productivity of the fabrication department may be severely affected. Few productivity measurement systems in place today would capture both the productivity of the purchasing department (i.e., internal productivity) and the contributions (positive or negative) of the purchasing department to the rest of the organization (i.e., external productivity). Conceptual research on organizational theory could be reframed in a productivity context to help explain the effects of the many intraorganizational relationships on the aggregation of productivity data from the individual to the organizational level.

Aggregation

Individual measures of productivity can be summed to form group productivity data only if the group members are working at independent, parallel jobs. Such is seldom the case, however. To the extent that the members of the group are interdependent or performing different tasks, aggregation of the measures is problematic. It may make more sense to identify the inputs and outputs of the group, which may be different from the inputs and outputs of any individual, and form a unique measure for evaluating group productivity.

Although unique group measures are feasible and useful, they may lead to discontinuities. If individual productivity rates are high but group productivity is low, explanations are difficult to derive, and managerial control becomes an onerous task. The problem is most likely based in the incompatibility of the measures used at different levels of analysis, but it is also possible that group dysfunctions and interferences are influencing factors. Research on the development of internally consistent measurement systems is needed to supplement and clarify existing knowledge of work behavior and interactions within groups. A first step in this direction is taken in the section below on productivity linkages, which outlines seven possible types of linkages that should be considered before attempting to aggregate measurement data.

Goal Alignment

As noted above, measures of individual productivity or other dimensions of performance should be selected to align behaviors with organizational goals. The same should be true of business units (e.g., departments and divisions) within the organization. Strategic planning involves ensuring that the goals at one level of the organization are consistent with those at each higher level so that the elements of the organization do not work at cross-purposes. An ideal productivity measurement system for an organization would align individual behaviors with group and organizational goals.

WORK GROUP STRUCTURES AND PRODUCTIVITY LINKAGES

As discussed above, the aggregation of productivity measures is one of the major considerations in the study of the relationships among individual, group, and organizational productivity. If the mathematics of aggregation is ever to be determined, the nature of the linkages within the work group must be identified and classified.

Types of Work Group Structures

McGrath's (1984) comprehensive work on the interaction and performance of groups provides many insights as to why the output of the group may not be a simple summation of the output of the members. In his review of Steiner's (1966, 1972) work, McGrath stated:

[Steiner] notes that groups seldom perform up to the level of their best member. Often, the quality or quantity of their performance is about what the second best member's ability would predict. Steiner considers the combined abilities of individual members—combined according to whatever rule is suitable for that type of task, disjunctive, conjunctive, or additive—as representing the group's potential productivity. Actual *group productivity, he argues, falls below potential productivity because of "process losses," losses incurred in the process of performing the task. He identifies two main types of process losses: motivation losses (or, potentially, gains) and coordination losses (p. 58, emphasis in original).*

Much of the work of McGrath and others he cites has dealt with the type of task or the interaction of the group with the type of task to be performed. McGrath classified tasks into eight basic types: planning tasks, creative tasks, intellective tasks, decision-making tasks, cognitive conflict tasks, mixed-motive tasks, conflicts/battles, and performances. He then related the types of tasks to the conceptual or behavioral skills needed for task accomplishment and the conflict or cooperation required within the group.

Separate from the type of task assigned to the work group, however, is the structure of the group itself. *Structure* refers to the roles that each member of the group plays and the way in which the elements of the task are assigned to the members of the group, that is, the organization of the work within the group. Attempts to aggregate individual measures of productivity meet with varying degrees of success depending on the structure and relationship of the workers in the group. Different structures create different linkages between individual and group productivity, and those linkages must be recognized in the aggregation process.

A simple example illustrates alternative structures for the accomplishment of a given task. Imagine a bucket brigade composed of five members whose objective is to transfer water from vat A to vat B. In the classic bucket brigade, team member 1 dips from vat A and passes the bucket through successive stationary members to member 5, who empties the bucket into vat B. (Assume that there is an unlimited number of buckets or that empty buckets can be tossed back to member 1.) With this structure, the productivity of the group is dependent on the slowest member, and if anyone on the team stops, the entire process stops.

An alternative structure would be to assign each member the job of dipping from vat A, walking with the full bucket to vat B to empty it, and then returning to vat A with the empty bucket. In this case, the team members are decoupled (they become a cooperating group rather than an interdependent team) so that a change in the productivity of one member does not affect the productivity of the others directly (indirect effects on the motivation of the others may occur). The productivity of the group is the simple summation of the productivity of the members.

Consider one other alternative structure: Team member 1 dips from vat A and sets full buckets on the ground. Team members 2, 3, and 4 pick up the buckets two at a time and carry them to a staging area near vat B, where they leave them and pick up two empty buckets for the return trip. The job of team member 5 is to pour the water from the full buckets into vat B. In this structure, performance of the team members is not as inexorably linked as in the first structure, but it is not as independent as in the second. The productivity of the group is dependent partly on the productivity of each member but also on the proper balance of the three different jobs of dipping, carrying, and emptying.

Several conclusions follow from these examples:

1. Many alternative structures exist for the accomplishment of a given group task.

2. The structure of the group creates linkages from individual productivity to the productivity of the group that determine the effect of changes in one member's output on total group output.

3. Productivity measures at the individual level concentrate on the number of repetitions of a job within a time period (number of buckets passed per hour). At the group level, measures focus on task accomplishment (amount of water transferred from vat A to vat B) and on the total resources used (number of person hours *and* number of buckets used). (Note that each of the three structures used as examples above requires a different number of buckets.)

In an effort to help explain the relationship of group structure to productivity linkages, in the next section I identify seven basic types of linkages. In practice, many combinations of the basic types of linkages are possible and lead to a large number of variations.

Types of Productivity Linkages

Direct

The simplest, but perhaps least common form of work group structure is one that is directly linked, that is, an increase or decrease in the productivity of one individual has an immediate and corresponding effect on the productivity of the group. This can happen when the work group is essentially a composite of independent workers considered as a collective. Examples include salesmen, postal carriers, some maintenance personnel, and others who can determine their own pace and are essentially independent of intraorganizational influences.

Indirect

Often, some members of a work group do not create the group's output directly (the accounting classification of "indirect labor" may or may not apply, depending on the level and unit of analysis). For example, a team formed to create computer software may be composed of six programmers, two clerical support personnel, and a project manager. The productivity of the programmers is directly linked to the output of the team, but the effect of the clerical personnel and the project manager is indirect, albeit necessary and important.

Proportional

In many instances, an increase in the productivity of one member of a work group will have an amplified or dampened effect on the productivity of the group. For example, in a competitive atmosphere, a productivity increase by one member may spur others to higher levels of performance. Conversely, a drop in productivity by one member may make the job of the other members more difficult by creating an imbalance in the work load.

Unidirectional

Sometimes, a change in the productivity of one member affects the productivity of the group in only one direction of change. For example, in an assembly line or any directly interdependent work team, an increase in productivity of one member may have the effect of creating additional idle time for that worker but have no effect on the output rate of the group. A decrease in productivity by that worker, however, could create a bottleneck that directly lowers the productivity of the entire group.

Temporal

The effect of the change in productivity of one worker may be realized in the productivity of the group or organization only after a time delay. For example, a decrease change in productivity of a worker creating a component of a composite product (such as an automobile or computer software) may not be felt until the stage in the process when the complete product cannot be assembled because of a shortage of that component.

Stochastic

Some work groups are loosely coupled and the degree of interdependence among the members varies. In this circumstance, and perhaps in many others, the effect on the group from the change in productivity of one worker can be estimated only in a probabilistic relationship. For example, in a construction crew, one member's increase in productivity may have little or no effect on group performance in one instance, and a direct or even amplified effect in another instance, depending on the nature of the task.

Nominal

To make the classification complete, the case of "no effect" must be included. Many jobs within a group or organization are necessary but have no direct effect on the measurable output of the unit; they enable the direct workers to be productive. Security, custodial services, and food services are examples of such jobs. For each of these jobs (security, for example), the productivity of the workers can be measured, but the linkage to organizational productivity is difficult, if not impossible, to establish.

RESEARCH NEEDS

Despite the widespread use of productivity measurement systems in all types of organizations today, many unresolved problems remain. In this section I discuss a number of the important problems in order to stimulate further study of ways to reduce the adverse effects of these problems on the measurement of individual productivity.

Determining the Unit of Output

Ideally, the output being measured should be physical units of a valued finished product. For some standardized manufacturing operations, counting the units produced approaches this ideal. For most jobs, however, problems of combining dissimilar outputs and identifying intangible outputs arise.

Dissimilar outputs can be combined by using a common surrogate unit or through some form of weighting. Beech Aircraft, for example, aggregates across different types of airplanes by using tons of aircraft produced. As strange as this may sound, the company found that, generally, a plane that weighed twice what another plane weighed was more complex and took twice as many resources to produce (personal communication between author and Beech Aircraft executives). In many instances, this same reasoning can be applied to individual production jobs.

Programming operations, in an effort to get away from counting lines of code, have experimented with "function points" (i.e., number of functions performed within a program) as a measure of output. Computer manufacturers may use units of computing capacity produced to enable them to aggregate large and small systems delivered. If engineered standards are available, total production expressed in standard hours is a legitimate measure of output, no more or less accurate than the standards used. Price weighting, using discounted prices, may be the most common form of combining dissimilar outputs.

Identifying intangible outputs common to many white-collar and service jobs requires ingenuity and a clear knowledge of objectives and process parameters. Transactions completed, customers served, and reports processed are common measures in these circumstances. Often, the measures of output are unique to the particular job, as in briefs filed, claims processed, or copy machines cleaned. Knowledge work, such as supervision, management, R&D, and consulting, presents special problems in measuring output. Although some progress has been made in this area, much productivity measurement research remains to be done to develop relevant measures of output for nonmanufacturing applications.

Determining the Unit of Input

Individual jobs require labor, material, capital, and energy. As noted above, however, at the individual level of analysis the focus is generally on the labor component. Energy is seldom associated with an individual job because of the difficulty of identifying energy use for a particular operation. Capital and material may be ascribed to the individual level (as in units produced per machine-hour or per pound of raw material) if the capital and material are dedicated to the individual job and are under the control of the operator. Mainly, the unit-of-input problem centers on the appropriate way to measure labor.

Labor can be measured in physical terms as hours worked, hours at work (includes breaks, for example), or hours paid (including vacations, holidays, and time off), depending on the purpose and the time horizon of the measurement system. Like outputs, labor inputs can be weighted by their discounted wage rates to reflect the different skill levels of workers and to permit aggregation.

Limiting individual productivity measures to the labor input is commonly accepted. However, it must be understood that the productivity of labor can be profoundly influenced by changes in capital, material, or energy, which are not captured by the measure. Research using only labor productivity as a dependent variable should establish controls for possible effects on productivity of other factors of production.

Productivity Versus Quality

The productivity-quality debate often stems from definitions of the two terms. If *quality* is defined in its broadest sense as meeting or exceeding customer expectations, then a document printed on a laser printer is of higher quality than one printed on a dot matrix printer even though both documents are error free. An alternative definition of quality, meeting technical specifications, would count errors in the document as defects but would consider the laser-printed document as a completely different product from the one printed on a dot matrix printer. The productivity paradox in information systems may derive to a great extent from this point. The investment in information technology may not increase the quantity of documents produced (it may, in fact, greatly reduce it), but the quality (in both meanings of the term) of the information may have been improved greatly. If the information is more timely, more accurate, and in a more meaningful and usable form, has productivity increased? Resolution of this debate will depend on better definitions and measures of output that take into account changes in customer expectations for quality.

If quality is limited to the definition of meeting technical specifications, the idea that improved productivity is achieved only at the expense of reduced quality is a misconception. First, the definition of productivity and its associated measures must reflect the production of acceptable products and services meeting all quality specifications. Reduced quality, therefore, would automatically reduce productivity. Second, reduced quality leads to returns, scrap, rework, and production disruptions, all of which consume resources without producing valued outputs. Elimination of the causes of defective products and services releases resources for more productive uses.

Although this idea is now well understood, industry's measures of productivity at the individual level seldom contain a quality component. As firms accept quality as a higher priority and redesign jobs to include quality checks, this problem will be relieved somewhat. But many individual productivity measurement systems should be revised to account for defects that are produced but not detected until later in the process.

The controls afforded the researcher in the design and conduct of experiments permit the development of productivity measures that systematically account for quality variations on a number of dimensions. Omission of quality as an integral part of productivity measurement is a serious flaw in the research design.

Productivity Versus Performance

At the individual level, productivity measurement tracks how well the worker applies talents and skills, using materials and equipment, to produce products and services within a specified time period. Although this is fundamental to success, it is not total performance. If the design of the jobs, the measurement systems, and the evaluation and reward systems are not aligned with the corporate strategy and reinforced at all levels of management, productivity is hollow. It is at best efficient, but it may also be inconsistent with the overall direction of the organization and therefore useless in the long run.

Even if jobs are properly aligned with organizational strategies, counterproductive behaviors by workers, such as poor attendance, tardiness, unauthorized breaks, socializing, and performing personal work, may not be captured by a particular productivity measure. Absenteeism, for example, may not be counted as an input even though the firm pays for the hours missed.

On the positive side, however, every employee has the opportunity to make contributions to the organization that may be recognized only by observation. Workers may make suggestions for improvement or may be exceptionally effective at satisfying customers in direct contact positions, yet those contributions may not be reflected in the productivity measure. "Has a positive influence on fellow employees" and "has an outstanding record of problem solving" are examples of factors that should be recognized over and above basic productivity.

Productivity research should take these basic differences into account. At the very least, the research study should clearly delineate between measures of productivity and measures of performance rather than using the terms as vague synonyms.

Productivity Measures Versus Financial Measures

At the organizational level, a firm may be highly productive but fail because of its inability to manage prices, costs, cash flows, and debt. A firm, therefore, will track many aspects of performance besides total firm productivity.

At the individual level, however, the emphasis usually is on productivity and cost per unit produced. Currently, a major thrust in cost accounting research is attempting to revise methods for assigning overhead costs to products and services produced (Cooper and Kaplan, 1991). These efforts may make the connection between productivity and cost more compatible and more meaningful at the individual level of analysis. Productivity researchers, however, should continue their efforts to develop individual-level productivity measurement systems that can be integrated with these new developments in unit cost analysis.

Measurement Error

No measurement system is perfect; a variance between actual and measured results will likely always exist. The variance can be reduced, however, by reducing simple errors (not counting correctly), reducing conceptual errors (not counting the right things), checking the reliability and validity of surrogate measures, and verifying the logic of using pseudoproductivity measures (such as measuring activities as an indicator of results).

Two dangers arise in attempting to reduce measurement errors, however. First, by trying to meet all criteria, the measurement system may become so complex that it loses its practicality. Second, the near-perfect measurement system may generate such high demands for data gathering and analysis that the cost of the system is not justified and the results are not timely enough to be useful. Although reducing measurement error should be a continuing goal, a compromise between this goal and the usability of the measure is generally in order.

Misuse of Measures

Much has been written about developing systems for measuring individual productivity; less has been said about how the results of the measures are to be used. A number of the considerations raised in this section imply misuses of productivity data, such as measuring a worker for factors outside his or her control. Other common misuses include using the results as a whip to speed the pace of work or to place blame on a worker for poor performance. Unfair comparisons, such as using the same measure under vastly different circumstances, can also cause problems.

Research into the development of a system for measuring individual productivity should not stop when the system is implemented. The integration of productivity measures with other measures of performance should be documented, and the effective and ineffective uses of productivity data should be explored.

CONCLUSION

The challenge before researchers and practitioners is to develop internally consistent and comprehensive productivity measurement systems that account for the productivity of individual workers, work groups, business units, and organizations. The degree to which this goal can be achieved will determine the ability of organizations to manage resources effectively and direct human effort toward organizational goals. It may help them regain the industrial leadership they have lost and understand the apparent paradoxes that ensue when expected productivity gains are not realized. Consistent productivity measurement systems will enable researchers and practitioners to speak a common language as they each play their role in solving the problems associated with poor productivity growth.

The difficulty in developing a comprehensive productivity measurement system stems from a number of factors, in particular the following:

• The concept of productivity is still often misunderstood; discussions of the relationship of productivity to effectiveness, efficiency, quality, innovation, and financial or behavioral measures of performance take the form of debates. A common definition of productivity, at all levels of organizational analysis, is a prerequisite for the development of a comprehensive measurement system.

• Attempts to aggregate individual productivity measures or to disaggregate organizational measures are thwarted by the dissimilarity in measures of output. At the individual level, output is often counted in physical units of product produced or service provided. At higher levels of analysis, different outputs from different sources are combined in some form of weighting scheme, sometimes using cost or price data that are incompatible with financial measures at the individual level, given current cost accounting methods.

• On the input side of the productivity ratio, individual productivity is often measured only against labor input, and labor may be counted in a number of different, but acceptable, ways. At the organizational level, a total factor approach is often used, that is, inputs consist of labor, materials, capital, and energy.

• In most organizations today, the amount of indirect or managerial work far exceeds the direct labor associated with producing products and services. The productivity of indirect labor and, to a lesser extent, managerial efforts can be measured in terms of results achieved and resources consumed. Often, however, the contribution of these activities to the productivity of the organization is unclear. If the organization was evaluated strictly by the value of products produced relative to inputs, it would have, for example, no training function; but such myopic views would never be accepted by the enlightened manager. Current productivity measurement systems suffer from an inability to capture and integrate the contribution of indirect functions, such as training, into the productivity equation for the organization.

• When individuals are formed into work groups or teams, linkages are formed between the effort of the individual and the output of the group. The nature of the linkage is dependent on the structure of the group, characteristics of the individuals, psychological factors, sociological factors, technological variables, and system variables. The complex interactions that take place in cooperative productive behavior, however, are seldom captured in common productivity measurement systems. In their efforts to understand and control work group behavior, managers and researchers alike are hampered by inadequate measurement systems.

Progress toward the goal of developing internally consistent and comprehensive productivity measurement systems will require a joint effort between practitioners and researchers. Greater understanding of the concept of productivity, common definitions of terms, and the building of conceptual models of productivity provide the requisite framework to develop and refine productivity measures. Better productivity measurement will help to organize and unify the building of a common body of knowledge on productive behavior.

REFERENCES

Cooper, R., and R.S. Kaplan
    1991   Profit priorities from activity-based costing. *Harvard Business Review* 69:130-135.
Forrester, J.W.
    1961   *Industrial Dynamics*. Cambridge, Mass.: The MIT Press.

Hershauer, J.C., and W.A. Ruch
  1978   A worker productivity model and its use at Lincoln Electric. *Interfaces* 8:80-
          89.
Lawler, E.E.
  1971   *Pay and Organizational Effectiveness: A Psychological View.* New York:
          McGraw-Hill.
McGrath, J.E
  1984   *Groups: Interaction and Performance.* Englewood Cliffs, N.J.: Prentice-Hall.
Ruch, W.A., and J.C. Hershauer
  1974   *Factors Affecting Worker Productivity.* Tempe: Arizona State University.
Steiner, I.D.
  1966   Models for inferring relationships between group size and potential group pro-
          ductivity. *Behavioral Science* 11:273.
  1972   Evils of research—or what my mother didn't tell me about sins of academia.
          American Psychologist 27:766.
Sutermeister, R.A.
  1969   *People and Productivity*, 2d ed. New York: McGraw-Hill.
Werther, W.B., Jr., W.A. Ruch, and L. McClure
  1986   *Productivity Through People.* St. Paul, Minn.: West Publishing.

6

The Influence of Organizational Linkages and Measurement Practices on Productivity and Management

D. Scott Sink and George L. Smith, Jr.

There are at least three world views regarding the productivity paradox:

1. There is no paradox. Information technology (IT) and other improvement interventions are improving performance. Researchers and practitioners simply cannot measure the improvement.
2. There is a problem but not a paradox. Improvement initiatives are not being driven by rationality or profound knowledge (defined below). They are more like random-walk processes, initiated on the basis of what is in vogue or what is easily available, not on the basis of what makes sense or will work best. Thus, the problem is not necessarily with measurement but with the quality of decision making.
3. There is a paradox, and addressing it is confounded by the lack of systems thinking, lack of profound knowledge, and inadequate measurement methodology.

We believe the third view is the most accurate.

The productivity paradox has a threefold nature. It is a measurement problem, a management and decision-making problem, and a combined problem of strategy, action, and measurement. In this chapter we present a conceptual model that portrays the organization, its management system, and the planning process in a way we hope will stimulate a thorough reexamination of managerial planning and decision making and some of the fundamental notions regarding performance. We explore the relationship of the measurement function to performance at the individual, group, and organizational levels in a way that integrates measurement, planning, and managing the organization. We also discuss research issues associated with the use of measurement to support improvement and to address linkage questions. The alignment of strategies, actions, and measures is a key theme in this chapter.[1]

LINKAGES AND PROFOUND KNOWLEDGE

Many organizational improvements are undertaken without knowledge of cause-and-effect relationships. Some are undertaken because they are the "in" thing to do; others are undertaken because they are believed to be the "right" thing to do. Some improvements, however, are initiated based on evidence that they will improve performance. Sometimes the interventions do improve the performance of certain subsystems, but the improvement cannot be tracked either horizontally or at higher levels of the organization. One expects that the interventions will cause a change in performance because there are linkages among entities within levels as well as between levels of the organization.

Deming (1986, 1991) and Goldratt (Goldratt and Cox, 1986; Goldratt and Fox, 1986) provide good examples of how failure to understand linkages can lead to interventions at one level having neutral or negative outcomes, particularly at the level of the macro system. Defining specifically what linkages are expected is critical in developing a performance measurement methodology. Much evaluation research simplistically assumes that an improvement at one organizational level will automatically cause an improvement at another level. Linkages are far more complex, however. Implementing an intervention in a given entity can cause multiple dimensions of performance to improve within the entity itself and, then, in other entities through linkages.

Deming (1986, 1991) suggests that making an improvement intervention in one entity and projecting positive performance linkages at

---

[1]We would like to express our appreciation to sponsors and collaborators of the Virginia Productivity Center (VPC) for continuing support of this research and development. This chapter was prepared in part with funds from a Virginia Productivity Center Internal R&D Grant 438566 focusing on the Organization of the Future. In particular, National Grocers of Canada; RHODIA, S.A.; Naval Aviation Depot, North Island; Department of Energy, Office of New Production Reactors; Norfolk Naval Shipyard; and Naval Sea Systems Commands 05, 06, and 07 have supported our R&D in the area of planning and measurement through grants and contracts.

the next higher level or within other entities at the same level require profound knowledge. He describes profound knowledge as comprising theory of systems, theory of variation, theory of psychology, and theory of knowledge. It is the blending of wisdom, experience, conceptual and operational understanding, skill, and judgment. We would add that it also includes understanding the organizational system and well-founded beliefs concerning cause-and-effect relationships. This is the crux of the paradox, in our opinion. Many managers involved in performance improvement do not have profound knowledge. Often, improvement interventions are implemented not with the aim of optimizing the larger system's performance, but rather with the aim of maximizing the performance of an individual or a subsystem. It can be argued that lack of systems thinking is at the heart of the productivity paradox.

A SYSTEMS MODEL OF ORGANIZATIONAL PERFORMANCE

A management system comprises three elements: who manages, what is managed, and how managing is done (i.e., the "tools" and methods used to convert data to information). An organizational system is a component of a management system; it is "what" is being managed. An organizational system has upstream systems (suppliers, vendors, other providers); inputs (labor, capital, energy, materials, and information and data); value-adding processes; outputs (goods and/or services); downstream systems (customers); outcomes (profits, customer satisfaction); and up-line systems (parent organizations, hierarchically superior systems). The Management Systems model shown as Figure 6-1, which was adapted from Kurstedt (1986) and Sink and Tuttle (1989), depicts a systems view of an organizational system.

The management team (i.e., "who" does the managing) makes decisions and takes actions aimed at improving the performance of the organizational system. Performance is multidimensional, and ambiguity and inconsistency regarding the criteria for measuring are major problems common to researchers and practitioners involved with the measurement of organizational performance. Operational definitions, which express the performance criteria in measurable terms, are sorely lacking in the literature and in practice. Thus, confusion reigns in the field of measurement as it relates to organizations. Less confusion exists regarding individual-level performance because industrial psychologists have established more specificity in the terminology used. Nonetheless, considerable variance exists among disciplines such as industrial engineering, industrial sociology, industrial psychology, organizational behavior, and human factors engineering when it comes to measurement terminology.

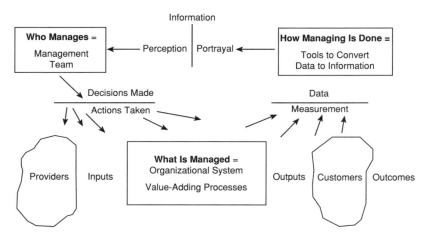

FIGURE 6-1 The Management Systems model. SOURCE: Adapted from Kurstedt (1986); Sink and Tuttle (1989).

In the absence of accepted operational definitions of performance and its components, the task of measuring and evaluating improvement is difficult. Researchers and practitioners become "wrapped around the axle" because there is no agreed language of performance measurement. They operationalize performance criteria differently because they have not grasped the fundamentals. Yet their hypotheses regarding what will actually improve if an intervention is made (e.g., IT) are crucial to understanding the productivity paradox.

Our ongoing and recently updated review of the literature (in preparation) confirms that there are at least seven interrelated and interdependent performance criteria for an organizational system: (1) effectiveness, (2) efficiency, (3) productivity, (4) quality, (5) quality of work life, (6) innovation, and (7) profitability (profit center) or budgetability (cost center). These seven criteria are substantially inclusive but not necessarily mutually exclusive. They represent level zero in a measurement-breakdown structure. An intervention to improve the performance of an entity may be expected to improve one or more of the seven basic criteria. For example, is it reasonable to expect that a specific IT intervention will increase productivity (output/input), or might it be more reasonable to expect that it will improve the quality of the output, which may be difficult to discern in measurements of productivity? Below we define each of the seven performance criteria. Their integration in the Management Systems model is depicted in Figure 6-2.

As seen in Figure 6-2, *effectiveness* focuses on the output side of an organizational system. An example of an indicator of effectiveness is

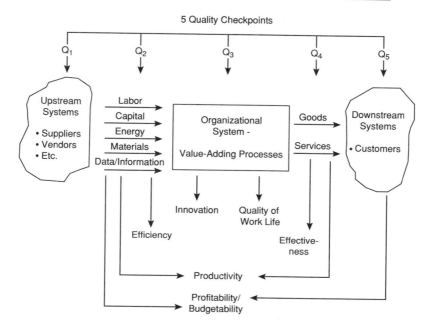

FIGURE 6-2 The Management Systems model integrating quality checkpoints and performance criteria. SOURCE: Adapted from Kurstedt (1986); Sink and Tuttle (1989).

actual output versus expected output. Attributes commonly used to refine the effectiveness criterion are timeliness, quality, quantity, and price/cost (i.e., value). An example of an operational definition is *accomplishment of the right things on time, within specifications or expectations*. The word *right* highlights the fact that effectiveness often incorporates elements of judgment, uncertainty, and risk.

Efficiency focuses on the input side of an organizational system. An indicator of efficiency would be resources actually consumed versus resources expected to be consumed. The same four attributes of timeliness, quality, quantity, and cost/price are often used to refine the measurement of efficiency.

Quality is pervasive throughout the organizational system. One can stop short of a thorough operational definition of quality by espousing the overly simplistic but often-cited adages "quality is conformance to requirements" and "quality is making the customer happy." However, one can do business with an operational definition (Deming, 1986). It is a definition from which one can measure. Assigning a number to each element of the Management Systems model shown in Figure 6-1 yields five quality checkpoints (see Figure 6-2). Quality checkpoint 1 (q1) is the selection and management of upstream provider systems; quality checkpoint 2 (q2) is incoming quality assurance; quality checkpoint 3 (q3) is in-process quality management; quality checkpoint 4 (q4) is outgoing quality assurance; and quality checkpoint 5 (q5) is proactive and reactive assurance that the organizational system is meeting or exceeding customer needs, requirements, expectations, specifications, and desires (perhaps even including understanding the customer's latent quality desires). These definitions, at the checkpoint level of specificity, get one closer to an understanding of total quality. The extent to which an organizational system is measuring and managing the performance of quality at each of the five checkpoints, over time, is an indication of whether total quality is being managed. This is not circular reasoning; it is the application of systems thinking to quality management.

Productivity is the relationship between what comes out of the organizational system and what is consumed to create those outputs. It is a set of ratios and indices comparing output to input. Taking a static, snapshot approach to measuring productivity yields ratios that can be analyzed over time (e.g., a run chart). Taking the dynamic approach yields indices (ratios over ratios) that provide rate-of-change information. The definition of productivity is one of the simplest of the seven criteria; operationalizing it is the difficult part. The problem most researchers and practitioners have with measuring productivity is that of capturing all the outputs of an organizational system (inputs are relatively easier to capture). People often allow their emotional and intuitive understanding of productivity to cloud their attempts to measure this criterion.

Quality of work life is the affective response of the people in the organizational system to any number of factors, such as their job, pay, benefits, working conditions, coworkers, supervisors, culture, autonomy, and skill variation. Measuring quality of work life suggests that one must measure these affective responses and evaluate changes in them over time. Standard instruments have been devised to do this. However, surrogate indicators, such as turnover and absenteeism, are often used as correlates of quality of work life.

Innovation is the reactive, proactive, creative, and successful response to changes (perceived or otherwise) in the internal and external environments of an organizational system. Innovation can include problem solving or opportunity capturing. The linkage issue is particularly salient for this aspect of performance. Organizations in the United States have traditionally attempted to encourage innovation largely through individual-based suggestion systems. World-class organizations, however, have developed group processes for sparking quality proposals for improvement. Today, world-class organizations monitor the quantity and quality of team-generated proposals that are developed and implemented. Team-based processes build quality in, reduce reject rates, improve motivation, make sustaining the process of employee involvement in innovation and improvement easier, and yield much higher payoffs. The U.S. levels of performance in this area pale by world-class standards: 1 to 2 proposals per employee per year with a 10 to 50 percent implementation rate versus 40 to 50 proposals per individual/team per year with an 80 to 90 percent implementation rate. By *world class* we mean best of best, best in class, highest level of performance for a given system or process regardless of industry. Clearly, there are world-class performances in North America; however, in key industries and for key processes and systems and at an aggregate level, North American business and industry have clearly been faltering over the past 30 years (Grayson and O'Dell, 1988; Kottler et al., 1985). This is clearly a linkage issue relative to individual- and group-focused performance improvement processes. Historically, U.S. managers have had difficulty in distinguishing between situations in which groups are appropriate and situations in which an individual approach is more applicable. The result has been weakened linkages among individual, group, and organizational performance (Kanter, 1983; Kanter et al, 1992; Lawler, 1986; Mohrman et al., 1989; Weisbord, 1991).

Profitability (relevant for profit-center organizational systems) measures the relationship between revenues and costs. An analogous criterion, *budgetability* (relevant for cost-center organizational systems), measures the relationship between what the organizational system said it would do and the cost, and what it did and the actual cost.

Figure 6-3 portrays the relationships among the seven criteria. The model is conceptual and provides only rough-order relationships. The approach we advocate is to consider these seven criteria as variables that explain variation in performance. One might benefit from being able to pull certain variables in and out of an analysis to see which ones explain variation in performance for a given organizational system, much as one would do in a multiple regression analysis. In defining and understanding each of the seven criteria, one might attempt to "partial out," as in a stepwise regression analysis, the other six. Lacking precise tools, this is difficult to do. However, once all seven criteria have been defined and are understood individually, the seven together can be used to examine linkage effects.

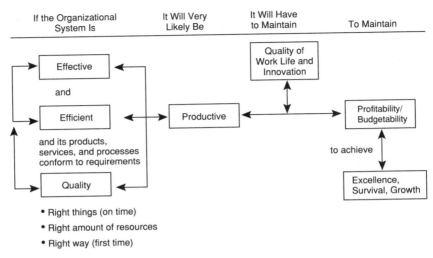

FIGURE 6-3 A conceptual model of the relationships among performance criteria. SOURCE: Sink (1993).

MEASUREMENT, LINKAGES, AND MANAGING ORGANIZATIONAL PERFORMANCE: FOUR GUIDELINES

A management team makes decisions and takes actions aimed at (1) ensuring that the organizational system performs, (2) ensuring that the organizational system continually improves its performance, and (3) responding to problems and crises. To ascertain whether its decisions and actions are working, the management team measures for the purpose of obtaining selected data. Those data are then converted into information, which is portrayed and perceived by the management team.[2] The management team formulates or reformulates decisions and ac-

---

[2]By *portrayal*, we mean the manner in which data are presented to a user. Examples of different portrayals would be tables, run charts, histograms, bar charts, and spreadsheets. By *perception*, we mean the process by which users convert data to information, that is, what they perceive to be the information content in portrayed data. A little is known about how cognitive styles influence the portrayal-to-perception interface; for example, the Myers-Briggs Type Indicator provides insights into how users prefer to collect data (sensory versus intuition) and how they prefer to process data (thinking versus feeling; Benfari, 1991). Visible management systems are currently popular for operationalizing the interface between informational portrayal and information perception and for supporting decisions and actions aimed at improving performance (Akao, 1991; Greif, 1989).

tions based on this feedback. We address this cycle, known as the improvement cycle, or the PDCA cycle (plan, do, check, act; see Deming, 1986; Shewhart, 1939), in more detail later in this chapter.

The transformation of performance data into management information requires an understanding of the linkages that relate the activities of individuals, groups, and the organization as a whole. In the process of identifying and then modeling those linkages, one must pay particular attention to the way in which performance is measured and productivity is assessed at the different levels of the organizational hierarchy. The literature and our own experience suggest the following four guidelines for constructing performance measurement systems for organizations. Each of the guidelines is examined in turn below.

1.   An organization's system of performance and productivity measures should be designed to support and complement the organization's mission and objectives. Strategies, actions, and measures should be aligned.

2.   The system of performance measures should reflect the differing needs and perspectives of managers and leaders at various levels of the organization. Measurement systems should be user driven.

3.   Measures of performance should be flexible and dynamic in light of changes within the organization and its operating environment.

4.   Reliance on traditional performance and productivity measures can be problematic because they are unlikely to provide all the information needed to model the relationships across organizational levels, or even to assess organizational performance and productivity completely.

Guideline 1: The Measurement System Should Support the Organization's Mission and Objectives

In the preface to their book *The New Performance Challenge*, Dixon et al. (1990:5) state, "The goal is to achieve better alignment among the organization's strategies, actions, and measures." The alignment sought by Dixon et al. is especially critical because an organization involves, first and foremost, the coordinated actions of individuals and groups. Understanding the effect measurement has on individuals and groups can provide the organization with a powerful key to unlocking the performance and productivity of sociotechnical systems. The mechanism that controls this effect is contained in the principles of behavior modification.

Measuring performance has a dual effect. According to the principles of behavior modification, measurement not only generates data regarding individual or group performance on a particular task, it can also help to modify the performance that is being measured. Powerful motivation can be provided by feedback on one's performance, often referred to as knowledge of results (KOR). Feedback is one of the five core job dimensions in job characteristics theory (Hackman and Oldham, 1976). Measuring and feeding back the results of positively regarded behavior can increase its frequency of occurrence, and measuring and reporting unacceptable behavior can decrease its frequency of occurrence (Fitts and Posner, 1968:26-31).

Designers and users of management information systems must realize that performance measures provide KOR and must take positive action to take advantage of their effects. Regardless of whether they do or not, the effects will be present, and the results can be disastrous if inappropriate KOR is given. For example, designers and users of management information systems typically focus their attention on generating business or financial information. But in doing so, their exclusive view is that these measures of performance and productivity are the raw data from which decision makers extract the information needed to perform managerial functions. They ignore the behavioral consequences that accompany measurement. As organizations become more willing to locate operational and tactical decision making closer to the point of production, an interesting phenomenon appears. In an empowered work group, the user of performance data is often also the one whose performance is being measured and portrayed. To the extent that the system of measurement simultaneously reflects and reinforces the personal goals of the individual workers and the operational and tactical objectives of the organization, the system generates data for decisions and motivates individual or work group effectiveness (i.e., the accomplishment of unit objectives) (Akao, 1991; Dixon et al., 1990; Hall et al., 1991; Mali, 1978; Sink and Tuttle, 1989:143-152). When the measurement system is not designed in a way that achieves this positive alignment, the organization's productivity can be sabotaged by its own information system (Goldratt and Cox, 1986; Sink and Tuttle, 1989:143-152).

In an era of increasing lower-level empowerment to make decisions and solve problems, congruency of strategy, actions, and measurement, at all levels of the organization, is paramount. Lack of such congruency will become more crucial in the future. As organizations deploy quality policy and empower teams at all levels to solve problems and make decisions aimed at improving performance, ensuring alignment is crucial to coordination and cooperation. If that local optimization and global suboptimization will be the result. Clearly, effective information and knowledge sharing is key to achieving congruency. Lawler (1986) has argued that sharing information, knowledge, power, and then rewards, in that order, will be in the future to creating congruency. As the premium on flexibility, adaptability, responsiveness, and innovation increases, sharing information and knowledge to ensure that strategies, actions, and measures are aligned will become more important. The nonexistence of measurement in most office, professional, and technical settings and, where measurement exists, the noncongruence of goals and actions may well be part of the productivity paradox. This is clearly the case in academic settings. The measurement and reward systems, perhaps unwittingly, seek to optimize the performance of the individual faculty member. When a departmental chairperson complains that the faculty members do not think departmentally and urges them to work as a team, it is simply an exhortation. (Deming [1986, 1991] defines an exhortation as a goal that is set in the absence of a method by which to achieve the goal. In this sense, seeking to improve the performance of the department when the measurement system focuses on the individual is merely an exhortation.)

In light of the foregoing discussion, the system of measurements adopted by the organization must be viewed as a part of the total system of performance portrayal and incentives provided by the organization. The system of measurements must be designed as a total system; otherwise, the organization will optimize a subcomponent and often thereby suboptimize the system. This phenomenon seems to be widespread in U.S. organizations (Deming, 1991; Dixon et al., 1990; Hammer and Champy, 1993; Senge, 1990). If organizations fail to do a better job of integrating strategy, action, and measurement, the best that can be said will be that they passed up an opportunity to increase organizational effectiveness. In the worst case, they might elicit or reinforce counterproductive behavior. Case examples of counterproductive performance are fairly frequent in the literature (e.g., Deming, 1991; Kerr, 1975; Senge, 1990) and common in personal experience.

Guideline 2: A Performance Measurement System Should Reflect the Differing Needs and Perspectives of Managers and Leaders at Various Levels of the Organization

A brief set of examples will illustrate the differences in the information needs of decision makers at various levels of the organization. Consider first the operational level, typically the individual level of the organization. Whether on the shop floor, at a retail sales counter, or in a classroom, the operational decisions that must be made are typically for action in the immediate planning horizon. Making a process adjustment, responding to a customer complaint, or finding a new way to explain a particularly difficult concept requires knowledge of the situation at hand and calls for application of expertise in real time. At the work-group level, planning a monthly production schedule, determining the number of additional clerks to call in for the upcoming sales period, or establishing the annual roster of course offerings is a tactical issue and has a longer planning horizon (typically measured in weeks or months). On the other hand, an executive-level or organizational-level decision to pursue a new line of products, establish an advertising campaign to attract a new class of customer, or develop a program of evening courses to serve the needs of nontraditional or working students is a strategic matter and has a planning horizon that can be several years in length. These three levels of decision makers—first-line employees, management teams or work groups, and executives—are typically positioned at the three levels in the organizational hierarchy. Even though these distinctions are being blurred by attempted shifts to self-management, the distinctions still exist.

Not only do the decision makers at various levels of the organization deal with different planning horizons, but more often than not, they need very different and very specific kinds of information to support the decisions for which they are responsible. Finally, their organizational objectives are expressed in differing degrees of specificity, and the type of information they need to determine whether their decisions are moving their particular unit toward the accomplishment of those objectives may differ radically on many dimensions. The following list summarizes some of the attributes performance measures should have and the way in which the measures relate to the organizational hierarchy.

As a basis for motivation and incentives, measures should

- allow for disaggregation of outcomes as a result of human effort (controllable factors) versus external (uncontrollable) factors;
- be relevant to the desired behaviors;
- be comprehensive enough to ensure balanced performance; and
- be accepted by those whose performance is being measured.

For assessing and evaluating organizational entities, measures should

- be specific to the mission of a given individual or unit; and
- be sensitive to the idiosyncrasies of the particular unit entity being controlled, scheduled, or managed.

For strategic planning and policymaking, measures should

- provide information regarding change over time so trends can be ascertained and
- be sufficiently standardized to allow comparison among entities and also to establish benchmarks for comparison with other organizations.

Regardless of the application, measures should

- measure what they are supposed to measure (be valid);
- reflect the actual content of the activity measured (be unbiased);
- reflect the full range of states of the particular attributes or variables being measured (be representative);
- move when "things change" and not move when they do not change in the appropriate direction;
- be intelligible to the users of the measures;
- give the same value when assessed by different people (be verifiable/reliable); and
- enhance statistical thinking and avoid errors of attribution.

Guideline 3:
Measures of Performance Should be Flexible and Dynamic

Dixon et al. (1990:vii) also state in the preface to their book that "the solution to the performance measurement problem lies not in creating some new monolithic system of measurement, but in institutionalizing a process for continuously changing measures." Later, they conclude that true global competitiveness requires that organizations establish and continuously redefine goals for all levels of the organization that are consistent with winning customer orders and achieving ever-increasing levels of excellence. McNair et al. (1986:137) concur with Dixon et al. (1990): "Translating the strategic goals of the organization into the performance measurement system provides management with a means to manage change and channel employee behavior. Proactive management suggests that changing measurements and incentives are critical."

For both sets of authors above, the ability of an organization to adapt its system of measurement is a seminal feature of the management information system and a key to success. One obvious reason for continually changing the system of performance measures will become clear below when we discuss material velocity management, in which one attempts to maximize the flow of materials through a manufacturing facility and minimize in-process inventories. The principles of material velocity management presented in Goldratt and Cox's (1986) highly acclaimed and widely read work *The Goal* dictate that manufacturing cells only produce in quantities demanded by customer orders, not to the capacity of the cell. The result is that workstations that are not on the critical path or do not represent "bottlenecks" would produce at a "sub optimal" or "unproductive" pace (when viewed individually) so as to not exceed the (system) optimal pace dictated by customer demand. The question that is raised is whether one seeking to evaluate the introduction of IT would apply similar logic to achieve "information velocity management."

As discussed in *The Goal*, the measures for success for the more capital-intensive operations in the plant under consideration were altered drastically when management began to think "systems." When the organization's leaders began to think seriously about the success of the plant (the system), they altered their measures. Maximizing the utilization of the most expensive piece of technology was no longer the aim. The aim was optimizing the performance of the system. Even though the setting for *The Goal*, and hence the example, is manufacturing, the principle also holds for office, professional, and technical settings. The inability to change paradigms and systems of measurement and rewards over time is clearly a key element in the productivity paradox. In retrospect, focusing improvement and measurement efforts on bottleneck elements in the office, professional, and technical settings makes sense.

Also inherent in the notion of flexible measurement systems is the realization that to be effective organizations must continually redefine their purpose. The successive redefinition of purpose must, in turn, be followed by a review of the system of measures to ensure that the factors being recorded are still indicators of effectiveness and provide the necessary reinforcement to ensure that workers' activities are consistent with the redefined goals. Vaill (1989) suggests that today's managers are managing and leading in "permanent white-water." As such, the balancing of strategy, action, and measurement is fast becoming a prerequisite for survival.

Guideline 4:
Reliance on Traditional Measures Can be Problematic

It follows from guideline 3 that traditional performance measures, which tend to focus directly on financial-related data, can be a problem. Traditional measures also typically stress efficiency as the principal criterion for evaluation. That managers tend to blame the failure of accounting systems for many of their problems is one symptom of rising discontent with the utility of financial measures.

According to McNair et al. (1986:144), cost accounting traditionally serves three purposes: (1) financial reporting to outside groups (e.g., shareholders, creditors, and regulatory agencies); (2) managerial reporting and cost modeling for planning (e.g., one-time studies to determine pricing, product line evaluations, make-or-buy decisions); and (3) feedback and control of factory operations (e.g., productivity assessment, incentive pay). But as Dixon et al. (1990:118) point out, "For control of factory operations, the traditional accounting measures are too irrelevant due to allocations, too vague due to 'dollarization,' too late due to accounting period delays, and too summarized due to the length of the accounting period." The problem of inappropriate cost-based measures that confronts manufacturers also applies to the service sector and to office, professional, and technical settings.

Of particular concern is the effect created when managers focus on the financial performance and productivity of direct labor. First, as noted in Chapter 5, a great many organizations operate in an environment in which the direct labor component of their products and services is continually shrinking. This is certainly the case in manufacturing, perhaps less so in the service sector. In this regard, one aspect of the productivity paradox seems to stem from assumptions that the introduction of IT would improve direct labor productivity. We question this assumption and argue that IT might improve aspects of performance but not necessarily productivity or even efficiency.

Second, in an era when throughput time (responsiveness) has been widely identified as a key to productivity, management attention should be focused on bottleneck operations. Goldratt and Cox (1986) provide convincing arguments that full utilization of workers and equipment may well be the enemy of organizational productivity. This concept is clearly counterintuitive to managers who are operating on the basis of traditional performance measures.

DESIGNING AND DEVELOPING MODERN MEASUREMENT SYSTEMS

Measurement is inextricably interwoven with the management process. Indeed, the control function implies measurement. Deming (1986); Dixon et al. (1990); Hammer and Champy (1993); Imai (1986); Juran (1988); Kanter (1983, 1989); Kilmann (1989); Mali (1978); Wheeler (1993); and others, have argued for systematic efforts to improve the quality of management systems and processes. Deming has gone so far as to state that 85 percent or more of the quality and productivity problems in the United States are caused by management. He further explains that management is to blame because it "owns" the management systems and the management systems are inadequate.

Management Systems

What is a management system? The model shown in Figure 6-1 provides a viewpoint that can lead the way to developing measurement systems required for world-class competition. Figure 6-4 combines Figures 6-1 and 6-2 and illustrates the components and interfaces of the management system that Deming and others are challenging managers to improve. To reiterate, the management system model comprises three components: (1) who manages (the management team), (2) what is managed (the organizational system), and (3) how managing is done (tools and methods to convert data into information). The management system also involves three interfaces: (1) the interface between decision and action, (2) the interface between information portrayal and information perception, and (3) the interface between measurement and

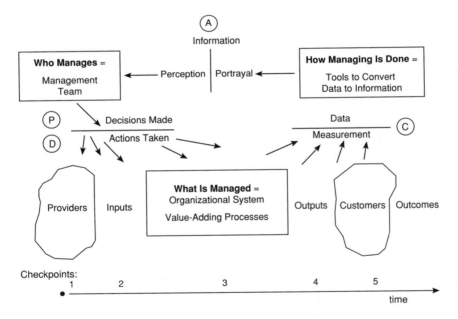

PDCA = Plan, Do, Check, Act (Deming, 1986; Juran, 1988; Shewhart, 1939)

FIGURE 6-4 Improved management systems are required to ensure continuous performance improvement. SOURCE: Adapted from Kurstedt (1986); Sink and Tuttle (1989).

data. The PDCA cycle is also superimposed on the composite model in Figure 6-4.

The organizational system (e.g., department, work group, section, branch, division, plant, company) has providers, inputs, value-adding processes, outputs, and customers. The five lines passing through the decision-to-action interface represent improvement interventions being made at the five key quality checkpoints in the management system. (Recall that the quality checkpoints are (1) selection and management of providers, (2) incoming quality assurance, (3) in-process quality management, (4) outgoing quality assurance, and (5) proactive and reactive assurance that the organization meets or exceeds its customers' needs, expectations, desires, requirements, and specifications.) If the organizational system manages and measures performance at each of the five quality checkpoints, total quality is managed.

A shortcoming of this model is that it is descriptive, not prescriptive. To overcome this, the measurement activity must be integrated with the planning process. Deming (1986) has suggested that, in actuality, the United States is the most underdeveloped nation in the world—it does so little with so much, particularly its human resources. Americans have spent much of the past two decades searching for quick fixes (Kilmann, 1989)—roaming from one quick fix to another, in almost a "random-walk" process. What is needed are more comprehensive and integrated initiatives aimed at improving overall performance.

Strategic Planning for Performance Improvement

When the goal is continuous performance improvement, no organizational management process is more important than planning. We believe the productivity paradox is as much a planning and action problem as it is a measurement problem. Strategic planning is not done very well in the United States (Sink and Tuttle, 1989). The problem is not so much that the plans are bad, rather that the process leading to the plans is rarely well designed or executed. In addition, strategic plans are not accompanied by commitment. Hence, there is a significant discontinuity among the plan, the planners' expectations, and the actual implementation. To achieve commitment, the planning process must be executed in a way that establishes positive linkages between levels in an organization. The process must (1) involve more people; (2) achieve better balance among the business plans, policies and strategies, and the performance improvement plan; (3) be structured, yet flexible and responsive to user needs and preferences; (4) be led from the top down and implemented from the bottom up; (5) be focused on the process as well as the plan; (6) provide for sharing significant amounts of information and knowledge; and (7) be alive, comprehensive, and well integrated. (We do not discuss the mechanics of strategic planning for performance improvement here because that is not the thrust of this chapter and has been detailed elsewhere, for example in Sink and Tuttle, 1989.)

Measurement should be viewed as a key step in a strategic management process, not the reverse. Too often, measurement has been viewed as an end in itself. Measurement is a means to an end; the end is survival, made possible by constant improvement and best-of-best class performance. The aims of the organization are to make good products, provide good services, provide stable employment, keep the customer happy, and stay in business. The introduction of IT to increase productivity is an example of an intervention that can be made at the individual, group, or organizational level with the goal of accomplishing these aims. However, IT, like any other intervention, has to be understood in the context of strategy, cause-and-effect relationships, and current performance levels.

Figure 6-5 depicts how performance measurement and continuous improvement are built into a strategic management planning process. Measurement supports and enhances strategic plans aimed at performance improvement. Note that planning corresponds to steps 1 and 2 of the process (Figure 6-5), actions are represented by step 3, and measures are reflected in step 4.

Organizations must institutionalize a process of continuously improving performance, and measurement systems must be an integral component of that effort. In doing this, the linkages issue must be addressed. That is what the planning process illustrated in Figure 6-5 can do for an organization when developed in the recommended fashion. Systematic planning, action, and measurement enhance the probability that there will be congruency across levels and ensure that linkages are positive. The following section focuses specifically on step 4 of the strategic management planning process.

Developing Enhanced Measurement Systems

In this section we describe the information portrayal-to-perception interface, the conversion of data to information, and the measurement-to-data interface. These elements characterize the measurement process within a management system.

Developing measurement systems for world-class competition entails the following: (1) identifying users and their information requirements as they support performance improvement; (2) identifying data requirements for the information needed; and (3) developing collection,

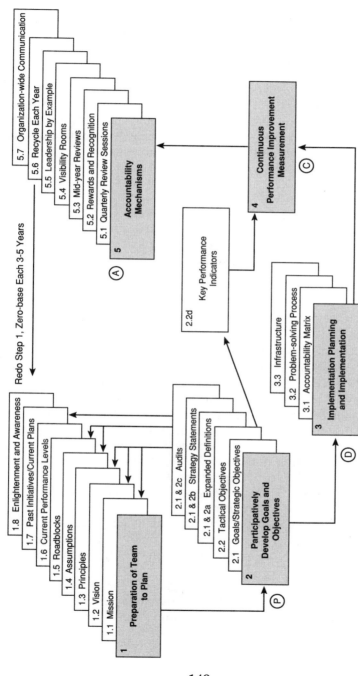

FIGURE 6-5 A detailed portrayal of the strategic management planning process, including the PDCA cycle. SOURCE: Sink (1993).

storage, retrieval, processing, and portrayal tools and techniques. Dixon et al. (1990) have identified three phases that organizations are likely to go through on the road to improved performance measurement systems: (1) tinkering with the existing measurement system (e.g., the cost accounting system); (2) cutting the "Gordian knot" between accounting and performance measurement; and (3) embracing change in strategies, actions, and measures.

Building measurement systems to support continuous improvement and address the productivity linkage paradox is a significant departure from the traditional orientation of organizational control. As such, some underlying issues and principles should be noted.

Key Issues, Principles, and Assumptions

Many measurement problems and failings can be traced to attitudes about measurement that are based on paradigms of the past. Listed below are issues, principles, and assumptions associated with the development of measurement for world-class competition, many of which challenge existing paradigms:

• The goal is to design, develop, and implement successfully measurement systems that share information and thereby support and enhance continuous performance improvement.

• Organizations that learn faster than their competitors have little to fear. Continuous learning must be cultivated through strategies, actions, and measures and must evolve over time (Dixon et al., 1990).

• Control-oriented measurement systems often hinder continuous improvement efforts. It is important to distinguish who is doing the controlling to understand this issue fully. The aim is to move toward control and improvement by those doing the work, to build quality in versus inspecting it in. It is the overreliance on external control that is hindering the rate of improvement.

• Measurement is often resisted due to fear of negative consequences: Visibility of good performance might lead to diminished resources. Visibility of poor performance might lead, initially, to more resources but eventually to punishment. Visibility of performance might promote catering to crises, excessive measurement, and micromanagement.

• Measurement biases and paradigms are dominated by disciplinary (industrial engineering, industrial psychology, accounting, corporate finance, statistics, quality control) and often myopic thinking.

• Measurement is complex. Once this is accepted, measurement can become less difficult.

- Any measurement system should consist of a vector of performance measures, not a single comprehensive measure. Much of the controversy and lack of acceptance of measurement stems from attempts to make a very complex problem appear too simple (Morris, 1979).

- Acceptance of the measurement process is essential to its success as a performance improvement tool. The process by which an organization determines what to measure, how to measure, and how to utilize measures is more important than the actual product of the measurement.

- The greater the participation in the process of creating a performance measurement system, the greater the ease of implementing future changes based on performance measurement, and the greater the resulting performance change (Morris, 1979).

- Organizations must measure what is strategically important, not just what is easy to measure.

- An experimental approach to developing measurement systems must be adopted—fear must be driven out (Deming, 1986).

- The arbitrary use of numerical goals, work standards, and quotas must be eliminated (Deming, 1986).

- What is needed is a method by which measurement teams and their various "customers" can create and continually modify performance measurement systems suited to their own special needs and circumstances, not a standard set of measurements created by experts or obtained from a "shopping list" and imposed on the organization (Morris et al., 1977).

- A performance measurement system must not appear to those involved as simply a passing fad (Morris et al., 1977).

- The measurement system must clearly fit into the management process and be acknowledged as decision making and problem solving aimed at supporting performance improvement.

- The behavioral consequences, unintended and potentially dysfunctional, of performance measurement must be anticipated and reflected in system design and implementation.

- The measurement system must be seen by those whose behaviors and performance are being assessed as being nonmanipulative and nongamed (Morris et al., 1977).

- An effective measurement system is built on consistent and well-understood operational definitions for a set of performance criteria.

- The unit of analysis/target system of a measure must be defined clearly if measurement is to succeed. A necessary precondition is an input-output analysis, which essentially "models" the system by identifying customers/users, outputs, value-adding processes, inputs, and upstream systems, suppliers, vendors, customers, and so on.

• Visibility, ownership, and line of sight must be created for resulting measurement systems in order to ensure effective utilization. *Line of sight* is a term used to represent understanding and/or visibility for cause-and-effect relationships on the part of the person performing. "To what extent is it clear that if I do this, this will result?" "What is the relationship between my behaviors and my performance?" Visibility often leads to control, and it certainly leads to improved understanding of cause-and-effect relationships (Wheeler, 1993).

• The process of measurement must be separated from the process of evaluation. For example, the difference between a control chart and specifications, requirements, and standards must be understood.

• The processes from measurement to data, data to information, portrayal to perception, and decisions to actions must be thoroughly understood in the context of performance measurement.

This rather long list characterizes the "new thinking" about measurement. In many respects, the concepts are consistent with ideas discussed by Deming (1986), Hackman and Oldham (1976), Kanter (1989), Lawler (1986), and others, with regard to the transformation from control-dominant to commitment-oriented organizations. The requirements for developing measurement systems for world-class competition are substantially different from those on which traditional performance measurement systems are based. The productivity paradox is caused, in part, by an inability to deal with these new requirements. To remedy this, the people participating in the process of improving measurement systems must be "masters," that is, they must possess profound knowledge of the new requirements. Further, the design principles for performance measurement systems have been altered substantially. The task of designing management systems, particularly performance measurement systems, has become more complex and challenging. In order to understand linkage issues, to measure their effects, and to predict their impact so that valid performance evaluation can be conducted at various organizational levels, the design of the measurement systems will have to be approached much more systematically.

Identifying Suitable Measures

Designers of a measurement system must be aware of the attributes of numerous possible performance measures. This will ensure that there is a suitable match between the measure selected and the requirements of the measurement system regarding a particular attribute. Four attributes of particular interest are sampling rate, character, precision, and ease of observation. They give rise to the following measurement issues:

1.   Performance measures differ in appropriate sampling rate. Flying a plane, for example, requires that altimeter readings be available on a continuous, real-time basis. However, deciding whether to purchase an additional Boeing 767 might require data from several years of monthly reports on passenger demand to support such a decision.

2.   Performance measures differ in character. Deciding whether parts being produced meet specifications may require only a numerical value from a dial or a red or green signal from a go-no-go gauge. On the other hand, deciding whether to purchase an additional machine for the shop floor or contract out for the additional orders requires data about allocation of overhead or equivalent annual cost estimated from discounted cash flow calculations.

3.   Performance measures differ in precision. Decision makers from different organizational levels typically have different requirements for precision. A decision maker at the organizational level might forecast demand for computing services as part of a long-range planning effort, which would be expressed in thousands or tens-of-thousands of hours per planning period. A scheduler, on the other hand, would require estimates precise to within minutes, or possibly hours.

4.   Performance measures differ in ease of observation. Some phenomena (e.g., sizes, speeds) can be measured directly, whereas phenomena such as comfort and timeliness may require referred indicators. A matter of great importance in measuring organizational performance stems from the difference between measures of inputs and outputs. In general, input measures are more easily observed. On the other hand, it is more likely that a truly useful system of performance measurement will focus on output measures.

These issues and examples are not exhaustive, but they are representative of measurement attributes that must be considered in developing the information system that will help address the productivity paradox. They illustrate the basic principle that performance measurements must be uniquely appropriate to the individual, group, or organization in their most elementary attributes.

Key Design Variables

The foregoing issues and principles translate into design variables for developing an organizational performance measurement system. Several aspects of measurement consistently bog down the process, however. The method commonly used by organizations is analogous to buying a tool off the shelf and simply installing it. It is not uncommon, for example, for a data center to buy a software package, install it, generate the reports the package provides, and simply expect the user to figure out how to use the reports. This is the "hammer looking for a nail to pound" approach to measurement. Tinkering with the existing measurement system is another common approach. Systems approaches to designing a performance measurement system are rare.

It will take a systems approach to develop the measurement systems that organizations need. Key design variables, such as the unit of analysis, user purpose, and operational definitions of measures, must be addressed and specified if the measurement system is to be successful. Specifying the unit of analysis entails defining the organizational system for which the performance measurement system is being established. What are the organizational system's boundaries? What are the outputs? What are the inputs? Who are the providers and the customers? What are the value-adding processes? Input-output analysis is a tool designed to provide answers to these questions. Once the questions are answered, the unit of analysis will have been adequately defined. One of the most common mistakes made when developing a performance measurement system is failing to define the system of interest. This is a key element of the linkage issue. For a given unit of analysis, measures are frequently developed outside the context of the larger system. An example would be evaluating the payoff of an IT intervention at the individual or group level without considering linkages to higher organizational levels. In other words, measures should be specific to a given unit of analysis, but the data should be interpreted in the light of other unit-of-analysis perspectives.

The users of the measurement system and their purposes also must be defined clearly. Who are the end users of the measurement system? What do they need from measurement to help them improve how they solve problems and make decisions? These questions may seem simple and obvious, yet it is quite common for measures to be specified without these questions ever being addressed. Again, the implication for the linkage issue is significant. Who is trying to confirm that improvement has taken place—the IT vendor, the manager who purchased the IT product, the critic who is against IT and therefore has a hidden agenda, the IT user who is skeptical of the benefits and is resistant to something new, or the analyst who is attempting to understand organizational performance over time? At the heart of the linkage issue and the productivity paradox is this question of user and purpose.

Operational definition of the aspects of performance to be measured is another important design variable. The seven performance criteria articulated previously are analogous to categories of instruments on an airplane control panel. For example, there are engine performance instruments, spatial location instruments, and communication instruments. In the well-designed measurement system, there will be a hierarchy of "instruments," "indicators," and "gauges." At the highest level in the model proposed herein is the measurement construct called performance. At the level below performance, we have postulated seven performance criteria. It might require a half dozen levels of detail in a measurement system in order to understand and model both system and subsystem performance on these criteria. This is not dissimilar to a multilevel work-breakdown structure for tasks. The difference here is that the breakdown is done for measurement. Once the hierarchy of measures is determined, specific indicators must be established, operational definitions written, the measurement-to-data interface determined, and ultimately, the user interfaces and utilization completed.

In the final analysis, however, examining the organization and designing the measurement system and the management information system can only do so much. The strategies employed by the decision makers and the decisions they make ultimately determine the success or failure of the organization.

APPLYING MEASUREMENT TO MANAGEMENT

Goldratt and Cox's (1986) *The Goal* provides a valuable insight into the relationship of measurement to management. When discussing the optimal production technique strategy (also referred to as material velocity management), they emphasized the need for identifying and managing bottleneck operations in systems with coupled, or linked, elements. The extraordinarily simple key is that the production level of the bottleneck operation must be managed in light of customer demands. Once this relationship is established, all other production units, in turn, must operate at the pace dictated (pulled) by the pace of the bottleneck operation. Idle people or machines are not arbitrarily considered "waste." In fact, nonbottleneck operations can only be understood and evaluated in light of the productivity of the total system. Production at any rate greater than that dictated by the pull of the bottleneck operation simply adds to unnecessary inventory.

In a subsequent work *The Race*, Goldratt and Fox (1986) provide more technical detail. They demonstrate that forcing workers or facilities in nonbottleneck operations to "be productive" not only generates unneeded inventory, but increases costs, reduces product quality, degrades system flexibility, and restricts the ability to respond to customer demands. However, for the purposes of this discussion, a later section of *The Race* makes an even more relevant point: "We are not dealing here with a change in the foreman's culture, but *a culture controlled by how management* measures *a foreman's performance*" (p. 112; emphasis added).

Why do organizations measure? Many of the references we have cited and much of our own experience suggests that traditional managers measure for control. However, world-class organizations measure not for control, but to drive continuous improvement. The management information system and, in particular, the performance measurement and portrayal system that support it are key to total productivity and world-class competitiveness. Foreign competitors of U.S. industry may not have worked out the theory or the underlying mechanisms, but in material velocity management, for example, they have sensed one of the keys to achieving "the goal." Organizations can put the information system to work to enhance their ability to achieve that goal.

We have discussed how the performance measurement system can provide management with information and a mechanism to reinforce behaviors consistent with organizational goals. To achieve these ends, organizations must become much more sophisticated in designing and implementing portrayal systems that display performance. If the portrayal system encourages local maximization and suboptimization of individual and group performance, the organization's total productivity falls. Local optimization can occur at the individual or group level. Further, there can be horizontal variation in local optimization (one individual is optimized another suboptimized) and almost infinite variations in next-level performance. This is what makes the linkages issue so complex to model and to analyze. If the system shapes the behavior of the entire work force toward the common goal, total productivity is enhanced.

The foregoing observations suggest that an alternative to precise control of direct labor, with its attendant dysfunctional consequences, can be found in the adoption of an organizational perspective that views measurement as an integral part of the managerial process. A key objective in adopting this new perspective is to establish a system of measures that tracks progress toward achieving the organization's strategic goals. Why haven't these changes occurred?

Goldratt and Cox (1986) see the goal as "making money," but we regard profitability as a means to an end. In the final analysis, Chester Barnard (1938:44) said it most decisively: the only true measure of organizational performance is its "capacity to survive."

CONCLUSION AND NEXT STEPS

In this chapter, we have not addressed organizational linkages and the productivity paradox methodologically or quantitatively. Our aim has been to spark systems thinking about the origins of the paradox. Some elements of the paradox may be explainable, others may not. But we strongly believe the methodological issues are much more tractable if systems principles, theories, and concepts are understood and put into practice. In order to address the productivity paradox and organizational linkages methodologically or quantitatively, several prerequisites must be resolved. First, profound knowledge of productivity and quality improvement is necessary to model and predict improvement in an entity. We believe that profound knowledge did not exist for much of the work being evaluated in the literature. Thus, it is impossible to rely on existing research and evaluation work as a basis for verifying that there is, in fact, a paradox. It is just as reasonable to conclude there is no paradox, only the perception of one based on poor measurement and evaluation.

Second, the lag between when an improvement intervention is made in an entity and when actual (predicted) improvement is seen, felt, and measured in the entity or in other entities as a result of linkages must be understood and dealt with methodologically. It is widely accepted that many short-term (tactical) operational improvements have long-term (strategic) consequences. The evaluation research that has been done to date, however, does not appear to be sufficiently longitudinal. Thus, researchers and practitioners may not be waiting long enough to see their beliefs in cause-and-effect relationships come to fruition. The lag between the time a potential improvement is made and when true improvement can be seen, felt, and measured presents a challenge for researchers and practitioners. Macroeconomic methodology does not have enough *granularity* to address this issue at the level of an organizational system.

Third, a science and methodology of measurement for performance improvement for organizational systems must be developed. Performance must be operationally defined and a theoretical measurement-breakdown structure developed and utilized so that evaluation results are comparable. Defining predicted linkages from entity to entity on the basis of beliefs in or, better yet, knowledge of cause-and-effect relationships is crucial to resolving the apparent paradox.

The viewpoint we expressed in this chapter was threefold: (1) a fixed system of performance and productivity measures cannot meet the informational needs of management in a modern production organization, (2) macro performance cannot be deduced from micro measures, and (3) measurement-driven suboptimization poses a significant threat to organizational productivity. Further, we believe that (1) a common set of measures cannot be used to assess and compare performance and productivity at all levels of the organization; (2) a particular system of measurement cannot serve the organization's needs indefinitely; and (3) total system performance cannot be deduced from measures of individual performance.

Researchers and practitioners should rethink and eventually abandon the strategy of measuring, rewarding, and attempting to maximize the "productivity" of virtually all individuals and production subsystems. Rather, productivity drivers should be pinpointed and useful portrayal mechanisms introduced to ensure that managers and practitioners accomplish the desired end of world-class organizational productivity.

The next steps to be taken include the following:

• Investigate whether potentially useful interventions are being forgone as a result of the productivity paradox.
• Determine if the reluctance to make performance improvement interventions is due to lack of information. If so, concentrate on evaluating candidate performance improvement interventions from a systems perspective.
• Model organizational linkages and analyze the productivity paradox for a selected set of specific examples in an effort to generate tangible theories about cause-and-effect relationships and frame the problem in a manner susceptible to solution.

The paradox of unrealized productivity improvements from IT interventions seems to us an example of incomplete systems thinking and failure to understand the nature of linkages at the individual, group, and organizational levels. Questions that need to be answered include the following:

• At which level would one expect performance to improve as a result of IT or any other productivity improvement initiative?
• Which aspects of organizational performance will be quantifiable and which will require qualitative assessments?
• To what extent have researchers and practitioners clarified what they *know* versus what they believe or feel about cause-and-effect relationships as they evaluate the linkage issue?

These are central questions that have been stimulated by a systems perspective and that demand concentrated study as part of the effort to unravel the productivity paradox.

REFERENCES

Akao, Y., ed.
 1991   *Hoshin Kanri: Policy Deployment for Successful TQM*. Cambridge, Mass.: Productivity Press.
Barnard, C.I.
 1938   *Functions of the Executive*. Cambridge, Mass.: Harvard University Press.
Benfari, R.
 1991   *Understanding Your Management Style: Beyond the Myers-Briggs Type Indicators*. Lexington, Mass.: Lexington Books.
Deming, W.E.
 1986   *Out of the Crisis*. Center for Advanced Engineering Study. Cambridge, Mass.: M.I.T. Press.
 1991   Four day workshop, by W.E. Deming. Atlanta, Georgia.
Dixon, J.R., J. Nanni, and T.E. Vollmann
 1990   *The New Performance Challenge: Measuring Operations for World Class Competition*. Homewood, Ill: Dow Jones-Irwin.
Fitts, P.M., and M.I. Posner
 1968   *Human Performance*. Belmont, Calif.: Brooks/Cole.
Goldratt, E.M., and J. Cox
 1986   *The Goal: A Process of Ongoing Improvement*, rev. ed. Croton-on-Hudson, N.Y.: North River Press.
Goldratt, E.M., and R. Fox
 1986   *The Race*. Croton-on-Hudson, N.Y.: North River Press.
Grayson, C.J., Jr., and C.S. O'Dell
 1988   *American Business: A 2-Minute Warning*. New York: Free Press.
Greif, M.
 1989   *The Visual Factory: Building Participation Through Shared Information*. Cambridge, Mass.: Productivity Press.
Hackman, J.R., and G.R. Oldham
 1976   Motivation through the design of work: Test of a theory. *Organizational Behavior and Human Performance* 16:250-279.
Hall, R.W., H.T. Johnson, and P.B.B. Turney
 1991   *Measuring Up: Charting Pathways to Manufacturing Excellence*. Homewood, Ill.: Business One Irwin.
Hammer, M., and J. Champy
 1993   *Reengineering the Corporation: A Manifesto for Business Revolution*. New York: Harper Business.
Imai, M.
 1986   *Kaizen: The Key to Japan's Competitive Success*. New York: Random House.
Juran, J.M.
 1988   *Juran on Planning for Quality*. New York: Free Press.
Kanter, R.M.
 1983   *The Change Masters: Innovation for Productivity in the American Corporation*. New York: Simon & Schuster.
 1989   *When Giants Learn to Dance: Mastering the Challenges of Strategy, Management, and Careers in the 1990s*. New York: Simon & Schuster.

Kanter, R.M., B.A. Stein, and T.D. Jick
    1992   *The Challenge of Organizational Change.* New York: Free Press.
Kerr, S.
    1975   On the folly of rewarding A while hoping for B. *Academy of Management Journal* 18:769-783.
Kilmann, R.H.
    1989   *Managing Beyond the Quick-Fix.* San Francisco: Jossey-Bass.
Kottler, P., L. Fahey, and J. Jatusripitak
    1985   *The New Competition.* Englewood Cliffs, N.J.: Prentice-Hall.
Kurstedt, H.
    1986   The Industrial Engineer's Systematic Approach to Management. MSM Working Draft and Articles and Responsive Systems Article. Management Systems Laboratories, Virginia Polytechnic Institute and State University, Blacksburg.
Lawler, E.E.
    1986   *High Involvement Management.* San Francisco: Jossey-Bass.
Mali, P.
    1978   *Improving Total Productivity.* New York: John Wiley & Sons.
McNair, C.J., W. Mosconi, and T. Norris
    1986   *Beyond the Bottom Line: Measuring World Class Performance.* Homewood, Ill.: Dow Jones-Irwin.
Mohrman, A.M., S.A. Mohrman, G. Ledford, T.G. Cummings, and E.E. Lawler
    1989   *Large-Scale Organizational Change.* San Francisco: Jossey-Bass.
Morris, W.T.
    1979   *Implementation Strategies for Industrial Engineers.* Out of print; available from Virginia Productivity Center, Virginia Polytechnic Institute and State University, Blacksburg.
Morris, W.T., G.L. Smith, and D.S. Sink
    1977   *Productivity Measurement Systems for Administrative Computing and Information Services.* Grant No. APR 75-20561. Columbus, Oh.: The Ohio State University Productivity Research Group.
Senge, P.M.
    1990   *The Fifth Discipline: The Art and Practice of the Learning Organization.* New York: Doubleday.
Shewhart, W.
    1939   *Statistical Method from the Viewpoint of Quality.* Washington, D.C.: U.S. Department of Agriculture, Graduate School.
Sink, D.S.
    1993   Developing measurement systems for world class competition. In *Handbook for Productivity Measurement and Improvement.* Cambridge, Mass.: Productivity Press.
Sink, D.S., and T.C. Tuttle
    1989   *Planning and Measurement in Your Organization of the Future.* Norcross, Ga.: Industrial Engineering and Management Press.
Vaill, P.B.
    1989   *Managing as a Performing Art.* San Francisco: Jossey-Bass.
Weisbord, M.R.
    1991   *Productive Workplaces: Organizing and Managing for Dignity, Meaning and Community.* San Francisco: Jossey-Bass.
Wheeler, D.J.
    1993   *Understanding Variation: The Key to Managing Chaos.* Knoxville, Tenn.: SPC Press.

7

Decomposing the Productivity Linkages Paradox

Robert D. Pritchard

The productivity paradox can be stated as follows: How can improvements in performance that occur at one level of analysis seem to disappear when performance is measured at broader levels of analysis?

Many interventions developed by behavioral science and the more technological disciplines are geared to improving the performance of individuals and groups. Those disciplines have frequently been satisfied with claiming success for an intervention when it can be shown that measures of the performance of the users have improved. Thus, if a group-based intervention shows that group output has improved, the claim is made that the intervention will help organizations function better. The assumption is that if the group performs better, the organization will function better.

The productivity paradox calls this assumption into question. Indeed, it calls into question the very foundation of much of the work done to improve organizational functioning. Typically, the ultimate justification for work in such areas as personnel selection, training, equipment design, motivation, task design, group structure, and feedback systems is that it will help the organization function better. The paradox suggests the possibility that "successful" interventions can actually have no effect on organizational functioning in that the positive effects of the intervention are somehow being absorbed or negated somewhere in the organization.

The panel's focus on organizational linkages is based on the premise that to understand why the paradox occurs, one must look to the linkages between the levels of analysis. If performance improves at one level but does not show up in the next, there is something about the linkage between the levels that is causing the disappearance of the effect. Understanding the linkages between levels of analysis can lead to a much better translation of improvements at lower levels in the organization into improvements at higher levels in the organization. In other words, if the design and evaluation of improvement interventions are grounded in an understanding of the linkages and their effects, they will have a more positive impact on overall organizational performance.

LINKAGES DEFINED

An organizational linkage occurs when the outputs from one organizational subsystem are combined with the outputs of another subsystem into broader outputs. Consider the example of a small manufacturing firm of the type exemplified in Figure 7-1. The firm has three levels of analysis above the individual: the unit, the division, and the total organization. The firm comprises a production division, a marketing division, and such other divisions as personnel, maintenance, purchasing, and accounting. The production division includes a design unit and a manufacturing unit. All units and divisions are managed by a top management group. If a new product is being considered, top management makes the decision to allocate resources to develop the new product. The design unit develops the design for the product, the manufacturing unit makes it, and the marketing division sells it.

This organization can be thought of as a set of linked subsystems. There are several levels of subsystems in this organization. According to Katz and Kahn (1978) and Naylor et al. (1980), as well as Chapters

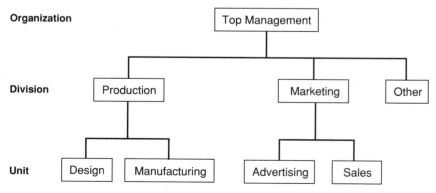

FIGURE 7-1 Example of an organizational structure.

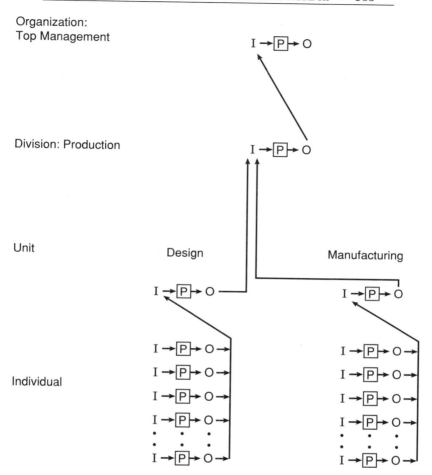

FIGURE 7-2 Organizational subsystem structure. NOTE: I = inputs; P = processing of inputs; O = outputs.

4-6, a subsystem has inputs, it does processing of some sort with those inputs, and it generates outputs. The individuals in each unit are themselves systems that become subsystems for the broader organization. This is depicted graphically in Figure 7-2, which shows the production division from the example above. At the bottom of the figure are the individuals. These individuals have inputs (I) in the form of materials, equipment, training, information, and so on. The individuals process (P) the inputs to produce outputs (O). An individual in the design unit might produce the output of an idea for one aspect of the new product's design.

The design unit is also a system in itself. An important part of its inputs is the outputs produced by the individual. This is shown in the figure by the line going from the outputs of the individuals to the inputs of the design unit. These and other inputs are processed by the design unit, which produces outputs in the form of designs for the product.

The design unit is also a subsystem in the production division. The outputs of the design unit are combined with the outputs of the manufacturing unit to be inputs to the production division. Finally, there is the entire organization as a system. One major source of its inputs is the outputs of the production division. Thus, the organization can be considered as a series of related systems from the individual to the entire organization. The outputs of the more molecular subsystems become inputs for the next-level system.

To return to the definition, a linkage occurs when the outputs of one subsystem are combined with the outputs of another subsystem into the outputs of broader organizational units. In the example, a linkage occurs when the outputs of the individuals must be combined to produce the inputs the design unit uses to produce a new product design. Another linkage occurs when the outputs of the design unit must be combined with those of the manufacturing unit to produce a product of sufficient quality to meet customer needs. Finally, a linkage occurs when the outputs of the production division must be combined with outputs of other parts of the organization to form the outputs of the total organizational system.

It is important to recognize that this definition indicates that what is combined in a linkage is the *outputs* of a subsystem. It is the outputs that are combined with other subsystems' outputs to generate broader organizational outputs. The refrigerator is made by combining compressors with electric motors and painted panels. It is not outputs relative to inputs (efficiency) or outputs related to expectations (effectiveness) that are being combined in the linkage. While one might measure efficiency, effectiveness, or one of the other aspects of performance discussed in Chapter 6 and aggregate it across organizational levels, that is a measure of organizational functioning, not what is being combined across a linkage.

In order to understand why the productivity paradox occurs, the paradox must be decomposed. In order to decompose it, the factors that could produce it must be examined. Many of the factors that could produce it have been discussed in earlier chapters. In Chapter 3, for example, Goodman and his colleagues identified a series of intra- and intertask factors that could produce the paradox.

My approach in this chapter is to break down the possible factors into three groups. The first group contains structural characteristics. These factors are fairly permanent organizational characteristics that by their very nature would produce the paradox. The second group involves side effects from organizational interventions that could reduce or eliminate the positive effects of an intervention. The third group comprises measurement issues. The first two groups of factors have been discussed in earlier chapters and thus are only touched on briefly here for the sake of completeness.

Structural Factors

Structural factors are characteristics of the organization itself that could produce the paradox. Time lag is one such factor. Because of the structure of tasks in an organization, improvements in one subsystem sometimes take considerable time to show up in the combined outputs of the broader system. Other structural factors are slack, bottlenecks in the availability of needed inputs, the centrality of the task to the overall functioning of the organization, and the degree of interdependence of people and subsystems in producing the output. (See Chapters 2-4 for discussions of structural factors.)

Structural factors have two important things in common. First, they are natural and unavoidable aspects of organizational functioning. Second, they all reduce the one-to-one correspondence between the outputs of one subsystem and the outputs of a broader subsystem. That is, they will in and of themselves produce data that look like the productivity paradox. Thus, to the extent that the paradox is caused by structural factors, there is no real paradox. This leads to the following hypothesis:

• The greater the presence of structural factors that naturally reduce the one-to-one correspondence between the outputs of subsystems that combine their outputs, the greater the likelihood of the appearance of a productivity paradox.

Intervention Side Effects

The second group of effects that could produce the paradox consists of unintended consequences of the intervention. It could be that direct measures of the effects of an intervention indicate improvement, but other effects of the intervention have a negative consequence at a broader level of analysis.

There are several types of such side effects. One type occurs when the intervention changes the focus of the effort from one unit of analysis to another. For example, giving each person in a unit a personal computer could result in people working individually rather than in groups. If the task for the unit requires high interdependence if it is to be done effectively, the shift from group to individual activity could decrease the combined, integrated output of the group while increasing the output of each individual. Another type of side effect is that the intervention could lead to changes in communication patterns. The new technology or work process could result in changes in the work structure that would disrupt a well-established informal communication pattern. It might take considerable time to reestablish a new pattern that is as efficient as the old one. Thus, although some output measures increase due to the changed technology, the decrease in communication effectiveness could decrease the unit's overall output.

These and other unintended side effects were discussed in Chapters 2-4. The important thing to note for the purposes of this chapter is that this class of factors exists and can be part of the paradox. Unintended side effects can produce the paradox in that performance can improve in one aspect of the work, but decreases that occur in other aspects of the work can eliminate the positive effects when the aggregation to a higher level of analysis occurs.

This leads to the following hypothesis:

• To the extent that unintended negative side effects of a successful intervention occur, they will reduce the overall output of the subsystem and thereby produce the appearance of a productivity paradox.

Measurement Issues

The third group of factors that can explain the paradox involves measurement issues. A major point in this chapter is that measurement issues are a critical key to decomposing the productivity paradox. There are two classes of measurement issues. The first comprises issues that are natural phenomena in organizations, and although they should be recognized and understood, they are not a cause for particular concern. The second class of measurement issues comes to the fore when there are actual errors or conflicts in the measurement of organizational performance. This class of measurement issues is much more critical to organizational functioning than the first class and much more problematic for decomposing the productivity paradox. In the next two sections, I examine each class of measurement issues in detail.

MEASUREMENT ISSUES: NATURAL PHENOMENA

Different Measurement Purposes

Organizational performance is measured in different ways for different purposes. This is true whether what is being measured is productivity, effectiveness, efficiency, or any other aspect of performance. There are five major purposes in measuring organizational performance, each of which has very different implications for what is measured (Pritchard, 1992).

The first purpose of measuring is to compare large aggregations of organizations to each other. Examples would be comparing the national economies of the United States and Japan and comparing the health care and computer industries. This type of performance measurement may be used by government agencies in determining how to control monetary policy, by government officials who are negotiating trade agreements with other countries, or by researchers studying broad organizational trends. A typical measure used for this purpose is price-deflated gross national product divided by the number of worker hours used (e.g., Kendrick, 1984; Mahoney, 1988).

The second purpose of measuring is to evaluate the overall performance of individual organizations for comparison with other organizations or with some standard. In this type of measurement, yearly sales figures, profit and loss margins, price/earnings ratios, and percentages of market share would typically be used. Performance measurement of this type might be used by individual investors to determine where to place their investment dollars.

The third purpose of measuring is for use as a management information system. Here, the focus is on a single organization, and the measurement deals with the functioning of the human-technological system. The question to be answered is how the entire organization or major parts of it are functioning, and whether that functioning is improving or declining. This type of measurement is used by upper management to determine major resource allocations, long-range goals, strategic plans, and the like.

The fourth purpose of measuring is to *control* parts of the organization. Although this type of measurement is often overlooked (Weiss, 1989), the control of the movement and timing of material resources and products is quite important to the efficiency of an organization. Under this heading are included such activities as production engineering and scheduling, quality control, materials distribution and management, and inventory control. The goals of this type of measurement include identifying whether problems are developing and assessing the effect of changes made in operations.

The fifth purpose of measuring is for use as a motivational tool (e.g., Algera, 1989). The objective is to improve performance by encouraging behavioral changes in individuals. The assumption underlying this type of measurement is that the human resources of an organization can have a significant impact on the organization's performance. In other words, personnel can exert more effort, be more persistent in their efforts, and spend their efforts in more optimal ways, thereby working more efficiently and effectively.

Although the last three purposes appear to be somewhat similar, there are important differences. Each measures performance in a single organization, but they focus on different things and at different levels of the organization. The management information system is concerned with the overall functioning of the organization or its major subsystems and deals with macro measures, such as the profitability of the total organization or the contribution of different units to some type of overall effectiveness. The measurement information is rarely given to lower-level personnel in the form of feedback. Data gathering for the *control* purpose is typically done on smaller-sized organizational units than for the management information system, and it uses less macro measures, such as the flow of resources to various units and how well work is being scheduled. In addition, it does not attempt to separate the effects due to personnel from the effects due to technology. Measurement for motivation is concerned with the performance of individuals or work groups and gathers data on the accomplishment of specific work objectives. It is done, ideally, so that the effects due to personnel can be separated from the effects due to the technology, and the results are typically given to unit personnel in the form of feedback.

Different Measurement Purposes Require Different Measures

What is most critical for the discussion here is that measuring for different purposes involves measuring different things. As one moves from measuring for motivational purposes to measuring the total organization, new causal factors come into play that will affect the values produced by the resulting measurement. This is illustrated in Figure 7-3. The middle section of the figure represents the transformation of outputs that is made from individual to unit, to division, to total organization. As noted above, the outputs of the more molecular levels become the inputs of the more molar levels. However, other inputs are added at each level in addition to the outputs of the more molecular level. The upper section of the figure shows some of the many factors

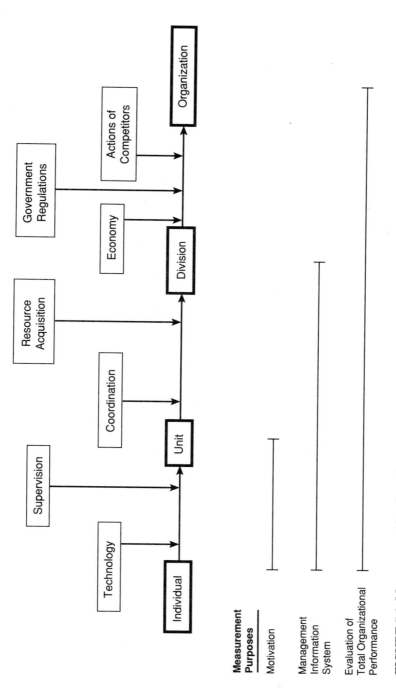

FIGURE 7-3 Measurement levels and sources.

that are added at each level of analysis in the form of inputs or constraints. In Figure 7-3, the behavior of the individual, the most molecular level, is combined with the existing technology to produce unit-level outputs. The supervision of the individual also influences the transformation of individual outputs to unit outputs. As an example, design engineer using a computer-assisted design (CAD) system produces specific designs for parts of a new product. Individual or subunit outputs are combined through an integration and coordination function that is overseen by the supervisor. The combined effects of individuals, the technology, and the supervision function produce the unit's outputs. Thus, the designs of individuals or small groups are combined into an integrated, final design for the new product, which is the output of the design unit.

The outputs of the manufacturing unit would be finished products. The outputs of the design and manufacturing units are then combined into outputs for the production division. To accomplish this, a coordination function is required so that the outputs of the units can be integrated effectively. The plans developed by the design unit, for example, must be manufacturable at a reasonable cost. In addition, a major resource acquisition process occurs when the person in charge of the division must acquire resources from top management. The more effectively this is done, the greater the outputs of the division tend to be.

The entire division has its own outputs that relate to the finished product. To measure the performance of the division, measures might be taken of how long it took to develop a manufacturable product, how economically the product can be made in the future, and how well the product meets customer needs. What is critical here is that the measures of the division's performance include not only the outputs of the two units forming it, but additional causal factors as well. Specifically, the effectiveness of division management in getting resources, how well those resources are divided between the two units, and how well the coordination is done between the two units will all influence how well the division performs on its measures.

The same process occurs for higher levels in the organization. One division's outputs are combined with those of other divisions to be inputs for the total organization. In this example, the outputs of the production division are combined with those of the marketing division to produce sales and revenues for the total organization. These are combined with the costs and revenues of other divisions to produce the organizational-level outputs. If the total organization is measured on such factors as return on investment, total revenues, net profits, and so on, new causal factors are again added to the performance measure. In Figure 7-3, the factors shown are the strength of the economy, government regulations, and actions of competitors. These are factors that will influence the overall performance of the organization on its measures, but they are not a function of the actions of the organization's divisions.

At the bottom of the figure, some of the different measurement purposes are listed. They indicate graphically that different factors are included when measurement is done for different purposes. Measurement for motivational purposes should measure only what the individual or the unit has control over. It will frequently measure up to the level of unit output, but it should try to remove the effects of the technology. The management information purpose encompasses individual behavior, the performance of the technology, how well supervision is done, the effectiveness of coordination of the individual units, and the effects of resource acquisition. Measuring total organizational performance typically includes all the factors shown in Figure 7-3, including those outside the organization.

One should expect the productivity paradox to occur when measures collected for different purposes are compared. For example, suppose an organization introduces CAD technology and finds that its design engineers are able to create better designs and in less time. It then measures overall organizational outcomes, such as return on investment and gross profit and finds no change. This is an example of the paradox, but it really makes no sense that the two measures *should* be related. As Figure 7-3 illustrates, measures at the organizational level of analysis will be influenced in a very minor way by the design unit's producing the better designs. This leads to the following hypotheses:

- The more factors that are added to a measure of organizational functioning when it is aggregated from lower to higher levels of the organization, the weaker the relationship between the original measure and the composite measure will be.
- The more factors that are added to measures of organizational functioning when they are aggregated to higher levels of the organization, the greater is the likelihood of finding evidence of a productivity paradox.

Different Aggregation Strategies

The problem being discussed here can be seen as an issue of aggregation. The concept of linkages is by definition a cross-level issue—measures are aggregated across levels of analysis. In order to deal with cross-level questions, measures must be developed that go across levels

(Hulin et al., 1978; Rousseau, 1985). If one wants to know the effects of, for example, computer technology on organizational functioning, one is raising a cross-level question. Computers are typically used at the level of individuals or small groups. Measuring overall organizational functioning requires a much broader unit of analysis. A key problem is how to go about this aggregation process so that the question can be answered.

In dealing with the productivity paradox, it is important not to confuse two very different aggregation strategies. The first strategy is to construct measures that add many sources of influence into the final, more global measure. That is the typical strategy, and the one described in this section. It amounts to adding error (uncontrolled variance) to the more molar measure. It will by definition reduce the relationship between the more molecular and the more molar measures and yield the productivity paradox.

The second strategy is to measure for one purpose and aggregate by *using the same measurement purpose* in going from the more molecular to the more molar level. For example, if an organization is measuring to see how well its personnel are doing the work, it wants measures that are predominantly determined by the behavior of the personnel. It does not want the measurement to be influenced by factors outside the control of the personnel. To obtain aggregate measures, it must find a way to express individuals' or groups' performance in a measure that can be combined across levels. Thus, the measure must allow the performance of individual designers to be aggregated to produce the performance of the design unit. An analogous measure must be developed to summarize the performance of individuals in the manufacturing unit. These two unit-level measures must then be combined to form a division-level measure, and division measures combined into total organization measures. If the organization achieves this, it will at least avoid the almost certainty of producing a productivity paradox. However, there is still a problem. The broader the aggregation, the less effect any one subsystem will have on the final aggregated total. If the performance of the design unit improves by 25 percent, but the design unit is only 1 percent of the total organization-level aggregation, the improvement in the design group will have a negligible effect on the total. This also will give the effect of a productivity paradox.

This leads to the following hypothesis:

• The greater the number of separate elements that are aggregated, the greater and more pervasive must be the change in performance to avoid the appearance of a productivity paradox.

CONFLICTS IN MEASUREMENT

The discussion of natural phenomena that could give the appearance of a productivity paradox was not meant to suggest a complete explanation for the paradox. The second class of measurement issues is also most likely involved, that is some type of measurement conflict.

One type of measurement conflict occurs when there are differences in the objectives of units that must cooperate with each other to produce the output. Another type occurs when there is conflict in objectives across different levels of the organization. These conflicts come about when the performance of different units is formally or informally measured in a way that produces a problem, and as discussed below, correcting what is measured is ultimately the key to correcting the problem.

Conflict Between Local Objectives

Different subsystems at the same level in the organization may have objectives that are not congruent. For example, the design unit in an organization may have as its objective producing an elegant design for a new product that uses the most cutting-edge technology. If this is done, the designers believe they have met their objective and done a good job. In contrast, the manufacturing unit has the objective of developing a manufacturing methodology that will produce the product as inexpensively as possible, and with the highest possible quality. The problem is that the objectives of the two units are not completely compatible. Elegant and cutting-edge designs are frequently difficult to produce. To add more complexity, the sales unit wants a product that meets customer needs. A finished product that is a compromise between design's desires for elegance and manufacturing's ideas of an easy product to make may not meet customer needs at all.

The above situation can produce the paradox. If the objectives of units that must work together are inconsistent, improving one or all units' ability to meet *their own objectives* does not improve the broader subsystem's performance. For example, suppose the design unit receives new, more advanced CAD equipment and it indeed helps designers to do their work better. If their improved performance is directed at making designs that are even more elegant and cutting edge, that could make it even more difficult for manufacturing to make them. Thus, the outputs of the design group go up, the outputs of the manufacturing unit go down, and there is no net change at the level of the production division. This is an example of the productivity paradox.

The example leads to the following hypotheses:

- Improving the ability of one subsystem (e.g., an individual, group, unit, division) to achieve its objectives will result in improvement in measures of broader organizational functioning only if that subsystem's objectives are consistent with the objectives of units with which it must coordinate to produce the broader subsystem's outputs.
- The greater the inconsistency in the objectives of units whose outputs must be coordinated to produce the outputs of the broader subsystem, the greater the possibility of a productivity paradox.

Inconsistency Across Organizational Levels

A second type of measurement conflict is related to the first, but it occurs when measures and objectives are not consistent with each other *across* organizational levels (e.g., Tuttle, 1981). That is, what are seen as the objectives for one subsystem are inconsistent with those at a higher level. For example, suppose a sales unit is trying to develop a strong and permanent customer base. Key objectives of the unit are to satisfy the customer no matter how small the order and never to sell the customer something not needed just to make a sale. The unit believes that this approach is an appropriate strategy and in the long run will produce a strong and permanent customer base. Top management, however, is evaluated on short-term measures, such as return on investment and profits. In this situation, the objectives of the different levels are inconsistent. Greater *immediate* revenues and profits would be generated by the sales unit if it would focus on the larger customers and sell whatever it could, regardless of customer needs.

The paradox can occur here as well. If the objectives are inconsistent, making a change that helps the sales unit meet its objectives more effectively can, in fact, reduce how well the broader organization performs on its measures of return on investment and immediate profits.

This phenomenon leads to the following hypotheses:

- Improving the ability of one subsystem to achieve its objectives will result in improvement in measures of broader organizational functioning only if that subsystem's objectives are consistent with the broader organization's objectives.
- The greater the inconsistency in the objectives of units in a hierarchical relationship to each other, the greater the possibility of a productivity paradox.

POTENTIAL SOLUTIONS TO THE PARADOX

Given the above explanations for why the paradox occurs, what implications do the explanations have for how the paradox and the linkage issues it highlights should be dealt with? In this section I suggest some solutions.

The basic approach to understanding what to do about the paradox problem is to look at the causes of the problem. Several groups of possible causes were discussed above, and the solution depends on the particular cause. Table 7-1 summarizes the causes discussed and indicates the solution to each.

Structural Factors and Intervention Side Effects

The first set of causes in Table 7-1 is structural factors. Recall that these are factors such as time lag, slack, and bottlenecks. To the extent that structural factors are producing the paradox, the solution is to measure those factors directly. This means directly tracking what happens to the output of one subsystem as it is combined with that of other subsystems. If an increase in output occurs across individuals, it might take some time before an increase occurs in the unit's outputs. Being aware of this lag and measuring appropriately could cause the apparent paradox to disappear. Measuring factors such as slack and bottlenecks would be done in a similar fashion. Thus, when an intervention occurs, the effects of the change in performance must be measured more broadly and more carefully.

The second set of causes is the side effects of an intervention. These occur when the intervention improves some aspects of performance but decreases performance in other parts of the subsystem. To assess these causes of the paradox, it is also necessary to measure the effects of the intervention more broadly. That is, one must not only measure aspects

TABLE 7-1   Causes and Solutions to the Productivity Paradox

Cause	Solution
Structural Factors	Measure Intervention Effects More Carefully
Intervention Side Effects	Measure Intervention Effects More Broadly
Measurement Effects	
Different Measurement Purposes	Aggregate Consistent Measures
Measurement Conflicts	
Conflict between Local Objectives	Resolve Conflicts and Replace Measures
Inconsistency Across Organizational Levels	Resolve Conflicts and Replace Measures

of performance that should be directly affected by the intervention, but also measure other aspects of the functioning of the broader subsystem that could be affected. For example, if a new CAD system is introduced, one should not only measure the quantity and quality of designs produced by the individual and groups using the new equipment, but also measure the overall outputs of the broader design unit.

Measurement Effects

The next major set of causes comprises direct measurement effects that could produce the paradox. This set of effects stems from the way productivity is measured. The first effect discussed is the natural phenomenon of measuring for different purposes.

Measuring for Different Purposes

The primary problem here is that improvements in measures taken for one purpose will not necessarily produce improvements in measures taken for another purpose. As measures are taken at higher and higher levels in the organization, more and more causal factors are being included in the measures that are not affected by lower levels in the organization. Thus, one should not expect much of a correspondence.

The solution to decomposing this aspect of the paradox is to aggregate measures that include the same causal factors. That is, one should not add new causal factors to the measures in aggregating up the organization. Consider the case of measuring for the motivational purpose. The organization's executives may want to know how well the personnel are doing the organization's work (i.e., producing their outputs). They can measure this in a particular unit but when they aggregate it, they should aggregate it with measures from other parts of the organization that reflect how well those personnel are producing their outputs. When the aggregation is complete, they have a measure of how well the personnel in this broader section of the organization are performing their work. If an organization introduces computer technology and expects it to improve how well people are producing their outputs, that is the measure it should use to evaluate the intervention. If the intervention is evaluated using traditional measures of overall organizational functioning, the organization is making the tacit assumption that factors such as economic conditions, actions of competitors, effectiveness of resource acquisition, coordination of units, and quality of supervision should also be affected by the introduction of computer technology.

One difficulty with this solution to the paradox is that of finding measures that can be aggregated across different types of units. That is, the measures must be on some common metric that can be combined. This is a challenge, but it can be done. Later in the chapter I summarize a technique that allows for this.

Conflict Between Objectives

The next two measurement effects deal with linkage/paradox problems that come about because of differences in objectives either (1) between subsystems that must coordinate with each other or (2) across organizational levels. If such differences exist, some of the outputs of one subsystem are in essence lost or wasted because they are not needed or valued by other subsystems. If the design unit produces elegant designs and the manufacturing unit requires simple, easy-to-make designs, some effort is going to be lost. This is an example of a conflict among coordinating subsystems. A conflict across levels would occur if the marketing division wanted to build a stable customer base over time and top management wanted immediate revenues.

Both of these situations are quite common. Sometimes there is a clear, openly acknowledged conflict in objectives. However, more typically, people recognize there is a problem, but they do not realize that it involves a conflict in objectives. The solution to this situation is to resolve the conflict in objectives and then develop new measures of organizational performance that are consistent with the agreed objectives. Such a solution is easy to propose but more difficult to implement. Essentially what is required is the development of a good performance measurement system. Below, I describe one such system in some detail because it offers a methodology for dealing with these measurement factors.

Developing a Performance Measurement System

A number of performance measurement systems have been proposed over the years (e.g., Craig and Harris, 1973; Kendrick, 1984; Mali, 1978; Riggs and Felix, 1983; Tuttle and Weaver, 1986). The system described here is called the Productivity Measurement and Enhancement System, or ProMES (Pritchard, 1990; Pritchard et al., 1989). (Note that for this system the term *productivity* is used in the broader sense. It encompasses the seven performance criteria discussed in Chapter 6.) The major conceptual base for this system is Naylor et al.'s (1980) view of behavior in organizations. When Pritchard and his students (Pritchard et al., 1988) applied this theory to the problem of measurement productivity, a new approach was developed. The new ProMES method not only produces a way to measure performance, it suggests ways that the information can be optimally fed back to employees so as to help improve their performance. The approach is designed primarily to be used for the motivational purpose in measuring performance or productivity.

The development of ProMES is done in a series of steps that start with identifying the primary objectives and end with providing performance information to the group in the form of a written feedback report that the group uses to improve its performance. To illustrate the steps, I use the example of a manufacturing setting in which a team of four or five persons assembles electronic printed circuit boards of the type found in computers. Each step in the process of developing ProMES is done by a design team composed of three to five job incumbents, one or two supervisors, and one or two facilitators who are familiar with the process and guide the group's activities. A more detailed description of the process can be found in Pritchard (1990, 1995).

Step 1: Develop Products First, the unit's *products* must be identified. Products are the important objectives that the group is expected to accomplish. Products may consist of services, tangible items, or a combination of the two. The ProMES design team meets and, through a process of group discussion and consensus building, develops the list of products. Assume that the design team identified the following products for the assembly group: (1) maintain high production, (2) make high-quality circuit boards, and (3) maintain high attendance.

Step 2: Develop Indicators The next step is to determine a method for measuring how well each objective is being accomplished. These measures are called *indicators*. They are typically quantitative, objective measures, but they can also be other types of measures, such as customer attitudes. Each product must have at least one indicator. The same design team identifies the indicators through group discussion and consensus. Assume that the design team developed the following list of indicators for the three products:

1. Maintain high production
   - percentage of boards completed: number of boards completed divided by number of boards received
   - meeting production priorities: number of high-priority boards completed divided by the number needed
2. Make high-quality boards
   - inspections passed: percentage of boards passing inspection

3. Maintain high attendance
   - attendance: total hours worked out of the maximum hours possible

In an actual ProMES system there are typically 4 to 6 products and 8 to 12 indicators. The example here is abbreviated to simplify the explanation.

When the design team reaches agreement on a unit's products and indicators, it presents the list to upper management for review and approval. Once approval is obtained, the design team can begin the next step.

Step 3: Develop Contingencies   The next step is to determine the *contingencies,* or the relationships between the amount of the indicator and how that amount will be evaluated. Figure 7-4 shows the general form of a contingency. The horizontal axis represents the amount of the indicator, ranging from the worst possible level likely to occur to the best possible level. The vertical axis depicts the different levels of effectiveness for the indicator. This scale ranges from +100 (maximum effectiveness) to –100 (minimum effectiveness). The zero point repre-

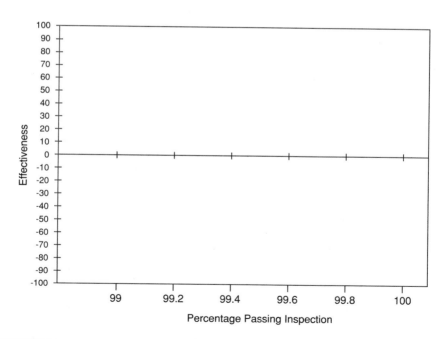

FIGURE 7-4 General form of a contingency.

sents the expected level of effectiveness. It is defined as the level of the indicator that is neither good nor bad. The basic idea of developing an indicator is to identify the function that defines what level of the indicator it takes to achieve what level of effectiveness.

A series of specific steps is used to develop each contingency. Through a process of group discussion and consensus, the design team identifies the end points of the indicator, determines the effectiveness scores for those end points, determines the zero point (expected level), and then completes the other points in the function. The process is somewhat complex conceptually, but in practice it is fairly easy. It also seems to produce contingencies that are reliable and useful over time (Pritchard et al., 1989).

In the example contingency, the design team determined that the best possible amount of boards passing inspection is 100 percent. This indicates that the team believes it is realistically possible for all the boards to pass inspection. The minimum, or worst feasible level of the indicator, was set at 99 percent of the boards passing inspection. Performance at or near this level was seen by the design team as a major production problem. The zero point, the expected level of the indicator, is 99.4 percent passing inspection. The effectiveness values that correspond to the maximum and minimum indicator levels are +70 and –80. The other values of the function are then determined.

This scaling process is done for all indicators so that each indicator has a contingency. Completed contingencies for all the indicators in the example are shown in Figure 7-5. Next, the contingency set is presented to higher management for approval. Frequently, disagreements arise about some of the contingencies; they are discussed and a compromise is reached. Once all the contingencies are approved by higher management, the contingency set is complete.

There are two particularly important aspects to note about contingencies. First, the overall slope of the contingency expresses the relative importance of the indicator. Steep slopes are produced for indicators that are very important to the functioning of the unit. Indicators with flatter slopes are less important to the functioning of the unit in that variations in these indicators will have a lesser impact on total effectiveness. Thus, the differential importance of the indicators is captured by the slope of the contingencies.

The second important aspect of contingencies is their nonlinearity. This is reflected in the completed contingency in Figure 7-5A. It shows that when the number of boards passing inspection is above the neutral point of 99.4 percent there is a large increase in effectiveness. However, once the passing rate reaches 99.7 percent, further increases do not represent as great a change. This nonlinearity is important be-

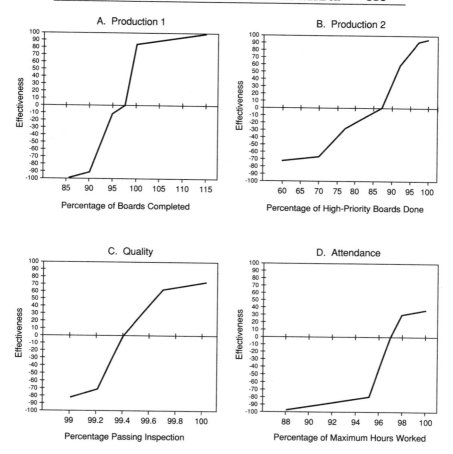

FIGURE 7-5 Completed contingency set.

cause a given amount of improvement at the low end of the measure may not have the same effect at the high end of the measure. It is quite common for improvements in the middle range of the indicator to result in large improvements in effectiveness, while improvements at the high end of the indicator result in smaller improvements in effectiveness. In other words, a point of diminishing returns is reached.

Put another way, once a certain level of effectiveness is reached, it may be more beneficial to focus on improving another area than to continue working on an area of performance that is already very good. For instance, if the unit producing circuit boards has completed a very high percentage of boards, it may be better to work on improving its only modest attendance even though attendance is not as important overall.

Step 4: Create the Feedback Report The fourth step in developing ProMES is to create a formal feedback report. Once indicator data are collected, effectiveness scores can be determined based on the contingencies for each indicator. As can be seen in Figure 7-5, if 99.8 percent of the group's boards pass inspection, it would achieve an effectiveness score of +62.

Continuing this process would result in an effectiveness value for each indicator. Once effectiveness values for each indicator are determined, they can be summed to determine the overall effectiveness score for that particular work group. This score represents the group's level of overall performance. A score of zero means that the group is meeting expectations; the higher the score is above zero, the more the unit is exceeding expectations. This information is presented to the unit in a formal written feedback report on a regular basis. Figure 7-6 shows an example of such a report.

Another overall measure that can be derived from the system is the group's percentage of maximum effectiveness, that is the overall effectiveness score the group would receive if it was at the highest possible level on every indicator. The unit's actual overall effectiveness score for the period can then be expressed as a percentage of this maximum. For example, summing the maximum values for each of the indicators in the example yields a total possible score of 300. The example unit received a monthly score of +97. Thus, its percentage-of-maximum score was 97/300, or 32.3 percent. The closer the unit is to 100 percent, the

Circuit Board Manufacturing Unit

Date: July 19xx

I. Production
    A. Percentage of Boards Completed   98%   +40
    B. Percentage of High-Priority Boards Done 85%   −5

    Total Effectiveness: Production = +35

II. Quality
    Percentage Passing Inspection   99.8%   +62

III. Attendance
     Percentage of Maximum Hours Worked   97%   0

     Overall effectiveness = +97

FIGURE 7-6 Sample feedback report.

closer it is to performing at the maximum performance level. If the unit's overall effectiveness is negative (i.e., below expectations), a negative value of the percentage-of-maximum score is calculated.

The advantage of the percentage-of-maximum index is that it allows the performance of groups doing very different things to be compared. The group with the highest percentage-of-maximum score is the highest-performing work group. This comparison is valid even if the groups have different indicators because the contingency process scales all indicators on a common metric, overall effectiveness. The comparison between different groups is then based on this common metric.

The ProMES methodology was first developed and evaluated in five units of an Air Force base (Pritchard et al., 1989). It resulted in large gains in productivity, and those gains were maintained for the entire time of measurement—at least 20 months. The methodology has also been successfully implemented in other organizations in the United States and Europe (Janssen and van Berkel, 1991; Jones, 1995; Kleinbeck et al., 1991; Kleingeld et al., 1991; Roth et al., 1995; Hedley et al., 1995; Schmidt, 1991; Stout and Jones, 1989; Thierry and Miedema, 1991; van Tuijl, 1991).

ProMES and Linkage Issues   ProMES is one methodology that can be used for dealing with conflicts in objectives that can produce the productivity paradox. The technique can be seen as a way of formally identifying organizational policy. Products, indicators, and contingencies reflect what the objectives of each subsystem are, what measures will communicate how well the subsystem is fulfilling those objectives, the relative importance of each measure, what is expected on each measure, and what level of output is defined as good or bad. This is a statement of policy. It is developed subjectively, but policy is by nature subjective. What ProMES does is to give organizational personnel a methodology with which to define policy in a way that people can understand, that people can agree with or not, and that can be communicated clearly.

By going through the process of developing the system, incumbents, supervisors, and managers can come to terms with the fact that there are disagreements in policy. These disagreements almost always occur somewhere in the development of a system. However, because the system gives personnel a structured method for dealing with the disagreements, it can make reaching a satisfactory compromise easier. This approach can be used across organizational levels and at the same level. Through the process of getting incumbents and supervisors to agree on the elements of the system and then presenting those elements to higher management and gaining approval, disagreements in objectives and policy across levels are made clear. Where possible, they are resolved and a new, more congruent policy is developed. If agreement is not possible, at least people know where the disagreements are and why they exist. This seems to make it easier to cope with the conflict.

The process of developing the system also helps resolve conflicts between units that must coordinate with each other. When the system is developed, it becomes clear where objectives are not consistent. In the design and manufacturing units in the example above, it would be clear from an examination of each unit's products and indicators that the two units are evaluating themselves differently. It then becomes the responsibility of higher management to work with the two units to bring products and indicators more in line with the objectives of the broader organization. One way this can be done is for each unit to have its own products, indicators, and contingencies as usual, but to have additional indicators that are a function of the joint efforts of the coordinating units. In the example, the common measures could be time to complete the final prototype, number of changes in the original design, and number of prototypes needed. These measures can only be highly favorable when the two units work closely together in developing the new product. These common measures would be added to the measurement system of each unit. If the two units want to look good on their measures, they must work together effectively.

ProMES and Aggregation The point has been made that one way of avoiding the productivity paradox is to aggregate only measures that are influenced by the same set of causal factors. The ProMES methodology offers a way to do this through the percentage-of-maximum measure. This is the index that is the unit's actual overall effectiveness divided by the maximum possible effectiveness for that unit. It is a metric that is common across all types of units, no matter what work they are doing.

One could calculate the percentage of maximum for a variety of different units. The mean percentage of maximum across the units would be the overall index of how well personnel are performing the organization's work.

TOWARD A COMPOSITION THEORY OF LINKAGES

While it is important to decompose the productivity paradox and suggest solutions for dealing with it, the larger objective must be kept in sight: learning about productivity linkages. The paradox is only an example of the importance of studying and understanding linkages between organizational subsystems. What is really needed is greater awareness and understanding of how outputs get combined and transformed across organizational levels.

The solutions to decomposing the paradox suggested above are a start in this direction, but they are just partial solutions. What is needed in addition is more conceptual work that will enable researchers and practitioners to understand better the nature of organizational linkages. Specifically, a sound theory of aggregation is needed, that is, a theory for how organizational levels are related to each other and how that affects organizational productivity.

Rousseau (1985) has cogently made the same point, arguing that when aggregation is done, what she calls a "theory of composition" is necessary. A composition theory specifies what the relationship is between the variables of interest at each level of aggregation. In the case of productivity, the composition theory would describe conceptually how productivity at the individual level is combined to produce productivity at the group level, and how the productivity of the groups are combined to produce divisional and organizational productivity.

A simplified example of such a composition theory is shown in Figure 7-7. The darker boxes in the middle of the figure show the linkages going from the individual to group to organizational level of analysis. Other levels would be needed for a complete theory, but the three depicted make the point. Above and below the middle of the figure are causal factors that will influence the transformation of outputs (i.e., linkage) from one level to the next.

The theory might suggest that an individual's output is a function of abilities, knowledge gained through training and experience, motivation, and availability of materials/resources to do the work. These variables combine to produce individual output, the first box in the figure. However, since the individual's efforts must be combined with those of others, how well individuals work together will influence how well the individuals' outputs are translated into group outputs and, ultimately, group performance. In addition, if the supervisor does not provide sufficient materials and information and does not handle intergroup and intragroup relations well, group performance will be affected. Thus, the *quality of supervision* is also involved in the translation of individual to group performance.

Another variable in this composition theory is the *degree of interdependence* of the individuals in the group. If each person works completely independently, moving to a higher level of analysis is more straightforward. Individual measures can be more easily aggregated because the work of one individual has little impact on the work of the others. If, however, there is a great deal of interdependence in the work, the situation is much more complicated. In this case, it is inap-

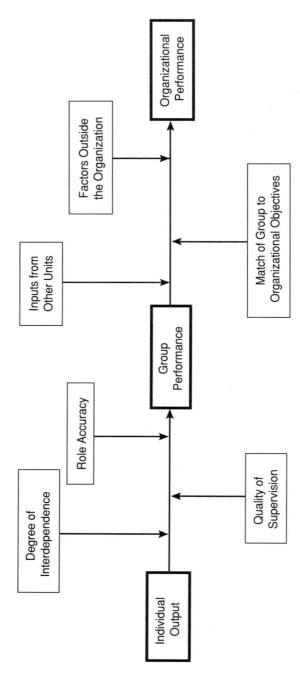

FIGURE 7-7 Simplified model of composition theory.

propriate simply to sum individual measures. Specific group-level measures that will capture the interdependencies would be needed.

Role accuracy is another variable that influences the translation of individual output to group performance. This variable is conceptualized as the accuracy of the match between what the individuals see as important in expending their time and effort and what is important to the broader group.

Other variables influence the translation of group-level performance to organizational performance. *Inputs from other units* are the outputs of other units that are needed to translate group-level performance to organizational performance. They could include other components of the final product, direct services (e.g., marketing), or staff functions of various types. *Match of group to organizational objectives* is analogous to role accuracy, but at the group level. It is the degree of match between group objectives and organizational objectives. Factors outside the organization include the economy and government regulations.

Once the variables in the theory of composition are identified and defined unambiguously, the next step would be to develop quantitative operationalizations of each variable. For example, degree of interdependence could be operationalized as the correlation of mean individual output and total group performance over time. If personnel in the group are truly independent, their individual outputs can simply be summed to arrive at total group output. In this case, if one calculated the correlation between mean individual output and group output over time periods, the correlation between the two measures over time would be 1.0. Thus, if this correlation is close to 1.0, the individuals are highly independent. If there is dependency between group members, the outputs of one individual influence the outputs of others. In a case of interdependence like this, the mean outputs of the individuals cannot simply be added to get total group output. Consequently, the correlation between mean individual output and total group output over time will decrease from 1.0. The greater the interdependency, the greater the decrease from 1.0 toward 0.

Once the operationalizations have been developed, the next step would be to estimate mathematical functions that capture how the separate variables are related to each other. For example, the interdependence coefficient, which ranges from 0 to 1.0, could be a multiplier between total individual output and group performance. An interdependence coefficient of, for example, .50 would mean that increasing individual output would improve group performance, but not as much as when interdependence is lower (e.g., a coefficient of .8).

Advantages of a Theory of Composition

While this theory of composition and the example functions are simplistic, they illustrate what a theory of composition for productivity linkages might be like. A great deal of work would be needed to develop a comprehensive theory, but the work would be well worth it because of the advantages of such a theory.

One major advantage of such a theory would be that it would enhance understanding of productivity linkages and cross-level organizational analyses in general. Researchers and practitioners have been very naive in their approach to organizations, assuming that changes in one level of the organization will automatically be apparent at higher levels of the organization. It is commonly implied, for example, that better selection of entry-level personnel will improve organizational productivity. The argument is that if the mean productivity of individuals is improved by, for example, 10 percent, the productivity of the unit will improve by 10 percent. This sort of argument ignores all the factors that the theory of composition indicates influence the translation of individual to group productivity. If the output of a group of programmers is increased by 10 percent through better selection, but the work flow between programmers is not managed so as to utilize the improved individual performance, the increase could easily be lost. A clear theory of composition would make the fallacy of the assumption very clear and indicate the factors that intervene in the linkages.

Once there is even a basic mathematical model of the linkages, several other benefits become possible. One advantage will be the ability to predict the relationships between components of the theory. Not only will this allow the theory to be tested, but once supported, the theory can then be used to predict what to expect when components of the model are changed.

One application of this capability of the model is to predict whether productivity gains at one level will be lost or wasted in their translation to higher levels. For example, it may be possible to predict that with the level of slack that exists in a given unit, improving the efficiency of one group will simply increase the amount of slack, not improve the broader unit's performance.

Another application is to do "what-if" and sensitivity analyses to compare productivity improvement strategies. For example, one could compare the expected gain in performance at the group and organizational levels from (1) improving personnel selection, (2) clarifying roles, and (3) changing technology. Being able to approximate the gains that would occur with different strategies could be of great benefit in deciding among alternatives.

DIRECTIONS FOR FUTURE RESEARCH

Attempting to understand linkage issues leads to a series of ideas for needed research. First, the most general need is for research that further explains the importance of linkages and the impact they have on attempts to improve organizational performance. It is easiest just to focus on a single intervention at a single level of analysis, but as this report makes very clear, such a strategy is overly simplistic.

Second, future researchers need to avoid the temptation to try to identify the "proper" criterion for assessing organizational performance. It make no sense to talk about organizational performance or effectiveness as if it is a concept that has a universal meaning. It is like asking whether an individual is a good performer. The obvious answer is a good performer at *what*? What constitutes organizational performance is what the measurer wants to assess the organization on. Researchers must be very careful that they do not fall into the trap of assuming that there is a set of agreed measures or even that one set of measures is somehow better than another.

Third, in order to attack the linkages problem in a systematic fashion, researchers should develop a master list of variables that could influence the translation of outputs across linkages. The chapters in this report are an excellent source for such a taxonomy. Such a listing could group the factors by type. For example, this chapter breaks down factors into structural effects, intervention side effects, and measurement effects. Within each type, the factors could be grouped by the type of solution needed to address the linkage issue. For example, variables that are the natural consequence of organizational structure (e.g., slack), which cannot and should not be considered problems, would be grouped together.

Fourth, empirical research is needed to identify the major linkage variables and their relative importance. To do such research, multiple units within multiple organizations must be studied in a longitudinal design. As a first step, improvements in outputs at the most molecular level must be shown to have occurred because of an intervention, and then those improvements must be traced through the various organizational linkages to the broadest organizational level. The idea would be to measure each explanatory factor as identified in the linkages taxonomy, along with the amount of loss of output across the linkage. For example, explanatory variables such as slack and conflict in objectives would be measured directly. Then, the importance of each could be assessed empirically. Ideally, the data would be collected so that the variance accounted for by each explanatory factor could be assessed.

The most important types of linkage variables are those that result in the actual loss of outputs from one level to the next. This represents waste, and to the extent it exists, its elimination will improve organizational functioning. Thus, the next step in the research program would be to use interventions to change the factors that are decreasing the translation of outputs across levels and assess the effectiveness of the interventions. For example, if conflict in the objectives of different units is causing the linkage loss, interventions to make the objectives consistent would be employed. The evaluation would be to assess the effectiveness of different types of intervention and to determine if the linkage loss can be eliminated.

Finally, a theory of composition is sorely needed. As argued in this chapter, this is a theory that indicates what the major linkage variables are and how they affect the translation of outputs from one level of the organization to the next. This would be a major research program that would take a great deal of work. However, if it could be done successfully, the payoffs would be enormous.

CONCLUSION

It is clear from the issues raised in this chapter that the productivity paradox is of great significance in that it highlights the importance of a much clearer understanding and appreciation of the linkages among levels of the organization. Researchers and practitioners have been very simplistic in thinking that changes at one level in the organization will be translated in a simple manner to higher levels. There are many possible explanations for the paradox, the importance of which is to enhance understanding of organizational linkages. This and other chapters in this report suggest many factors that must be considered in understanding these linkages. The challenge is to use these ideas to further understanding of linkages and, from that, to learn how efforts to improve productivity can be facilitated.

AUTHOR'S NOTE

I would like to thank Margaret Watson for her contribution to an earlier version of this chapter. Steven Worchel suggested several of the ideas in the section on unintended side effects of organizational interventions. I would also like to thank Amie Hedley-Goode, Karlease Clark, and Anthony Paquin for their helpful comments on an earlier draft of the chapter.

REFERENCES

Algera, J.A.
  1989   Feedback systems in organizations. In C.L. Cooper and I. Robertson, eds., *International Review of Industrial and Organizational Psychology*. Chichester: John Wiley & Sons.
Craig, C.E., and R.C. Harris
  1973   Total productivity measurement at the firm level. *Sloan Management Review* 14(3):13-28.
Hedley, A., J.E. Sawyer, and R.D. Pritchard
  1995   Development of a new performance appraisal instrument: An application of the ProMES methodology. In R.D. Pritchard, ed., *Productivity Improvement Strategies and Applications: Case Studies in Organizations*. New York: Praeger Press, forthcoming.
Hulin, C., C. Roberts, and D. Rousseau
  1978   *Developing an Interdisciplinary Science of Organizations*. San Francisco: Jossey-Bass.
Janssen, P.M., and A. van Berkel
  1991   ProMES in a Dutch Production Organization. Paper presented at the Academy of Management conference, Miami.
Jones, S.D.
  1995   ProMES with assembly line work groups: It's more than just a technology. In R.D. Pritchard, ed., *Productivity Improvement Strategies and Applications: Case Studies in Organizations*. New York: Praeger Press, forthcoming.
Katz, D., and R.L. Kahn
  1978   *The Social Psychology of Organizations*, 2d ed. New York: John Wiley & Sons.
Kendrick, J.W.
  1984   *Improving Company Productivity*. Baltimore, Md.: Johns Hopkins University Press.
Kleinbeck, U., K.H. Schmidt, and M. Przygodda
  1991   Participative Productivity Management (PPM) Using ProMES: Theory, Methods and Empirical Results from German Studies. Paper presented at the Academy of Management conference, Miami.
Kleingeld, A., H.F.J.M. van Tuijl, and J.A. Algera
  1991   The Management of Performance in a Dutch Organization: Introducing ProMES into a Service Organization. Paper presented at the Academy of Management conference, Miami.
Mahoney, T.A.
  1988   Productivity defined: The relativity of efficiency, effectiveness and change. Pp. 13-38 in J.P. Campbell and R.J. Campbell, eds., *Productivity in Organizations*. San Francisco: Jossey-Bass.
Mali, P.
  1978   *Improving Total Productivity*. New York: John Wiley & Sons.
Naylor, J.C., R.D. Pritchard, and D.R. Ilgen
  1980   *A Theory of Behavior in Organizations*. New York: Academic Press.
Pritchard, R.D.
  1990   *Measuring and Improving Organizational Productivity: A Practical Guide*. New York: Praeger.
  1992   Organizational productivity. Pp. 443-471 in M.D. Dunnette and L.M. Hough, eds., *Handbook of Industrial/Organizational Psychology*, 2d ed., Vol. 3. Palo Alto, Calif.: Consulting Psychologists Press.

1995   *Productivity Improvement Strategies and Applications: Case Studies in Orga-*
        nizations. New York: Praeger Press, forthcoming.

Pritchard, R.D., S.D. Jones, P.L. Roth, K.K. Stuebing, and S.E. Ekeberg
1988   The effects of feedback, goal setting, and incentives on organizational produc-
        tivity. *Journal of Applied Psychology Monograph Series* 73(2):337-358.
1989   The evaluation of an integrated approach to measuring organizational pro-
        ductivity. *Personnel Psychology* 42(1):69-115.

Riggs, J.L., and G.H. Felix
1983   *Productivity by Objectives.* Englewood Cliffs, N.J.: Prentice-Hall.

Roth, P.L., M.D. Watson, P.G. Roth, and R.D. Pritchard
1995   ProMES in an electronic assembly plant. In R.E. Pritchard, ed., *Productivity*
        Improvement Strategies and Applications: Case Studies in Organizations. New
        York: Praeger Press, forthcoming.

Rousseau, D.M.
1985   Issues of level in organizational research: Multi-level and cross-level perspec-
        tives. *Research in Organizational Behavior* 7:1-37.

Schmidt, K.H.
1991   Development of a Productivity Management System for Craftsmen.   Paper
        presented at the Second European Congress of Psychology, Budapest.

Stout, J., and S. Jones
1989   Using ProMES in the Insurance Industry. Paper presented at the Society for
        Industrial and Organizational Psychology meeting, Dallas.

Thierry, H., and H. Miedema
1991   ProMES in Dutch Banks: Performance, Productivity and Compensation Is-
        sues. Paper presented at the Academy of Management conference, Miami.

Tuttle, T.C.
1981   *Productivity Measurement Methods: Classification, Critique, and Implications*
        for the Air Force. Manpower and Personnel Division, AFHRL-TR-81-9. Brooks
        Air Force Base, Tex.: Air Force Human Resources Laboratory.

Tuttle, T.C., and C.N. Weaver
1986   *Methodology for Generating Efficiency and Effectiveness Measures (MGEEM):*
        A Guide for Air Force Measurement Facilitators. Manpower and Personnel
        Division, AFHRL-TP-86-36, AD-A174 547. Brooks Air Force Base, Tex.: Air
        Force Human Resources Laboratory.

van Tuijl, H.F.J.M.
1991   Productivity Measurement and Improvement in Photocopier Maintenance Per-
        sonnel. Development and Implementation of ProMES with Varying Degrees
        of Participation. Paper presented at the Second European Congress of Psy-
        chology, Budapest.

Weiss, L.G.
1989   Productivity Measurement Issues. Unpublished paper, Department of Psy-
        chology, Texas A&M University.

8

Models of Measurement and Their Implications for Research on the Linkages Between Individual and Organizational Productivity

John P. Campbell

As argued in the previous three chapters, measuring productivity is a very intrusive process. It makes goals very explicit, serves to identify the work to be done, influences individual and organizational choice behavior, and helps to define what will be rewarded and punished. That is, measurement is a powerful influence on individual and organizational productivity and performance.

My purpose in this chapter is to outline a substantive measurement model that has direct implications for future research on the linkage between individual and organizational productivity. The model is intended to be entirely consistent with Chapters 5 and 6 and to make the necessity of a substantive specification of information technology (IT) productivity even more explicit.

Measurement has two principal parts. The first concerns the substantive specification of the variables to be measured. The second is the specification of the rules and scaling operations by which different values of a particular measure will be assigned to different amounts of the variables under consideration. The substantive theory cannot be separated from the scaling model. Both are always present, if only by default. For example, a university may use student credit hours per faculty member as an indicator of the productivity of academic departments simply because "it is there." Use of such a measurement operation, however, implies something very concrete about what is meant by departmental productivity in that institution—teaching large classes cheaply is the way to be productive.

In any measurement model, there also should be a clear distinction between the latent variable, or construct, and the observed measure. By definition, a particular variable can be measured in any of several different ways. For example, quantity of code production for a programmer/analyst could be measured through archival production records (raw or adjusted), the amount of code produced in a specified time in a simulation exercise, or a supervisor's judgment. The distinction between the latent variable and the operational measure is of fundamental importance and is the crux of this chapter.

A basic axiom of measurement is that the validity of a measure can only be judged against the specific objectives or purposes of measurement (American Educational Research Association et al., 1985). In the current context, one major goal is to support the modeling of the linkage between individual and organizational productivity. That is, if both individual and organizational productivity can be measured, can the causal relationships between individual and organizational productivity be described? A second measurement objective is to assess the components of productivity that most directly reflect the effects of IT implementations. The two general goals of modeling the individual-organizational linkage and evaluating the effects of new information technologies may indeed require different measures.

Having said this, it should be noted again that measurement itself is a very powerful treatment (see Chapter 5). It defines goals and guides action. If it is based on a sound analysis of the variables to be measured and the measurement operations validly reflect the appropriate sources of variation, the effects on performance, effectiveness, or productivity can be dramatic (e.g., Pritchard et al., 1989). Perhaps for the first time, people would know where to direct their energies and the outcomes on which rewards and punishments will be contingent.

In the next section I outline a measurement model that could be used at the individual and organizational levels to guide research on measuring productivity and its antecedent. I discuss the model in the context of the individual first and then consider the organizational analog.

A SUGGESTED MEASUREMENT MODEL

As discussed above, any measurement theory must address the nature of the variable(s) to be measured and the appropriateness of the scaling procedures used to estimate "scores." Without a specification of the former, the latter cannot be evaluated. Consequently, the description of the model below focuses on the former rather than the latter.

Modeling the Latent Structure of IT Productivity: An Analogy from Individual Performance

What are the basic variables that constitute IT productivity and what is their basic form? That is, what is the latent structure of IT productivity? No one seems to know at the moment. Even a tentative specification has not been offered. Speculations seem to center around a variety of specific measures that happen to be available (e.g., lines of code per programmer per year).

Describing in the abstract what is meant by the latent structure of the basic variables that constitute productivity in a specific industry or organization is not easy. A quick rendition of a prototype model might be helpful (see Figure 8-1). Although the prototype to be described concerns the latent structure of individual performance (not productivity), it provides a useful stepping stone for talking about how to develop a measurement model of individual and organizational productivity in the IT industry (for a fuller discussion of the prototype, see Campbell, 1991).

The specifications for modeling the latent structure of individual performance begin with a definition of performance. *Performance* is individual action that has relevance for the organization's goals. A measure of performance reflects how well people execute the relevant actions. Also, performance is not one thing. It is composed of a finite, but not too large, number of major components, or factors. The covariances among the components probably are not zero, but neither are they so large as to allow highly accurate prediction of performance on one component from performance on another (e.g., teaching performance versus research performance).

In this model performance has eight components at the most general level (classes of things people do on the job). The eight components are intended to be sufficient to describe the top of the latent hierarchy in any specific job. However, the eight components have different patterns of subgeneral components, and their content varies differentially across jobs. Further, any particular job might not incorporate all eight components. A brief description and discussion of each of the eight components follows.

Job-specific task proficiency reflects the degree to which the individual can perform the core substantive or technical tasks that are central to his or her job. Core tasks are the job-specific performance behaviors that distinguish the substantive content of one job from another. Constructing custom kitchens, doing word processing, designing computer architecture, driving a bus through city traffic, and di-

Determinants of Job Performance Components: $PC_i = f(DK, PKS, M)^a$

Declarative Knowledge (DK)	Procedural Knowledge and Skill (PKS)	Motivation (M)
Labels	Cognitive skill	Choice to perform
Facts	Psychomotor skill	Choice of level of effort
Rules	Physical skill	
Principles	Self-management skill	Choice of duration of effort
Goals	Interpersonal skill	
Self-knowledge		

i = 1, 2 . . . k performance components. Performance components are the latent variables that represent the substantive content of what people should be doing in a particular job (e.g., conducting undergraduate classes). They are intended to fit a hierarchical factor model and to define a set of continuums along which individual proficiency can be measured. At the top of the hierarchy $k = 8$.

Predictors of Performance Determinants[b]

DK = f[(ability, personality, interests), (education, training, experience), (aptitude/treatment) interactions]

PKS = f[(ability, personality, interests), (education, training, practice, experience), (aptitude/treatment) interactions]

M = f[whatever variables are stipulated by the chosen motivation theory]

[a] Performance differences can also be produced by situational effects, such as the quality of equipment, degree of staff support, or nature of the working conditions. For purposes of this model of performance, these conditionals are assumed to be held constant (experimentally, statistically, or judgmentally).
[b] Individual differences, learning, and motivational manipulations can only influence performance by influencing declarative knowledge, procedural knowledge and skill, or the three choices.

FIGURE 8-1 A proposed model of job performance and its determinants.

recting commercial air traffic—all are categories of job-specific task content. Individual differences in how well such tasks are executed are the focus of this performance component.

Non-job-specific task proficiency reflects the fact that the vast majority of individuals are required to perform tasks or take actions that are not specific to their particular job. For example, in research universities with doctoral programs, the faculty must teach classes, advise students, make admissions decisions, and serve on committees. All faculty must do these things, in addition to "doing" chemistry, psychology, economics, or electrical engineering.

Written and oral communication, that is, formal oral or written presentations, is a required part of many jobs. For those jobs, the proficiency with which one can write or speak, independent of the correctness of the subject matter, is a critical component of performance.

Demonstrating effort reflects the degree to which individuals commit themselves to all job tasks, work at a high level of intensity, and keep working under adverse conditions.

Maintaining personnel discipline reflects the degree to which negative behavior, such as substance abuse at work, law or rule infractions, or excessive absenteeism, is avoided.

Facilitating peer and team performance reflects the degree to which the individual supports his or her peers, helps them with job problems, and acts as a de facto trainer. It also encompasses how well an individual facilitates group functioning by being a good model, keeping the group goal directed, and reinforcing participation by other group members. If the individual works alone, this component will have little importance. However, in many jobs, high performance on this component would be a major contribution toward the goals of the organization.

Supervision / leadership includes all the behaviors directed at influencing the performance of subordinates through face-to-face interaction and influence. Supervisors set goals for subordinates, teach them more effective methods, model the appropriate behaviors, and reward or punish in appropriate ways. The distinction between this component and the previous one is a distinction between peer leadership and supervisory leadership.

Management / administration includes the major elements in management that are distinct from direct supervision. It includes the performance behaviors directed at articulating goals for the unit or enterprise, organizing people and resources to work on them, monitoring progress, helping to solve problems or overcome crises that stand in the way of goal accomplishment, controlling expenditures, obtaining additional resources, and representing the unit in dealings with other units.

Next, performance *components* must be distinguished from performance *determinants* (the causes of individual differences on each performance component). As noted by the equation at the top of Figure 8-1, in this model individual differences on a specific performance component (PC) are a function of three major determinants: declarative knowledge (DK), procedural knowledge and skill (PKS), and motivation (M). Thus, $PC = f(DK, PKS, M)$. *Declarative knowledge* is simply knowledge about facts and things. Specifically, it represents an understanding of a given task's requirements (e.g., general principles for equipment operation). *Procedural knowledge and skill* is attained when declarative knowledge (knowing what to do) has been successfully combined with being able to actually do it (modified from Anderson, 1985, and Kanfer and Ackerman, 1989). The major categories of procedural knowledge and skill are (1) cognitive skills, (2) psychomotor skills, (3) physical skills, (4) perceptual skills, (5) interpersonal skills, and (6) self-management skills.

As a direct determinant of performance, motivation is defined as the combined effect of three choice behaviors: (1) choice to perform, (2) choice of level of effort to expend, and (3) choice of the length of time to persist in the expenditure of that level of effort. These are the traditional representations for the direction, amplitude, and duration of volitional behavior. The important point is that the most meaningful way to talk about motivation as a direct determinant of behavior is as one or more of these three choices.

Having summarized the general ingredients of the model, a few general points should be noted. First, the precise functional form of the PC = f(DK, PKS, M) equation is obviously not known and perhaps not even knowable. Further, spending years of research looking for it would probably not be of much use. Instead, the following is suggested. First, performance will not occur unless there is a choice to perform at some level of effort for some specified time. Consequently, motivation is always a determinant of performance, and a relevant question for virtually any personnel problem is how much of the variance in choice behavior can be accounted for by stable predispositions, how much is a function of the motivating properties of the situation, and how much is a function of the interaction. Performance also cannot occur unless there is some threshold level of procedural skill, and there may be a very complex interaction between procedural skill and motivation. For example, the higher the skill level, the greater the tendency to choose to perform. Another reasonable assumption is that declarative knowledge is a prerequisite for procedural skill (Anderson, 1985). That is, before being able to perform a task, one must know what should be done. However, this point is not without controversy (Nissen and Bullmer, 1987), and it may indeed be possible to master a skill without first acquiring the requisite declarative knowledge. Nevertheless, given the current findings in cognitive research, the distinction is a meaningful one (Anderson, 1985). Performance could suffer because procedural skill was never developed, because declarative knowledge was never acquired, or because one or the other has decayed. Also, some data suggest that the abilities that account for individual differences in declarative knowledge are not the same as those that account for individual differences in procedural skills (Ackerman, 1988).

Beyond the Basic Taxonomy of Performance Components

The eight performance components above are meant to be the highest-order components that can be useful. To reduce them further would mask too much. However, as noted, not all the components are relevant for all jobs.

The nature of the lower-order factors within the major components has been the subject of considerable research for some of the eight components (e.g., supervision/leadership, management/administration) and is a matter of speculation for others (e.g., communication, demonstrating effort). It is possible that the number of subfactors for the first component (core task performance) is equal to the number of different jobs in the occupational hierarchy. That is, specific determinants of performance on this component would be different for each job. This would be a very poor description of the latent structure. However, one would hardly expect the determinants of core task performance to be the same for jazz musicians, graphic artists, professional golfers, theoretical economists, the clergy, farm managers, and so on. Where between these two extremes is a more appropriate description of the subfactors of core task performance? The model assumes that the number of discriminable subfactors for this component is a manageable number, and that it would be quite possible to build a systematic body of knowledge around the major differences in the correlates for the subfactors.

Peak Versus Typical Performance

In a very illustrative study of supermarket checkout personnel, Sackett et al. (1988) obtained the correlation between a standardized job sample measure (see below) administered by the researchers, and an on-line computerized record of actual performance on the very same job tasks. Both measures were highly reliable, but the correlation between the two was surprisingly low. The authors called this a distinction between maximum and typical performance, and they reasoned that the cause of the low correlation was the uniformly high motivation generated by the research situation versus the differential motivation across individuals in the actual work setting. If such an explanation is accurate, attempts to model performance must address the issue of what to do with the distinction. The prototype model includes the two components of core task performance and level and consistency of effort in an attempt to keep these two aspects of performance ("can do" versus "will do") separate. If both components can actually be measured, so much the better. If they cannot, the typical performance measure is a fuller account of an individual's contribution.

Potential Measurement Methods

When it comes to the actual measurement of performance, the model allows only three, or possibly four, primary measurement methods. Ratings, or the use of expert judgments to assess performance, are considered by many to be a very poor method of measuring (Cascio, 1991), but they are probably not as bad as claimed. One advantage of ratings is that their content can be directly linked to the basic performance components by straightforward content validation methods (e.g., critical incident sampling or task analysis). Also, their reliabilities are usually respectable and can be improved considerably by using more than one rater, and they are as predictable as objective effectiveness measures (Nathan and Alexander, 1988; Schmitt et al., 1984). In the context of the performance model being described, ratings have the added advantage of being able to reflect all three kinds of performance determinants (DK, PKS, and M) and can be used for any performance component (i.e., the basic eight or their subfactors). The principal concern about ratings has always been their possible contamination by systematic variance unrelated to the performance of the person being assessed. Breaking performance rating into its sequential elements—sampling observations, perceptual filtering, encoding information, storage in memory, retrieval of information for a specific purpose, and differential weighting and composite scoring of the information retrieved—shows it to be a very complex cognitive process that allows many opportunities for unsystematic variance and contamination (Landy and Farr, 1980). Considerable faith is restored by the fact that the more thorough attempts to use the method have produced credible results (Campbell, 1991).

The second measurement method is the standardized job sample, in which the task content of the job (e.g., the supermarket checkout above) is simulated, or actually sampled intact, and presented to the assessee in a standardized format under standardized conditions. The content validity of this method can also be determined directly, but for the reasons discussed above, it may not reflect the influence of all three determinants (DK, PKS, and M), and it may be difficult to use it to measure some of the eight components. Also, there is always a question about whether the knowledge and skill required by the standardized sample are different in any major respect from those required in the actual job setting.

A third measurement method would consist of directly observing and measuring the task as it occurs in the job setting. This is what Sackett et al. (1988) were able to do for the supermarket checkout personnel. Using this method would require rather expensive observational or recording techniques for most jobs, and for complex jobs the difficulties in observation might be insurmountable.

In general, the fourth measurement method is not allowed because it equates performance and effectiveness, which includes factors outside the control of the individual. However, it may sometimes be possible to specify outcomes of performance that are almost completely under the control of the individual and to assess individuals on such indicators.

The Characteristics of Good Measurement

In general, a "good" measure has high content validity, allows the appropriate performance determinants to operate, has a high proportion of reliable variance, is not contaminated by systematic variance due to things such as race or gender bias, minimizes the influence of general method variance (e.g., the "ratings" method), minimizes the influence of instrument-specific method variance, and maximizes the estimated true correlation between the operational measure and the latent variable.

If validity is defined as the degree to which an indicator measures what it is supposed to measure, there are two major ways a measure could be invalid: (1) the definition/specifications for the variable(s) to be measured are wrong and (2) the measurement operations themselves do not capture the appropriate determinants. For example, when defined as the number of units produced divided by labor costs, individual productivity can be increased simply by cutting salaries, and the measurement operations can validly reflect the change. On the other hand, if the operational measure is insensitive to changes in output (i.e., the numerator), the measure would not be a valid one. This might happen if cutting salaries leads to more defects in the work produced but the quality control system cannot detect it.

Similarly, if reliability of measurement is defined as consistency over repeated measures, then unreliability can result from a lack of consistency in the way the variable is defined (either across time or across decision makers) or from a measurement method that contains too much random error. To say it another way, the validity and reliability of measurement depend on a good theory and a good measurement method.

MEASUREMENT ISSUES RAISED BY THE PROTOTYPE MODEL

The prototype model provided above has useful implications for the measurement of individual and organizational productivity. The following issues seem critical.

Goal Explication

Understanding the organizational goals to which a job should contribute is a fundamental issue for performance measurement. The same is true for measuring individual and organizational IT productivity against the goals of the IT enterprise. For example, some sources speak disparagingly about the effects (or lack of an effect) of the automatic teller machine (ATM) on bank productivity. This seems to imply that introducing a new technology to maintain market share or to keep customer satisfaction from decreasing is not a goal against which bank IT should be judged. Is this a correct inference? Certainly customers can do many things with an ATM system that they could not do before. Should this not be designated as an increase in productivity? In general, if one wants to make clear statements about the state of IT productivity and the rate at which it is changing, the goals for IT must be articulated.

The Definition of Productivity

As is often true in discussions of performance, the term *productivity* is frequently used without any attempt to say what it means. In the context of the individual-organizational linkage, what should it mean? Is it the value of the IT-using organization's output that is purchased by users divided by the costs of achieving that output? Is it the judged utility of the output to some larger organization or industry? Or is it the quantity or quality of the output itself? There is nothing sacred about any particular characterization. The requirement imposed by the model is to come to some agreement about the definition that would be most useful and to use it consistently. How best to do that is a research issue.

Unit of Analysis and Locus of Measurement

In the performance model, a major concern is whether individual differences on the performance measure(s) are in fact under the control of the individual. The same concern is relevant for productivity measurement. Are the quantity (quality?, value?) of output and the costs of achieving that output actually under the direct control of the individual (if the concern is individual productivity) or the organization (if the concern is organizational productivity)? If not, evaluating individuals or organizations by using such contaminated measures is counterproductive.

Components of Productivity

If performance is truly multidimensional such that the word should never be used in the singular without a modifier, the implication is that the same is true for productivity. What then are the major components of IT productivity?

There are at least two complicating factors. First, IT is not a monolith. At various places in this report, the word *productivity* has been modified by each of the following:

• software engineering/design productivity (e.g., the completion of software designs by software engineers);
• software development productivity (e.g., the writing of code to operationalize the design);
• software production productivity (e.g., the writing of code to meet specific user demands);
• software productivity (e.g., *PC World* magazine's standardized comparison of WordPerfect 4.2 versus 5.1);
• hardware productivity (e.g., the output versus costs for a 486/33 processor compared with a 286/25 processor under standardized conditions);
• hardware user productivity (e.g., replacing all 286/25 personal computers with 486/33 machines in a data analysis facility); and
• software user productivity (e.g., replacing WordPerfect 4.2 with 5.1 in an administrative/clerical operation).

One can think of the individual-organizational linkage within each of these contexts. However, the nature of the dependent variables to be measured would most likely be different, and certainly the sources of variation in a productivity indicator will not be the same across contexts. Which contexts are the most important? Are all of them?

The second complicating factor is that, by analogy to the prototype model, productivity within each of these contexts is multidimensional. That is, productivity is not singular for software engineering organizations or for any of the other contexts. The ability to specify the basic variables of interest is a function of the current accumulation of information within each context and the knowledge to be gained by future research. In some contexts there may indeed be enough information to propose a useful array of basic productivity components if the information has been summarized with such a purpose in mind. In other contexts, more research may be needed. The investigation of the productivity of computer-aided design (CAD) users in Chapter 10 is an example of such research.

The eight higher-order components in the individual performance model described earlier are meant to reflect the structure of performance that seems to be represented in the current theory, practice, and research evidence. The question here is whether the available literature on IT productivity would permit at least a tentative specification of its latent structure.

Productivity Determinants

The prototype measurement model says that variation in individual performance is a function of three determinants (DK, PKS, M). They are important ingredients of the model because an operational performance measure (e.g., supervisor ratings or scores from a job task simulator) could choose to control or not control for one or more of them. For example, the measurement objective could stipulate that individual differences in motivation (the three volitional choices noted above) should not contribute to individual differences in performance scores produced by the measure, as when evaluating the effects of a skills training program. In such an instance, the measurement goal is to determine whether the specified technical skills have in fact been mastered, not whether the individual chooses to use them in the actual job setting. In general, the critical issue is whether the measure allows the relevant determinants to influence scores.

Perhaps another example would help illustrate the point. It is generally agreed that many commercial airline accidents are the result of faulty "cockpit management." That is, at a critical time there is a breakdown in task delegation, communication, and teamwork. These specific variables seem to represent supervision/leadership and management/administration in the prototype model's taxonomy of performance components. If a simulator is used to measure performance, there are two major considerations at the outset. First, does the simulator allow performance on the two components to be observed? Second, what performance determinants should be allowed to operate and which should be controlled? For example, one frequently critical determinant in cockpit management is the hesitation of a junior crew member to question the actions of the senior pilot if he or she appears to be in error. To bring this determinant into the simulator, the simulator "crew" should reflect the established air crew hierarchy. To serve a different objective, the measurement procedure could choose to control for the motivational determinants so as to evaluate the effects of knowledge or skill differentials without being confounded with motivational differences. Again, the choice of measurement operations is very dependent on the measurement objectives.

Moving from individual performance to a consideration of individual and group productivity makes the explication of determinants a bit more complicated. Individual and group productivity are surely influenced by a number of other things besides individual knowledge, skill, and motivation, and legitimately so. For example, the translation of individual output to group output is a function of such things as the nature of the task, the structure of the organization, the nature of the technology, and a number of management considerations (e.g., coordination, planning, goal definition, feedback, and control) regardless of whether they are exercised by a manager or an empowered work group.

Chapter 3 provided an excellent summary of what is known, and not known, about how to model the linkage between individual and organizational productivity. Taken in concert with Chapters 5 and 6, Chapter 3 makes it possible to at least outline the basic determinants of organizational productivity. At perhaps the highest level of abstraction, the list of basic determinants might be as follows:

- Individual performance, as explained in this chapter.
- Technology, in this case IT, as discussed in Chapter 9.
- The interaction of technology and individual capabilities, in the sense that certain kinds of technologies, in combination with certain kinds of individuals, may have a much greater or lesser effect on productivity than would be expected from the sum of the main effects. For example, new technology A may be totally beyond the capabilities of the current users, but technology B may take full advantage of those capabilities.
- Organizational structure, as it applies to the individual-organizational linkage. The parameters of organizational structure were discussed in Chapters 3 and 5.
- The interaction between technology and organizational structure, that is, some technologies may be very inappropriate and even counterproductive when implemented within certain kinds of organizational structures, and vice versa. For example, installing and maintaining a computerized project managment system may detract from the performance of a nonhierarchical research and development team that interacts closely on a daily basis.
- The interaction between organizational structure and individual

capabilities, that is, individuals may need certain specific skills to be productive in certain organizational structures, or certain structures may differentially influence the motivation of certain types of people.

• Management functions, as in the expertise with which planning, coordination, goal setting, monitoring, control, and external representation are carried out. The overall effects of "management" on organizational productivity are very much a function of who does it and how well. Also, there are undoubtedly a number of critical interactions among individuals, technologies, and the procedures by which the management functions are executed. For example, the empowered work group may be an effective "manager" only for individuals at a certain level of performance.

Various chapters in this report provide a more detailed view of one or more of these productivity determinants. The critical issue is that the specific determinants of a specific component of organizational productivity constitute the linkage with which this report is concerned. For a productivity measure to be useful in studying linkage phenomena, it must be capable of being influenced by the appropriate determinants.

IMPLICATIONS FOR EVALUATING STRATEGIES FOR IMPROVING PRODUCTIVITY

If the above list captures the basic determinants of organizational productivity, a number of chapters in this report point to an array of basic strategies that could be used in an attempt to improve IT productivity by operating as one or more of the determinants. The basic change strategies might be outlined as follows:

- Change individuals by
    — selecting people who would exhibit higher performance,
    — increasing individual knowledge and skill through training,
    — more clearly identifying the tasks to be performed and the goals to be achieved, and
    — increasing the time individuals spend on the task and the level of effort they expend to accomplish goals.
- Change to a more appropriate organizational structure.
- Improve the technology itself.
- Improve the management functions.

For example, one of the most important topics for research and practice in organizational science during the past 20 to 25 years has concerned the implications of less hierarchical and more participative work groups and organizations as instruments of the management functions. On at least one occasion, even one of the largest corporations in the world (the Ford Motor Company) has been the unit of analysis (Banas, 1988). The pieces of this strategy go by various names, such as autonomous work groups, self-managed work teams, employee empowerment, and the high-involvement organization (Goodman, 1986; Goodman et al., 1988; Lawler, 1991). The central concern of this very large domain of research and practice is how the contributions of individuals to the effectiveness of the larger unit can be optimized by the strategy of decentralizing the management functions. Such a strategy should lead to better communication, coordination, and problem solving, and to higher motivation and commitment.

If a particular change strategy aimed at a particular determinant, or set of determinants, of organizational productivity fails to exhibit any effects, it is useful to keep in mind that such a result could occur for any of several reasons. Among them are the following:

- The strategy truly does not work.
- There is a certain lag between the time of implementation and the time the effect will be realized. The productivity indicator was measured too soon (see Chapter 3).
- Changes in the productivity indicator are a function of so many other things that even if the change strategy is a good one its efforts will be masked (see Chapter 4).
- The productivity indicator is so unreliable that differences in scores across units, between treatment strategies, across time, and so on, reflect nothing more than unsystematic error.
- The productivity indicator is not a measure of productivity. That is, it is a reliable measure of something else.

To cite one strategy of major interest, a question considered by a number of analysts (see Chapter 2; also Loveman, 1988) is whether the large investments in IT by firms or industries have improved the productivity of the firm or the productivity of the industry. In the opinion of many people, the investment has not yielded much of a return. However, from the perspective of the measurement model described here, most of the available data are not appropriate to the question. Besides the fact that most of the indicators used do not fit the definition of productivity (e.g., profit, return on investment), the indicators are so distant from the locus of technological change that it seems virtually impossible to interpret whatever relationship is found. So many other determinants can intrude that interpreting a strong relationship would be almost as difficult as interpreting a weak relationship. However, the difficulty is not symmetrical because the influence of a type II error (saying that a technological change has no effect on productivity when in fact it does) operates only one way. One could fail to find a significant relationship because of a low N (e.g., too few firms in the sample), because the observed indicator is not a valid measure of the appropriate dependent latent variable, or because the productivity measure is not really under the control of the information technology, no matter how good or bad the technology is. It is perhaps little wonder that so few relationships are detected.

These issues are not unique to the implementation of information technologies. The problems associated with the implementation of change have been major topics for research and practice for many decades (e.g., Bennis et al., 1962). Chapter 4 summarized a number of the issues and demonstrated that it is unreasonable to expect a specific intervention that is directed at part of the organization to affect substantially the overall productivity of the entire organization as reflected in a summary index several steps removed from the direct effects of the new technology.

Finally, there is sometimes an implication that the goal of modeling the individual-organizational productivity linkage is to be able to determine how much of the variance in group or organizational productivity is due to individual productivity and how much is due to other sources. That is, the goal is to account for all significant sources of variance in organizational productivity and to determine the proportion of variance accounted for by each source. Using such a comprehensive analysis-of-variance framework would pose measurement problems (e.g., specifying all the populations of interest and sampling from them) that are impossible to surmount. In reality, estimates of the variance in organizational productivity accounted for by individuals will always be a function of specific sample (i.e., organizational) characteristics that cannot be overcome, in any practical sense, by a randomized design. That is, by definition, there is no general answer to the question of how much of the variance in organizational productivity is due to variation in individual productivity. Instead, as pointed out in Chapter 3, the goal should be to learn as much as possible about how each determinant operates under various conditions. Knowledge of the interactions will always be incomplete, but knowing a fair amount about the most important effects will go a long way toward maximizing an organization's utilization of the contributions of individual workers.

SUMMARY OF THE CRITICAL IMPLICATIONS

In summary, the proposed model for the measurement of IT productivity incorporates the following notions:

• A guiding definition of IT productivity must be agreed on. For example, is the central concern performance, effectiveness, productivity in the conventional sense (Mahoney, 1988), utility, or something else? Are there different domains of IT that require a different definition?

• By whatever definition, productivity is composed of major components that are distinct enough to preclude talking about it in the singular as one thing.

• The better the specification of the latent structure of productivity in substantive terms, the more valid and useful measurement will become.

• Specification of the major determinants of each productivity component is of critical importance. In particular, for IT productivity, are the effects of differences in individual knowledge and skill, individual motivation, IT, job and organizational structure, and the management functions all of interest, or just some of them?

• A measure will be valid to the extent that (1) the variables to be measured are defined appropriately, (2) the content of the measure matches the content of the variable, and (3) the determinants of score differences on the measure accurately reflect the measurement objectives.

• The score variation on measures of individual productivity should be under the control of the individual. The score variation on measures of unit productivity should be under the control of the unit. Measurement should minimize the opportunity for productivity "scores" to be influenced by sources of contamination having nothing to do with the objectives of measurement. For example, one most likely does not want the scores on a productivity measure merely to reflect changes in the business cycle.

Given these implications, the next section outlines steps that should be taken to enhance understanding of the nature of IT productivity and its measurement.

RESEARCH NEEDS

The analyses of IT productivity measurement issues in this chapter point to a number of questions that can be addressed only through additional research and information gathering. To achieve truly effective measurement of IT productivity for purposes of modeling the linkage between individual and organizational productivity and evaluating the effects of productivity improvement strategies, the following steps should be taken.

First, a representative panel of relevant experts (i.e., individuals who are very knowledgeable about the IT industry) should consider the question of which domains of IT productivity are the most critical to address. The possibilities range from the productivity of software design organizations to the productivity of operational information processing systems themselves. A taxonomy of the critical types of IT organizations or systems and their relevant goals would add considerable clarity to all these issues.

Second, for each type of IT organization, an additional expert panel should be assembled to consider all available information and formulate an initial statement of what the basic components of productivity are within that context. These would be substantive specifications, not abstractions. To proceed with measurement, the enterprise simply must know what it wants to measure. As used here, *expert* does not refer to academics or other experts in organizational research or measurement. The experts of interest are the people who have responsibility for using IT itself.

To the fullest extent possible, the panel(s) should also attempt to specify the major determinants for each relevant component of productivity. If, for certain specific productivity components, it would be impossible for changes in a specific determinant (e.g., higher-performing individuals or new hardware) to affect productivity, such constraints should be identified.

In effect, these two steps would generate a working "theory of productivity" in each context for which IT productivity is a critical issue. The theory may change as more evidence accumulates, but there must be a starting place. Certainly, the people most involved with IT productivity issues can offer a theory of its latent structure that goes beyond identifying ad hoc measures that happen to be available and can provide some reasonable specification for the determinants of the basic IT productivity components.

Third, the above steps would feed directly into a program of research and development on productivity measurement itself. Chapters 6 and 7 outlined specific procedures for such measure development and offered relevant examples. The critical ingredient is the use of a designated group (or groups) of experts/decision makers to articulate the goals of their specific enterprise, develop a theory for what productivity is in that context, and construct valid measures that directly reflect the productivity of the unit being studied. It is the group's responsibility to make sure that the appropriate determinants are reflected by the measures and that there is no serious contamination by extraneous influences. That is, by design, output measures must be identified or developed that directly reflect the performance of the unit in question and are directly relevant for the organization's goals. There is really no way to sidestep these judgments. There is no standardized set of commercially available operational measures that can be purchased and used. This is as true for organizational productivity as it is for unit or individual productivity (Campbell, 1977). The ProMES procedure described by Pritchard in Chapter 7 is the most direct application of these notions. Pritchard et al. (1989) go one step further and ask that the marginal utility of different levels of output on each measure be scaled, given the goals of the enterprise. This might be a very eye-opening exercise for organizations. Achieving large gains on some components of productivity may be of little value, while even small gains on some other measure might be judged to have tremendous value; and the differences in marginal utility need not be highly correspondent with a dollar metric.

In an ideal world, the specific goals and specific measures that are specified for a particular organization would be congruent with the theory of productivity articulated in the second step above. If they are not, revisions to the model should be considered. Over time, this interplay between a conceptual framework and specific measurement applications should steadily increase understanding of IT productivity and how it should be measured. One way to aid such investigation would be to develop an IT productivity measurement manual that would incorporate the working model and a set of procedures such as those suggested in Chapters 6 and 7.

Fourth, to enhance understanding of the linkage of certain determinants to specific components of IT productivity, it would be useful to conduct two kinds of exploratory investigations, using the working theory developed in the second step above. Both kinds of studies would seek simply to describe the critical events in specific organizations that seemed to have a positive or negative effect on productivity. One type would be the straightforward case study. If an appreciable number of case studies are done and they are conducted within the same framework, the accumulated results relative to how the various determinants affect productivity should be both interpretable and informative.

The second type of study would collect accounts of critical incidents from several panels of people within each organization. The general instructions to the writers of the accounts would ask them to describe specific examples of incidents that illustrate positive or negative effects of "something" on productivity (as defined by the working model). This is a proven strategy for identifying specific individual training needs (Campbell, 1988). Taken together, the two kinds of studies should provide considerable information about why particular strategies that are used to improve IT productivity succeed or fail.

The two types of studies are exploratory in nature. By no means are they meant to supplant more controlled multivariate or experimental research, such as outlined in Chapter 9 and elsewhere. It is also true that some of the reasons why new technology does not have the intended effects are already well known. The case studies and critical incident data gathering are not meant to reinvent the wheel. The intent is simply to provide additional specific information as to how changes in IT can succeed or fail. Aggregating such information over a large number of instances may indeed lead to an expansion of the understanding of how to improve IT productivity.

REFERENCES

Ackerman, P.L.
  1988   Individual differences in skill learning: An integration of psychometric and information processing perspectives. *Psychological Bulletin* 102:3-27.
American Educational Research Association, American Psychological Association, and National Council on Measurement in Education
  1985   *Standards for Educational and Psychological Testing.* Washington, D.C.: American Psychological Association.
Anderson, J.R.
  1985   *Cognitive Psychology and Its Implications*, 2d ed. New York: W.H. Freeman.
Banas, P.A.
  1988   Employee involvement: A sustained labor/management initiative at the Ford Motor Company. Pp. 388-416 in J.P. Campbell and R.J. Campbell, eds., *Productivity in Organizations.* San Francisco: Jossey-Bass.
Bennis, W.G., K.D. Benne, and R. Chin., eds.
  1962   *The Planning of Change.* New York: Holt, Rinehart, & Winston.
Campbell, J.P.
  1977   On the nature of organizational effectiveness. Pp. 13-55 in P.S. Goodman and J.M. Pennings, eds., *New Perspectives in Organizational Effectiveness.* San Francisco: Jossey-Bass.
  1988   Productivity enhancement via training and development. Pp. 177-216 in J.P. Campbell and R.J. Campbell, eds., *Productivity in Organizations.* San Francisco: Jossey-Bass.
  1991   Modeling the performance prediction problem in industrial and organizational psychology. In M.D. Dunnette and L. Hough, eds., *Handbook of Industrial and Organizational Psychology.* Palo Alto, Calif.: Consulting Psychologist's Press.
Cascio, W.F.
  1991   *Applied Psychology in Personnel Management*, 4th ed. Englewood Cliffs, N.J.: Prentice-Hall.

Goodman, P.S., ed.
1982 *Change in Organizations.* San Francisco: Jossey-Bass.
1986 *Designing Effective Work Groups.* San Francisco: Jossey-Bass.
Goodman, P.S., R. Devadas, and T.L. Griffith
1988 Groups and productivity: Analyzing the effectiveness of selfmanaging teams. Pp. 295-327 in J.P. Campbell and R.J. Campbell, eds., *Productivity in Organizations.* San Francisco: Jossey-Bass.
Kanfer, R., and P.L. Ackerman
1989 Motivation and cognitive abilities: An integrative-aptitude- treatment interaction approach to skill acquisition. *Journal of Applied Psychology* 74:657-690.
Landy, F.J., and J.L. Farr
1980 A process model of performance rating. *Psychological Bulletin* 87:72-107.
Lawler, E.E.
1991 *High Involvement Management.* San Francisco: Jossey-Bass.
Loveman, G.W.
1988 *An Assessment of the Productivity Impact of Information Technologies.* Sloan School of Management. Cambridge, Mass.: MIT Press.
Mahoney, T.A.
1988 Productivity defined: The relativity of efficiency, effectiveness, and change. Pp. 13-39 in J.P. Campbell and R.J. Campbell, eds., *Productivity in Organizations.* San Francisco: Jossey-Bass.
Nathan, B.R., and R.A. Alexander
1988 A comparison of criteria for test validation: A meta analytic investigation. *Personnel Psychology* 41:517-536.
Nissen, M.J., and P. Bullmer
1987 Attentional requirements of learning: Evidence from performance measures. *Cognitive Psychology* 19:1-32.
Pritchard, R.D., S.D. Jones, P.L. Roth, K.K. Stuebing, and S.E. Ekeberg
1989 The evaluation of an integrated approach to measuring organizational productivity. *Personnel Psychology* 42:69-115.
Sackett, P.R., S. Zedeck, and L. Fogli
1988 Relations between measures of typical and maximum job performance. *Journal of Applied Psychology* 73:482-486.
Schmitt, N., R.Z. Gooding, R.A. Noe, and M. Kirsch
1984 Meta analyses of validity studies published between 1964 and 1982 and the investigation of study characteristics. *Personnel Psychology* 37:407-422.

9

Coordination as Linkage: The Case of Software Development Teams

Sara Kiesler, Douglas Wholey, and Kathleen M. Carley

This chapter examines coordination in software development teams as a practical context for talking about the linkages between individual and group productivity. We do not discuss individual-organizational nor group-organizational linkages, although many of the points we make pertain to those linkages as well.

Software development is a kind of technical work found in many organizations: the technical team project. Certain technical tasks transcend the ongoing functions of departments or the capabilities of individuals, and thus organizations create a project group or team to do the work. A software development project group can have two to several hundred members. Membership is typically diverse; the work may require the participation of programmers, software engineers, applications experts, researchers, requirements analysts, software testers, documentation writers, project managers, customer support personnel, and perhaps others. Project members may be drawn from different locations and different departments and may even work on the project in different places. The projects have predictable stages but also experience unpredictable changes in the organizational and technical environment—changes in personnel, modifications in available software and hardware technology, changing client expectations, and new economic constraints (Brooks, 1987).

In software development, productivity depends on teamwork. *Teamwork* refers to work done as a team and to the attitudes, skills, and behaviors that subordinate personal prominence to the efficiency of the

214

whole. Teamwork is crucial because every job and every stage is inter-dependent. High levels of individual productivity do not ensure success. Productivity depends on leveraging competencies through teamwork (Clark et al., 1987).

Coordination is the overt, behavioral instantiation (representation) of teamwork. That is, coordination is what people, technology, or organizations actually do to integrate team members and their work to form a group product. Measures of coordination include observations that different people and subunits working on a project agree to a common definition of what they are building, share information, hand off components of the work expeditiously, take responsibility for one another's performance, and mesh their activities. Coordination should be distinguished from exogenous forces—prices, monopoly position of the group, resources made available to the group, management priorities, and so forth—that affect group productivity directly rather than through linkages.

THE DOMAIN OF SOFTWARE DEVELOPMENT

Software development is a theoretically interesting context for examining linkages and it also has practical importance. The United States has more than 7,000 software firms; many other firms participate in the development of software systems (National Science Board, 1989). Business, education, government, and technical endeavors ranging from automated manufacturing to financial transactions to national defense require complex software systems. Most experts agree that the demand for software outstrips the ability of firms to produce it. Software systems are notoriously difficult to produce. Problems often force delays in the implementation of new applications, compromises in what those applications can do, and uncertainties about their reliability (National Research Council, 1990).

Coordination in Software Development

Simplified models of the software life cycle break its development into distinct phases. One such breakdown is that suggested by Davis (1987): (1) problem definition, (2) feasibility, (3) analysis, (4) system design, (5) detailed design, and (6) implementation and maintenance. A variety of tasks, each with its requisite skills, must be done during these different phases: analysis, design, coding, documentation, and testing. *Analysis* involves evaluating and translating organizational or individual needs into system capabilities. *Design* involves developing a set of distinct logical units, each of which can be developed and tested separately; choosing software and hardware; structuring a data base so as to minimize redundancy and improve ease of access; and so on. *Coding* means translating the design specifications into executable instructions that run reliably and efficiently on particular hardware. *Documentation* involves coordinating and maintaining consistency of the human-computer interface, writing manuals and specifications, and preparing the internal code description, as well as recording the rationale behind design and coding decisions. These tasks are highly interactive in that changes in requirements often require changes in design, code, and documentation. Design decisions often feed back to change or limit the capabilities that the system can offer. Changes in the hardware and software, or changes in a company's financial status, may force the team to return to the design phase. This process is iterative in that software systems must be enhanced and changed as the environments in which they exist change and as people put them to new uses.

Achieving a successful software system requires coordination among the various phases and tasks involved in the software development cycle and minimal backtracking. If the software system is small, and members are physically proximate and respect one another, effective coordination can occur because the group can work out problems together and keep all the implementation details in focus. This focus on sharing ideas through direct communication is what traditionally has been meant by teamwork; it is the main emphasis of cooperative team learning in high school and college classrooms (e.g., Bossert, 1988-1989). In many cases of modern technical work, however, this simple model of coordination is impossible. Kraut and Streeter (1990) discuss three reasons why this is so—project complexity, uncertainty, and interdependence.

Complexity

A fundamental characteristic of many software tasks is that they are too big for any one or two skilled programmers to undertake alone. Moreover, a single complex skill like programming is not the only skill required in the software development process. Software development also requires analysis to determine what the software should do; evaluation of alternative platforms; design to shape the basic structure of the programs and their communication with other programs, data bases, and users; tests to ensure that code meets requirements and that users understand the interface; creation of special tools for implementation; hardware and software maintenance procedures; written documentation; and an administrative infrastructure to set priorities on requests for features and to handle feedback from users.

Uncertainty

Complexity per se does not invariably lead to difficulties in coordination. As Kraut and Streeter (1990) note, automotive factories, textile mills, and tuna canneries employ hundreds of people to produce their products, yet many run smoothly. Software development is different in that it is more uncertain. Manufacturing involves routines, doing the same thing repeatedly. But the software development process is nonroutine activity, and specifications for it invariably are incomplete. Incompleteness partly results from limited knowledge of the software development domain (Curtis et al., 1988). At many points the information that designers or programmers need to make decisions is not available to them, although others in the project may have the knowledge needed for those decisions.

Software development is also uncertain because specification of what a software system should do changes over time (Brooks, 1987; Curtis et al., 1988; Fox, 1982). Competition, regulations, standards, company politics, plans, and financial conditions can lead to changes in specifications. Also, it is often only by using software that purchasers understand its capabilities and limitations. As they use the software, they often demand new capabilities that they were not able to envision at the software's creation.

Uncertainty in software development may be reflected in disputes among different groups involved in its development (Curtis et al., 1988; Kraut and Streeter, 1990). People associated with different parts of a project can have different beliefs about what the software should do. For example, analysts translate users' needs into requirements for system capabilities. As a result, they often adopt the point of view of the software's purchasers. On the other hand, designers and programmers may have more of an insider's focus and emphasize ease of development and efficiency of operation. These differences in points of view must be resolved for the team to succeed.

Interdependence

Complexity and uncertainty in software work would be less of a problem if software did not require integration of its components to such a large extent. Software consists of hundreds or thousands of modules or components that must mesh with each other perfectly for the software system as a whole to operate correctly. One mistake in part of a system can have disastrous, unanticipated consequences (Travis, 1990). This required integration, combined with complexity and uncertainty, requires in turn special coordination techniques that may not be necessary in more standardized manufacturing and in developing projects that are merely complex and uncertain (Ouchi, 1980).

Research on Individual-Group Linkages

Much of the existing research on software development and other technical teamwork does not deal with linkages. There has been considerable work on individuals' cognitive problems resulting from creating, understanding, and debugging programs, designs, and other aspects of systems, and on the individual-computer interface. (See Curtis, 1985, for a sample of this kind of research.) This approach ignores the linkage issues inherent in software development. Results from studies of individuals' problems in engineering and interaction with computers do not generalize simply to team problems (Scott and Simmons, 1975). Other research does address linkages, but typically indirectly. A great deal of work has gone into software and procedures that should promote coordination, such as code reuse, computer-aided software engineering (CASE) tools, object-oriented languages, and automatic code generation (Chase, 1987; Sims, 1989; Verastegui and Williams, 1988). However, the effects these developments have on linkages are rarely evaluated. Also, there are descriptive studies of labor costs and delays in software development. Generally, these studies use sophisticated simulation or models but not measures of coordination other than costs (Abdel-Hamid and Madnick, 1989; Beatty, 1986). Hence, much of the research on software development does not help one understand individual-group linkages in this domain.

Outside the domain of software development, in laboratory studies of group decision making and problem solving, there has been considerable research on individual-group linkages. These studies have long shown that group productivity usually does not equal the sum of individual group members' performance.[1] At the least, if individual labor

---

[1]The definition and measurement of performance and productivity at the group or organizational level are not addressed in this chapter. However, to understand the behavioral research on groups and teams, one must know that behavioral scientists primarily use behavioral rather than economic measures of performance. These may be of several kinds: (1) quantity, quality, or cost-effectiveness of per-person output, such as number of problems solved or service calls completed; (2) disruptive behavior, such as absenteeism, accidents, or labor disputes; and (3) attitudes, such as subjective ratings of the quality of work life (Guzzo et al., 1985). Those interested in improving individual productivity have estimated effect sizes for many interventions and the standard

is to be combined into a joint product, some resources must be invested in the combination process itself. For instance, planning as a group takes time and effort. Social psychologists who study small groups have called the transaction costs of coordinating work in a team "process losses" (Steiner, 1972). Three approaches have evolved as ways to reduce process losses and improve coordination: team member selection and training, team design, and team communication.

Coordination Through Selection and Training

In software teams, the top 10 percent of programmers are said to be more than four times as efficient as the bottom 15 percent (Boehm, 1987). These individual differences in ability are relevant to teamwork. If a team is staffed with highly skilled and experienced workers, team tasks such as training, job design, and management are made simpler. More important, because members of a team interact, they influence one another and the team as a whole (McGrath, 1984). Individual competency multiplies through intragroup learning and transfer of skills. Under a competency multiplier process, teams made up of highly competent members outperform other teams even beyond what their individual abilities would predict. The multiplicative effects of individual abilities are particularly important when the team's work is complex, uncertain, and interdependent. Highly able team members can solve nonroutine problems and teach those solutions to one another (Clark and Stephenson, 1989; Hill, 1982; Hinsz, 1990). These members contribute valuable nonoverlapping skills and cancel one another's errors, so team interaction bestows extra benefits on team performance (Porter et al., 1975; Tziner and Eden, 1985).

Competency multiplier effects also may be seen over time because competent members become better at what they are already good at

---

deviation of job performance in dollar terms. These estimates can be used to show the financial benefit of labor savings that would be achieved by introducing an intervention or even what the net dollar value of the intervention would be, taking into account all business costs and benefits (Hunter and Schmidt, 1983). Several difficulties stand in the way of doing this to estimate the effect of a coordination strategy or intervention on team productivity (Boehm, 1987; Jones, 1986). Agreed team goals may exist but have no metric because the work is unique (e.g., building a space platform). Time-based indices are popular: lead time, time to completion of project, and even time to profit (Clark et al., 1987; Abdel-Hamid and Madnick, 1989). These measures do not, of course, address the quality of work.

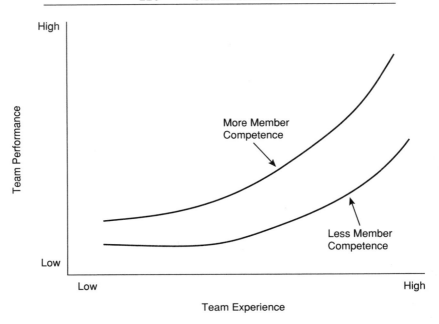

FIGURE 9-1 Competency multiplier effects.

and, together, more uniquely able than other teams (March, 1981). (See Figure 9-1.) Competent teams gain more from technological interventions and tools that increase individual competency and intermember learning, which contributes to an increasing gap between excellent and poor teams. In this manner, selection and training to acquire the most competent team members become a linkage factor, especially over time.

A strategy that focuses exclusively on individual selection and training to achieve teamwork is often impractical and has a number of disadvantages. Organizations often are prevented from hiring only the best people. The best people may lead to higher labor costs than are necessary. Moreover, those whose high talents are hidden initially cannot be discovered if the organization tries to hire only those with excellent resumes. Finally, even a group of highly qualified individual workers, placed on a team, may function poorly as a team unless attention is given to their organization as a team.

Coordination Through Team Design

Organization as a team, or team design, refers to the organizational structure and formal procedures that provide "built-in" solutions to coordination. These solutions may include task decomposition, lines of authority, centralization of control, and standard operating procedures, or they may include technologies to standardize or rationalize the work itself.[2] Team design through structure and formalization is theoretically an efficient alternative to direct communication when tasks are complex, uncertain, and interdependent (Aldrich, 1979; Cyert and March, 1963; Downs, 1967; March and Simon, 1958; Simon, 1962). For instance, instead of having to talk repeatedly about what each person should do, formal task decomposition allows a group facing a complex task to divide its work into manageable chunks. It should not be surprising, therefore, to find that recent solutions to effecting teamwork in software development and other kinds of technical work have emphasized team design.

A major emphasis in team design has been the development of formal procedures governing communication at various stages of the work. For instance, formal meetings may be held at predetermined times in order to consider decisions about changes in the design. Brooks (1987), Curtis et al. (1988), and Fox (1982) noted that problems in accurately and completely communicating stable software requirements to members of a software project are among the most difficult to resolve in software development. Formalization is thought to increase control and regulate information flow. Written specifications or plans, documentation, and formal meetings ensure adherence to the plan and system as they evolve and that all the components fit together.

Formalizing project management can also help managers monitor teams' work. Each phase of the work cycle, from planning through operation and maintenance, is supposed to have well-defined products

---

[2] Modern software practices (e.g., logical models, well-defined interfaces, modularity, layered architectures, hierarchical management, object orientation) can be considered team designs because they are meant to regulate the number of connections that people and software components have. Modularity and information hiding, hallmarks of object-oriented design and programming languages, are thought to promote independence in programming, ease adaptation, and minimize backtracking (Dietrich et al., 1989; Parnas, 1972; Rumbaugh, 1991). Object-oriented design and programming also directly incorporate team design principles through inheritance. In software engineering, computer-aided software engineering (CASE) tools have been developed to facilitate the development of logical models, coordinate project design through a shared data dictionary, and automate input/output analysis (Sodhi, 1991; Zarella, 1990). The degree to which current CASE tools actually facilitate team coordination still is under contention (Spurr and Layzell, 1990). In a recent comparison of software maintenance teams that did and did not use CASE tools, groups using CASE tools were less productive (Banker et al., 1991; see also Orlikowski, 1988).

and milestones. Thus, it is specified in advance what will be delivered at each stage and how the deliverables will be tested or scrutinized to ensure that they do what they are supposed to do. In software development, all official project documents may be under change control. For example, there are usually naming conventions that must be adhered to project wide. Similarly, code cannot be written without design reviews; code cannot be tested before code walk-throughs; changes cannot be made without issuing a modification request; no piece of code goes to system test without an integration test; and so on.

Another important element in team design is the authority structure, which can be used to resolve disputes and inconsistencies across units. There is some evidence from an extensive comparison of automotive product development teams that significant variance in the authority structure contributes to the superior performance of Japanese automobile design teams over their American and European counterparts. Japanese team managers had greater authority and independence than American and European managers did (Clark et al., 1987). A concomitant of this idea in software development is that a chief designer or architect is the one person in a complex project who has sufficient knowledge of both the application domain and the possible software architectures to integrate the two. Weinberg (1971) advocated the chief programmer role, in which a senior designer/programmer has control over a software project. Problems arise when the design is distributed in more than one head or, worse (and probably more typically), is not in anybody's head. According to Curtis et al. (1988), skilled designers often assume responsibility for communicating their technical vision to other project members and for coordinating the work of the project.

In sum, team design (including group structure, formal procedures, and hierarchy) is advocated in teams to routinize the transfer of information and increase control and reliability. Formality and written documentation also are attempts to reconcile differences of opinion, help people understand their goals and those of others, induce the evaluation of alternatives, and develop agreements that all can accept. The effort expended by a small group writing a formal design document can be more than offset by the communication forgone later when each project member does not need to describe his or her vision separately to the scores of people who need the information. Formal procedures also reduce errors. Thus, for example, in software development one might run automated consistency checks on a formal specification document (cited in National Research Council, 1990) or even use a computer-based system that tracks modification requests to trigger management intervention when a project schedule slips.

Benefits obtained from team design do not come without costs, however. Formal structures and procedures can place an extra burden on development costs by increasing the need for a coordination infrastructure: training, increased clerical and management staff, and increased project reports and archives. Fox (1982) estimated that in large software projects, 50 percent of the cost is for planning, checking, scheduling, managing, and controlling. Tools and techniques that formalize communication or management require that time and effort be spent in teaching people to use them and ensuring that they do. Change-control systems are potential time wasters or distractions from work. Management sometimes uses standardization and rationalization of tasks to increase control, which can sap motivation and increase dependency on outside experts. Design also can impede innovation by limiting the options explored by a team. Finally, the "care and feeding" of bureaucracy can become more significant to employees than the ultimate goals they are supposed to accomplish.

A particularly serious disadvantage of team design as a coordination strategy is that it can depersonalize interaction. For instance, with task decomposition, team members, or subgroups of the team, have different roles. Team members or subgroups working on their own tasks tend to develop divergent perspectives and habits of work (e.g., Brewer and Kramer, 1985; Tajfel, 1982). They may have little opportunity or eagerness to learn from others on the team, which will impede the exchange of expertise and discovery (Burns and Stalker, 1961; Carley, 1990, 1991, 1992; Faunce, 1958; Festinger et al., 1950; Jablin et al., 1987; Monge and Kirste, 1980; Newcomb, 1961). Task decomposition can also exacerbate demographic or skill differences that existed at the start (Barnlund and Harland, 1963; Dearborn and Simon, 1958; Jablin, 1979; Monge et al., 1985; Sykes et al., 1976).

Whether team design through structure, formalization, or technology actually works as well as it is supposed to theoretically, remains debatable. Boehm's (1987) analysis of software productivity indicates that productivity due to changes in team design increased by just 7 percent between 1981 and 1986. Card et al. (1987) reported that software engineering technology improved reliability 30 percent but had no impact on productivity. Chapter 2 reaches the same conclusions as Card et al. did in 1987.

Coordination Through Team Communication

Experience, organizational theory, and behavioral research suggest that team design does not by itself solve all coordination problems in teamwork. No matter how successfully task decomposition, authority structures, or standard operating procedures reduce the number of interfaces between team members, different members with different skills and perspectives still must negotiate what is to be built and fit together pieces of the design. Consensus formation, sharing of know-how, and integration of work outputs create communication demands that if not met at one level tend to surface at others.

Team design, while necessary for some purposes, is sometimes a misguided attempt to apply structure and formalization when they are not suitable. Formal coordination mechanisms are intended to simplify and disaggregate behavior and therefore increase group resiliency, but they can fail in the face of interdependence under uncertainty, which typifies much software work. Flexibility, texture, richness, expressiveness, and sometimes accuracy—all disappear during the codification of roles, rules, and procedures (Boisot and Child, 1988; Bruner, 1974). Under these circumstances, communication is needed for coordination (Clark et al., 1987; Daft and Lengel, 1984, 1986; Kraut and Streeter, 1990; Stohl and Redding, 1987; Van de Ven et al., 1976).

Direct communication is also referred to as coordination by feedback (March and Simon, 1958), mutual adjustment (Thompson, 1967), organismic communication networking (Tushman and Nadler, 1978), clan mechanisms (Ouchi, 1980), and informal communication (Kraut and Streeter, 1990). These terms convey the unique advantages of talking personally with others: spontaneity, interactivity, richness, friendliness. With communication, people develop deeper relationships and more opportunities to observe and learn from one another. Communication improves group commitment, socialization, and sometimes control. It makes possible the acquisition and maintenance of group culture, authority, and norms that people do not talk about overtly (Levitt and March, 1988; Nelson and Winter, 1982). Communication counters some of the costs to relationships of formal approaches to coordination. Research on communication in organizations has shown the heavy use made of communication in research and development teams where work is uncertain (e.g., Adams, 1976; Allen, 1977; Pelz and Andrews, 1966; Tushman, 1977).

Despite its advantages, constant communication in the traditional sense of face-to-face or telephone conversation is impractical in many software development teams. The ease of acquiring information is at least as important as the quality of the information in determining the sources that people use (Culnan, 1983; Zipf, 1935). Physical proximity is the major determinant of engineers' work-related information exchange and influence on projects (Allen, 1977). Constant communication may be undesirable as well as impractical—who can be reached conveniently is not necessarily the same as who can contribute high-quality information. Communication can be costly if highly skilled persons spend too much time communicating with others instead of completing their individual tasks (Scott and Simmons, 1975). New communication techniques can reduce the costs of direct communication. Computer networks with electronic mail and bulletin boards that allow for fast but asynchronous conversation permit project members to talk even though they are geographically dispersed or mobile. Nonetheless, as discussed in Chapter 2, communication networks that are installed to increase efficiency might actually encourage the proliferation of communications, leading people to spend more time screening messages, and thereby reduce the cost advantages of the networks. Also, these media are inefficient for some kinds of communication, notably for collaborative planning and problem solving under uncertainty (Finholt et al., 1990; Galegher and Kraut, 1990). Research on the coordination and productivity benefits and costs of network communication suggests that, appropriately managed, the net effect can be positive. However, networks and other new technologies for communication do not automatically bestow benefits on coordination.

The Dilemmas of Coordination as Linkage

As we have described, coordination does not have a simple one-to-one relationship with team performance and thus is not a simple answer to forming linkages between individual work in a team and productivity as a team. Three dilemmas characterize the linkages. First, too little or too much coordination impedes performance. Hence, the team has to invest in the right amount of coordination. Second, design and communication have different effects on teamwork; the team has to match the appropriate coordination strategy with the tasks and phases of the team's work. Third, any coordination strategy tends to become habitual. Hence, the team must find ways to undo or unlearn design or communication strategies that might have been successful in the past but become inappropriate for a new task. We discuss these dilemmas in turn.

Amount of Coordination

Most teams use design and communication. If a team puts little or no effort into these forms of coordination, its performance will be poor. The more coordination, the better, up to a point. But coordination is costly; in experimental studies, team performance typically is above the level of the average team member but below the level of the most competent member because of coordination costs. At high levels, the process of coordination is very costly in time, resources, hassles, and distractions (e.g., Abdel-Hamid and Madnick, 1989; Diehl and Stroebe, 1987). Thus, coordination has a curvilinear, inverted U-shaped relationship with performance.

Communication Versus Design

We propose, in addition, a dilemma of balancing approaches to teamwork. Communication and design are somewhat inconsistent with one another. For instance, teams may find task decomposition very efficient and comfortable. But if, because of their separate roles, team members do not talk to one another, friendships deteriorate and free riding increases. Members may begin to put their own prominence above the group's, which is a form of public goods problem.[3] Consider a 3×3 matrix, in which communication and design are orthogonal factors (see Figure 9-2). When communication and design are each low, performance is poor because the team is not coordinated. When communication is high, design should be only moderate to achieve high performance at low cost, and vice versa. Finally, when communication and design are each high, coordination costs interfere with performance (Figure 9-3). One can imagine this happening, for instance, in teams in which there are many direct working relationships, many meetings, and many formal procedures that have to be followed.

Most groups combine some measure of design and communication, but they may overemphasize one or the other. It may be that for every task and project, there is an appropriate level of design and an appropriate level of communication for every level of design.

In technical work, the timing of communication and design may be important. It has long been thought that group discussion is necessary at times when tasks are highly uncertain or equivocal—at the beginning of projects and during crises. Communication at these times can

---

[3]In public goods theory (Olson, 1971), a dilemma exists when contributions of effort and resources for a group are partly inconsistent with the self-interest of individual group members. Individual members may believe with good reason that they are better off letting others cope with unassigned group tasks, such as teaching new members and handling unplanned client interruptions. As long as someone else does the work, free-riding members still benefit from the group's success. Also, in a complex and interactive project, one person's contribution to the group at any particular moment may seem inconsequential. The public goods problem may increase when uncertainty is high and team design contributes to lack of communication (Macy, 1990).

Team Communication

	Low	Moderate	High
Little	Poor Performance	Poor Performance	Poor Performance
Moderate	Poor Performance	Good Performance	Good Performance
High	Poor Performance	Good Performance	Poor Performance and High Coordination Costs

(left axis label: Team Design)

FIGURE 9-2 Patterns of communication and team design leading to different levels of performance.

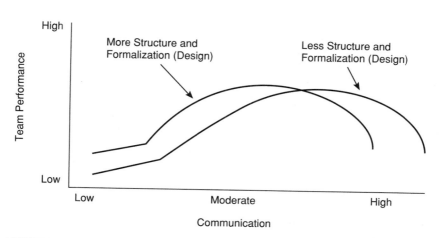

FIGURE 9-3 Complementarity of communication and team design at low levels of both, and substitution of communication and design at higher levels of both.

help create mutual understanding, commitment, and substitutability (because individuals have more common knowledge). Teams that communicate intensively initially and spend more time working out plans may do better than "fast starters" that begin coding and implementing quickly (see Hackman, 1987).

Team design might be a better strategy for coordination than direct communication once a team's plans are in place. Design allows members the most autonomy and time to do individual work. Programming probably is the most individual task in software development. A lead programmer doing coding might be working alone or perhaps with one or two others. Since coding is a conjunctive activity (i.e., the project cannot go forward without it), the programmer is needed by others and is less substitutable than those who have been working on other jobs and jointly with others. Over time, the influence of the programmer increases (assuming this work is individualized), and the rest of the team gets more dependent on the programmer because the work is central and the role is nonsubstitutable. Development of project-specific skills and overall understanding in the programmer can be seen as addressing coordination over time in two ways. First, as more pieces of a project get built, the programmer's competence becomes more critical to the rest of the group. Second, the programmer(s) will exert authority, which will lead to centralization and more design.

Design also addresses problems of heterogeneous skills in a team. Three elements of design are particularly important here: the role structure, the formal authority structure, and formal communication channels. The role structure specifies who does what. The formal authority structure specifies who reports to whom and who has access to what resources (Carley, 1990; Malone, 1987). Formal communication channels specify who is supposed to talk to whom. During coding and implementation phases of software development, these formal structures enable individuals to concentrate on their individual tasks and thereby successfully complete the project. These structures should be particularly useful when there is substantial heterogeneity among group members.

Entrainment

As teams develop ways of coordinating their work, they adopt habitual patterns of coordination, a process called *entrainment* (Kelly et al., 1990). Patterns of coordination become institutionalized and legitimated. As a consequence, it becomes more costly to renegotiate approaches to coordination. Particular styles of coordination and group cultures influenced by those styles emerge in all groups. With this emergence of a team coordination style, individual members are likely to become more similar to one another in their personal attitudes and ideas about teamwork (e.g., Kiesler and Kiesler, 1969). In experimental studies, entrainment is inferred from a group's tendency to use the same work methods even though the task demands change. In research with on-going groups, entrainment must be inferred by examining the extent to which coordination approaches become more similar and predictable over time.

Ironically, as teams become better at what they do and better coordinated, they also can become increasingly rigid in their approach to coordination. If their task assignments change, team members may be unable or unwilling to adjust their coordination strategies to the demands of the new tasks. They may be too internally focused and too comfortable, and their previous successful experience will not have suggested ways in which they should change. Research has only begun on this problem.

RESEARCH PROBLEMS AND DIRECTIONS

Much of the research discussed above was conducted with small, homogeneous groups working on well-specified collaborative tasks that can be done in one or a few sittings (McGrath, 1984). Except for the work on lateral coordinative mechanisms (which does not examine the role of groups in particular; e.g., Burns, 1989; Galbraith, 1972; Lawrence and Lorsch, 1967; Pfeffer, 1978), there has been relatively little research on coordination of large and ongoing teams within organizations. Also, little is known about technical teams in organizations that use computer-based technology. Such technology permits organizations to form large, dispersed, and diverse teams working on complex, uncertain, interdependent tasks that would not have been possible in the past. These teams have coordination problems that differ from those of traditional small groups and formal departments whose members are physically proximate. Laboratory and field research must employ technological and other resources to study the modern technical team.

Certain theoretical problems also must be solved if researchers and practitioners are to understand linkages between individuals and teams. Two of these problems are described in the next two sections.

Efficiency Versus Social Effects

Observations of today's technical projects (e.g., Curtis et al., 1988; Sproull and Kiesler, 1991) suggest that multilevel theories may be required to capture fully how coordination acts as a link between individuals and group productivity. In a two-level framework, for instance, coordination mechanisms are viewed as having efficiency effects and social effects.

Efficiency effects of coordination are the direct, intended benefits of coordination minus its direct costs. These are the benefits and costs discussed above. However, coordination mechanisms can also have systemic, long-term effects on the team, organization, or social system. (For this concept, see Maruyama, 1963; Mason, 1970.) For instance, suppose as a result of using electronic mail to coordinate work, dispersed teams also discover ways to mobilize to influence management policy. Here, communication initially intended simply as an efficiency amplifier for a team also has effects on employee participation and organizational politics. Or, as was observed in one study, management may realize that the communication system can be used to monitor individual team members' performance in ways that used to be too difficult, which changes its authority relationships with the team members (Rule and Brantley, 1990). Social effects can affect linkages and productivity qualitatively and in ways that were entirely unanticipated. For instance, while greater employee participation may have no direct effect on the performance within teams, it can increase interteam learning and exchange of expertise across teams.

Linkages and Scaling Up

Another theoretical problem in the study of linkages is the incomplete understanding of how to study behavior across individual, group, and organizational levels of analysis. Experimental studies of individual behavior and simple tasks are necessary to test causal hypotheses, but one cannot deduce from experimental findings what will happen with real groups in organizations. Experimental group behavior never replicates exactly that of ongoing groups in organizations.

One approach to scaling up from individuals and simple tasks to teams and more complex tasks is to add variables. Amount of discussion (a communication variable) and centralization (a design variable) are variables, for example, that would be appropriate at the group level. A more difficult scaling problem arises, however, when such variables do not scale at the same rate; then multivariate effects change, which causes a phenomenon in the large to look very different from the way it looks in the small. For instance, discussion between two persons working together seems qualitatively different from meetings of 100 or more members of a large team. Ship designers encounter this problem when they try to deduce the behavior of a full-size ship from tests of models. Two important factors in a ship's drag are waves made by the ship's prow and turbulence under the ship. Because wave effects and turbulence depend on fine details of the hull shape, designers cannot rely on mathematical calculations alone. Instead, they build scale models and tow them in water, measuring their drag. Although the model gives an estimate of drag, there is no way to measure how much of the model's drag is accounted for by turbulence and how much by making waves. To complicate matters, the two factors do not scale in the same way. The turbulence under the ship depends on the surface area and the speed to the 1.825 power, but the wave drag is a much more complex function of speed and ship size. Since the two effects are confounded in the model's drag and scale differently, scaling up from model tests is very hard. The ship in its full glory may act very differently than the model did, particularly if the model is small relative to the ship. Ship models and towing tanks are surprisingly large for that reason.

Based on evidence to date, the scaling problem is probably serious in researching the linkages between individual productivity and the productivity of large, dispersed project groups. For example, in asking how computer technologies and networks affect group coordination and productivity, researchers can test some hypotheses in the laboratory, but in reality, networks often inspire more groups, larger projects, more diverse groups, and more flexible group structures (Sproull and Kiesler, 1991). A social consequence of this is that peripheral employees, such as geographically or organizationally isolated employees, gain new opportunities to initiate and receive communication (Eveland and Bikson, 1988; Fanning and Raphael, 1986; Wasby, 1989). If management policies permit such interactions, peripheral employees can increase their membership in groups and their connections to groups. These interactions can increase information flow between the periphery and the center of the organization and among peripheral workers. In short, while increasing connections through network communication could increase the participation of everyone in principle, peripheral employees are likely to see a relatively greater impact than are central employees (Eveland and Bikson, 1988; Hesse et al., 1990; Huff et al., 1989). This chain of events looks very different from a linear scaling up from individual or even small group behavior in relatively simpler settings.

In sum, individual behavior and small group behavior may scale differently to organizational reality. Variables that seem trivial (perhaps because of low variance) in the laboratory may loom much larger in an organization—and vice versa. If so, one may see the same phenomena differently in the two settings, no matter how fine-grained and careful the research is. It is important to do both kinds of research, that is, to study individuals and small groups in the laboratory and in the field and to study large and ongoing groups in organizations. The purpose is not to discover exactly how variables and processes scale at each level, but to ensure that researchers are always attuned to scaling problems.

Studying Groups in Organizations

Understanding of linkages in group productivity might be more effectively advanced if the tests of models in this domain were more ambitious scientifically. For example, an Israeli study involved a true experiment in the field on the effects of selection on tank crew performance (Tziner and Eden, 1985). The study involved the assignment of 672 soldiers to 224 crews, using a complex Latin square factorial design to control for differential performance ratings by the 28 unit commanders. Assignment on the basis of ability was varied experimentally. No other interventions were made in the natural military environment, but considerable control was exerted on data collection to increase its reliability and validity. There were four waves of measurement using previously validated instruments. The study showed that "spreading the talent around" is an inefficient way to distribute staff for interdependent groups, and the researchers were able to provide empirically supported advice counter to prevailing practices.

A kind of sociological/microeconomic study needed in the domain of software productivity is exemplified by a comparative study of product development teams in the automotive industry (Clark et al., 1987). The unit of analysis in this study was a major car development project; three U.S., eight Japanese, and nine European auto companies participated in the research. The researchers collected data from the companies on 29 projects (6 in the United States, 12 in Japan, and 11 in Europe) involving the development of new sedans, micro-mini cars, and small vans introduced from 1980 to 1987. The researchers used questionnaires and interviews with project managers, heads of R&D groups, engineering administration staff, and engineers, as well as archival data on lead time, engineering hours, technology, subcontracting, and outcomes such as model prices. This study confirmed that Japanese projects were completed in two-thirds the time and one-third the engineering hours of the non-Japanese projects, and it reconfirmed that if schedules are kept under control, cost overruns also tend to be restrained. These results do not refute a time-cost trade-off. Rather, the study points to the potential importance of particular project strategies, kinds of project organization, leadership, and staffing.

CONCLUSION

A changing but mostly large proportion of the variance in the productivity of software development and other technical teams derives from how such teams coordinate their work. Without coordination, individual work cannot be integrated and turned into a group product. Technical teams use team design and communication to coordinate their work, each of which can be considered a linkage process. Research has contributed much to the understanding of the additive and interactive effects of team design and communication on coordination. They are, in part, substitutes for one another. Too much of either one, or of both, creates costs that outweigh the benefits of coordination. There are many unknowns in this domain, however, especially when one tries to predict the side effects and outcomes of linkages over time. The very meaning of productivity in software development has changed as approaches to coordination have changed. Improvements in IT and formal methodologies used for coordination have increased the scope of software engineering projects. In 1963 the Mercury space project required 1.5 million object instructions, whereas a space station of the 1990s requires at least 80 million. Today, software development teams are generally much larger, more diverse, better trained, and more dispersed than they used to be. Moreover, their tasks are more complex, more uncertain, and more fluid than they were in the past—all this despite improvements in hardware and software that have made individual work and coordination less onerous. Hence, as new technological and nontechnological approaches to linkages are developed, there are new efficiency and social consequences, including changes in one's expectations of team productivity.

REFERENCES

Abdel-Hamid, T.K., and S.E. Madnick
    1989   Lessons learned from modeling the dynamics of software development. *Communications of the ACM* 32:1426-1438.
Adams, J.S.
    1976   The structure and dynamics of behavior in organizational boundary roles. Pp. 1175-1199 in M.D. Dunnette, ed., *Handbook of Industrial and Organizational Psychology*. Chicago: Rand-McNally.
Aldrich, H.
    1979   *Organizations and Environments*. Englewood Cliffs, N.J.: Prentice-Hall.
Allen, T.J.
    1977   *Managing the Flow of Technology*. Cambridge, Mass.: MIT Press.
Banker, R.D., S.M. Datar, and C.F. Kemerer
    1991   A model to evaluate variables impacting the productivity of software maintenance projects. *Management Science* 17:1-18.

Barnlund, D.C., and C. Harland
1963   Propinquity and prestige as determinants of communication networks. *Sociometry* 26:466-479.
Beatty, C.A.
1986   The Implementation of Technological Change: A Field Study of Computer Aided Design. Doctoral dissertation, The University of Western Ontario, Canada.
Boehm, B.W.
1987   Improving software productivity. *IEEE Computer Society* 20:43-57.
Boisot, M., and J. Child
1988   The iron law of fiefs: Bureaucratic failure and the problem of governance in the Chinese economic reforms. *Administrative Science Quarterly* 33:507-527.
Bossert, S.T.
1988-   Cooperative activities in the classroom. *Review of Research in*
1989   *Education* 15:225-250.
Brewer, M.B., and R.M. Kramer
1985   The psychology of intergroup attitudes and behavior. *Annual Review of Psychology* 36:219-243.
Brooks, F.P.
1987   No silver bullet: Essence and accidents of software engineering. *IEEE Computer Society* 20:10-18.
Bruner, J.
1974   *Beyond the Information Given*. London: Allen and Unwin.
Burns, L.R.
1989   Matrix management in hospitals: Testing theories of matrix structure and development. *Administrative Science Quarterly* 34:349-368.
Burns, T., and G. Stalker
1961   *The Management of Innovation*. London: Tavistock Publications.
Card, D.N., F.E. McGarry, and G.T. Page
1987   Evaluating software engineering technologies. *IEEE Transactions on Software Engineering* 13:845-851.
Carley, K.M.
1990   Coordinating for success: Trading information redundancy for task simplicity. *Proceedings of the 23rd Annual Hawaii International Conference on System Sciences* 3:261-270.
1991   A theory of group stability. *American Sociological Review* 56:331-354.
1992   Organizational learning and personnel turnover. *Organization Science* 3:20-46.
Chase, M.L.
1987   *Altering the Application of the Traditional Systems Development Life Cycle for Software Programs*. NTIS No. AD-A181/1HDM. Maxwell Air Force Base, Montgomery, Alabama.
Clark, K.B., W.B. Chew, and T. Fujimoto
1987   Product development in the world auto industry. *Brookings Papers on Economic Activity* 3:729-781.
Clark, N.K., and G.M. Stephenson
1989   Group remembering. Pp. 357-391 in P. Paulus, ed., *Psychology of Group Influence*, 2d ed. Hillsdale, N.J.: Erlbaum.
Culnan, M.J.
1983   Environmental scanning: The effects of task complexity and source accessibility on information gathering behavior. *Decision Science* 14:194-206.

Curtis, B.
  1985   *Human Factors in Software Development*. Washington, D.C.: IEEE Computer
          Society.
Curtis, B., H. Krasner, and N. Iscoe
  1988   A field study of the software design process for large systems. *Communica-
          tions of the ACM* 31:1268-1287.
Cyert, R.M., and J.G. March
  1963   *Behavioral Theory of the Firm*. Englewood Cliffs, N.J.: Prentice-Hall.
Daft, R.L., and R.H. Lengel
  1984   Information richness: A new approach to managerial behavior and organiza-
          tion design. In B. Staw and L.L. Cummings, eds., *Research in Organizational
          Behavior*, Vol. 6. Greenwich, Conn.: JAI Press.
  1986   Organizational information requirements, media richness, and structural de-
          sign. *Management Science* 32:554-571.
Davis, W.S.
  1987   *Systems Analysis and Design: A Structured Approach*. Reading, Mass.: Addison-
          Wesley.
Dearborn, D.C., and H.A. Simon
  1958   Selection perception: A note on the departmental identification of executives.
          Sociometry 21:140-144.
Diehl, M., and W. Stroebe
  1987   Productivity loss in brainstorming groups: Toward the solution of a riddle.
          Journal of Personality and Social Psychology 53:497-509.
Dietrich, W.C., L.R. Nackman, and F. Gracer
  1989   *Saving a Legacy with Objects*. Research Report RC, Research Division 14792.
          New York: International Business Machines Corporation.
Downs, A.
  1967   *Inside Bureaucracy*. Boston, Mass.: Little, Brown.
Eveland, J.D., and T.K. Bikson
  1988   Work group structures and computer support: A field experiment. *Transac-
          tions on Office Information Systems* 6:354-379.
Fanning, T., and B. Raphael
  1986   Computer teleconferencing: Experience at Hewlett-Packard. Pp. 291-306 in
          Proceedings of Conference on Computer-Supported Cooperative Work. New York:
          The Association for Computing Machinery.
Faunce, W.A.
  1958   Automation in the auto industry: Some consequences for in-plant social struc-
          ture. *American Sociological Review* 23:401-407.
Festinger, L., S. Schachter, and K. Back
  1950   *Social Pressures in Informal Groups: A Study of Human Factors in Housing*.
          Palo Alto, Calif.: Stanford University Press.
Finholt, T., L. Sproull, and S. Kiesler
  1990   Communication and performance in ad hoc task groups. Pp. 291-325 in R.
          Kraut, J. Galegher, and C. Egido, eds., *Intellectual Teamwork: Social and Tech-
          nological Foundations of Cooperative Work*. Hillsdale, N.J.: Erlbaum.
Fox, J.M.
  1982   *Software and its Development*. Englewood Cliffs, N.J.: Prentice-Hall.
Galbraith, J.K.
  1972   Organization design: An information-processing view. Pp. 49-74 in J.W. Lorsch
          and P.R. Lawrence, eds., *Organization Planning: Cases and Concepts*.
          Homewood, Ill.: Irwin.

Galegher, J., and R.E. Kraut
  1990   Computer-Mediated Communication for Intellectual Teamwork: An Experiment in Group Writing. Unpublished manuscript, Sloan School of Management, Cambridge, Mass.
Guzzo, R.A., R.D. Jette, and R.A. Katzell
  1985   The effects of psychologically based intervention programs on worker productivity: A meta-analysis. *Personnel Psychology* 38:275-291.
Hackman, J.R.
  1987   The design of work teams. In J. Lorsch, ed., *Handbook of Organizational Behavior*. Englewood Cliffs, N.J.: Prentice-Hall.
Hesse, B., L. Sproull, S. Kiesler, and J. Walsh
  1990   Computer Network Support for Science: The Case of Oceanography. Unpublished manuscript, Carnegie Mellon University, Pittsburgh.
Hill, G.W.
  1982   Group vs. individual performance: Are $N + 1$ heads better than one? *Psychological Bulletin* 91:517-539.
Hinsz, V.B.
  1990   Cognitive and consensus processes in group recognition memory performance. *Journal of Personality and Social Psychology* 59:705-718.
Huff, C., L. Sproull, and S. Kiesler
  1989   Computer communication and organizational commitment: Tracing the relationship in a city government. *Journal of Applied Social Psychology* 19:1371-1391.
Hunter, J.E., and F.L. Schmidt
  1983   Quantifying the effects of psychological interventions on employee job performance and work-force productivity. *American Psychologist* 38:473-478.
Jablin, F.M.
  1979   Superior-subordinate communication: The state of the art. *Psychological Bulletin* 86:1201-1222.
Jablin, F.M., L.L. Putnam, K.H. Roberts, and L.W. Porter, eds.
  1987   *Handbook of Organizational Communication: An Interdisciplinary Perspective*. Beverly Hills, Calif.: Sage.
Jones, C.
  1986   *Programming Productivity*. New York: McGraw-Hill.
Kelly, J.R., G.C. Futoran, and J.E. McGrath
  1990   Capacity and capability: Seven studies of entrainment of task performance rate. *Small Group Research* 21:289-314.
Kiesler, C., and S. Kiesler
  1969   *Conformity*. Reading, Mass.: Addison-Wesley.
Kraut, R.E., and L.A. Streeter
  1990   Satisfying the need to know: Interpersonal information access. Pp. 909-915 in D. Diaper et al., eds., *Human Computer Interaction—Interact 1990*. Amsterdam: North Holland.
Lawrence, P., and J. Lorsch
  1967   *Organization and Environment*. Cambridge, Mass.: Harvard University Press.
Levitt, B., and J.G. March
  1988   Organizational learning. *Annual Review of Sociology* 14:319-340.
Macy, M.
  1990   Learning theory and the logic of critical mass. *American Sociological Review* 55:809-826.

Malone, T.W.
1987   Modeling coordination in organizations and markets. *Management Science* 33:1317-1332.

March, J.G.
1981   Footnotes to organizational change. *Administrative Science Quarterly* 26:563-577.

March, J.G., and H. Simon
1958   *Organizations.* New York: John Wiley & Sons.

Maruyama, M.
1963   The second cybernetics: Deviation-amplifying mutual causal processes. *American Scientist* 51(2):164-179.

Mason, R.O.
1970   Beyond Benefits and Costs: A Study on Methods for Evaluating the NASA-ERTS Program. Unpublished manuscript, Southern Methodist University, Dallas.

McGrath, J.E.
1984   *Groups: Interaction and Performance.* Englewood Cliffs, N.J.: Prentice-Hall.

Monge, P.R., and K.K. Kirste
1980   Measuring proximity in human organizations. *Social Psychology Quarterly* 43:110-115.

Monge, P.R., L.W. Rothman, E.M. Eisenberg, K.L. Miller, and K.K. Kirste
1985   The dynamics of organizational proximity. *Management Science* 31:1129-1141.

National Research Council, Computer Science and Technology Board
1990   Scaling up: A research agenda for software engineering. *Communications of the ACM* 33:281-293.

National Science Board
1989   *Science and Engineering Indicators—1989.* NSB 89-1. Washington, D.C.: U.S. Government Printing Office.

Nelson, R.R., and S.G. Winter
1982   *An Evolutionary Theory of Economic Change.* Cambridge, Mass.: Belknap Press.

Newcomb, T.R.
1961   *The Acquaintance Process.* New York: Holt, Rinehart & Winston.

Olson, M.
1971   *The Logic of Collective Action: Public Goods and the Theory of Groups.* Cambridge, Mass.: Harvard University Press.

Orlikowski, W.J.
1988   Information Technology in Post-Industrial Organizations. Doctoral dissertation, New York University.

Ouchi, W.G.
1980   Markets, bureaucracies, and clans. *Administrative Science Quarterly* 25:129-140.

Parnas, D.L.
1972   On the criteria to be used in decomposing systems into modules. *Communications of the ACM* 5:1053-1058.

Pelz, D.C., and F.M. Andrews
1966   *Scientists in Organizations: Productive Climates for Research and Development.* New York: John Wiley & Sons.

Pfeffer, J.
1978   *Organizational Design.* Arlington Heights, Ill.: AHM Publishing.

Porter, L.W., E.E. Lawler, and J.R. Hackman
1975   *Behavior in Organizations.* New York: McGraw-Hill.
Rule, J., and P. Brantley
1990   Surveillance in the Workplace: A New Meaning to "Personal" Computing. Unpublished manuscript, State University of New York, Stony Brook.
Rumbaugh, J.
1991   *Object-Oriented Modeling and Design.* Englewood Cliffs, N.J.: Prentice-Hall.
Scott, R.F., and D.B. Simmons
1975   Predicting programming group productivity: A communications model. *IEEE Transactions on Software Engineering* 1:411-414.
Simon, H.A.
1962   The architecture of complexity. *Proceedings of the American Philosophical Society* 106(6):467-482.
Sims, M.L.
1989   Review of the Suitability of Available Computer Aided Software Engineering (CASE) Tools for the Small Software Development Environment. NTIS No. AD-218176/4/HDM. Wright-Patterson Air Force Base, Ohio.
Sodhi, J.
1991   *Software Engineering: Methods, Management and CASE Tools.* Summit, Pa.: Tab Professional and Reference Books.
Sproull, L., and S. Kiesler
1991   *Connections: New Ways of Working in the Networked Organization.* Cambridge, Mass.: MIT Press.
Spurr, K., and P. Layzell, eds.
1990   *Case on Trial.* Chichester: John Wiley & Sons.
Steiner, I.D.
1972   *Group Process and Productivity.* New York: Academic Press.
Stohl, C., and W.C. Redding
1987   Messages and message exchange processes. In F.M. Jablin et al., eds., *Handbook of Organizational Communication: An Interdisciplinary Perspective.* Beverly Hills, Calif.: Sage.
Sykes, R.E., K. Larntz, and J.C. Fox
1976   Proximity and similarity effects on frequency of interaction in a class of naval recruits. *Sociometry* 39:263-269.
Tajfel, H.
1982   Social psychology of intergroup relations. *Annual Review of Psychology* 33:1-39.
Thompson, J.D.
1967   *Organizations in Action.* New York: McGraw-Hill.
Travis, P.
1990   Why the AT&T network crashed. *Telephony* 218:11.
Tushman, M.L.
1977   Special boundary roles in the innovation process. *Administrative Science Quarterly* 22:587-605.
Tushman, M.L., and D. Nadler
1978   Information processing as an integrating concept in organizational design. *Academy of Management Review* 3:613-624.
Tziner, A., and D. Eden
1985   Effects of crew composition on crew performance: Does the whole equal the sum of its parts? *Journal of Applied Psychology* 70:85-93.

Van de Ven, A.H., A.L. Delbecq, and R. Koenig, Jr.
    1976   Determinants of coordination modes within organizations. *American Socio-
            logical Review* 41:322-338.
Verastegui, R.J., and D.J. Williams
    1988   *Improving Software Productivity: The Selection and Administration of GSA's
            Programmers Workbench at Martin Marietta Energy Systems, Inc.* NTIS No.
            DE880011803/HDM. Washington, D.C.: U.S. Department of Energy.
Wasby, S.
    1989   Technology in appellate courts: The ninth circuit's experience with electronic
            mail. *Judicature* 73:90-97.
Weinberg, G.M.
    1971   *The Psychology of Computer Programming.* New York: Van Nostrand Reinhold.
Zarella, P.F.
    1990   *CASE Tool Integration and Standardization.* Technical report, CMU/SEI-90-
            TR-14. Software Engineering Institute. Pittsburgh: Carnegie Mellon Uni-
            versity.
Zipf, G.K.
    1935   *The Psycho-Biology of Language.* Boston: Houghton Mifflin.

10

Productivity Linkages in Computer-Aided Design

Douglas H. Harris

This chapter examines productivity linkages and influences within the domain of *computer-aided design* (CAD). Consistent with its use in the design community and by other researchers, CAD encompasses the entire process of creating, modifying, and verifying designs with computer-based tools. It also encompasses the three principal elements of the computer-based design workplace: designers, design tools, and design tasks. The central question addressed in this chapter is, when CAD technology increases the productivity of individual designers, under what conditions will those increases lead to increases in the productivity of the design team and, in turn, the design organization?

Many of the issues discussed in earlier chapters are relevant to this type of information work—particularly the inhibitors and facilitators of linkages discussed in Chapter 3 and the coordination and communications concepts discussed in Chapter 9. I examine these and other issues here as they relate to productivity linkages among designers, design teams, and engineering organizations. I also assess influences that are likely to operate through these linkages to affect CAD productivity at different levels of analysis. Finally, I identify the types of research needed to understand these linkages and influences better and to define their role in the productivity of organizations.

The observations made in this chapter are based in part on the findings of other researchers, and in part on the results of a study a colleague and I made of the effectiveness of CAD within the engineering design organizations of a large aerospace company (see Harris and Casey,

1987). Although our study did not address linkage issues directly, the data we obtained and the experience we gained in collecting them provide a rich source of information for examining linkage issues.

In exploring the CAD domain, it is important to recognize that CAD is but one part of a larger evolving industrial process. Companies throughout the world have been attempting to achieve productivity gains by introducing computer-based tools in their engineering and manufacturing organizations. Companies in the United States, in particular, have been investing in CAD as a means of meeting the challenge of foreign competitors. Increased productivity is expected to come from automating routine tasks, increasing the efficiency and accuracy of complex calculations and tests, replacing physical prototypes with electronic prototypes, and facilitating the sharing of design data and the products of design tasks. Despite these expectations, however, previous studies conducted in several countries suggest that, thus far, the productivity potential of CAD has seldom been realized (Beatty and Gordon, 1988; Liker and Fleischer, 1989; Majchrzak et al., 1987).

Another aspect of the evolving industrial process is the important interface between CAD and computer-aided manufacturing (CAM). Computer aiding for engineering design has evolved from the development of relatively simple computer-based tools for drafting into sophisticated computer-based systems intended to streamline the entire design process. Computer aiding for manufacturing has evolved from numerically controlled machines into entire computer-based production facilities. In reviewing this evolution, many industry leaders have concluded that significant productivity gains overall cannot be realized until the two become a totally integrated CAD/CAM process. For example, a special committee of the National Research Council (1984) studied companies that were utilizing both CAD and CAM and strongly recommended pursuing the productivity gains that it believed could be realized through better integration of the two. Thus, although the focus here is on CAD, productivity linkages extend as well to the industrial enterprise of which CAD is only a part.

THE CAD DOMAIN

As noted above, Harris and Casey's (1987) study of the engineering design activities of a major aerospace company provides the principal data for this examination of productivity linkages in CAD. At the time of the study, the aerospace company had spent hundreds of millions of dollars on CAD hardware, software, facilities, and training. In addition, the company's design engineers had accumulated several years of CAD experience. The main purposes of the study were to document the lessons learned in the implementation and utilization of CAD, define a benchmark of organizational effectiveness in the evolution of CAD, and identify avenues for increasing the effectiveness of CAD in the future.

The study was conducted by first analyzing the computer-based tools and the tasks for which they were being used, then observing and interviewing users of the tools, and finally, surveying the users of the tools on factors influencing CAD effectiveness. The study focused on the 250 designers who had been the most frequent users of CAD tools during the previous year (out of a design engineering population of about 1,500 in the organization studied). These designers were identified from logs maintained by the system for the previous year.

The CAD domain was defined by identifying the specific design tasks that were being performed and then categorizing the tasks into a set of principal activities. The 200 design tasks thus identified could be categorized relatively easily into four principal CAD activities. This four-activity definition of the CAD domain was consistent with the findings of other investigators (e.g., Liker et al., 1990; Majchrzak et al., 1987). These four activities are summarized in the four sections that follow.

Creation or Modification of Two-Dimensional Drawings

Creation or modification of two-dimensional drawings includes all tasks required for the preparation of two-dimensional drawings of various types, such as plan views and projections. These tasks are directly analogous to the tasks that, prior to the development of computer-based tools, were completed at drawing boards. Computer-based tools available in CAD automate many of the labor-intensive details of this process, such as providing lines of selected widths, creating and positioning text, providing dimensions, filling and shading, and manipulating and correcting drawing elements. Computer aiding of this activity does not really extend the capability of the designer, rather it automates drafting functions in an attempt to make them more efficient and to make their products more consistent.

Creation or Modification of Three-Dimensional Models

Creation or modification of three-dimensional models encompasses the development of three-dimensional formulations of designs and their manipulation on computer displays. This activity is analogous to the tasks that, prior to CAD, required the construction and direct manipulation of physical models. With CAD, many of the manipulations that were previously performed physically, such as checking the fit of parts and examining the movement of working parts, are now performed electronically. Models can be constructed with varying degrees of sophistication, from simple wire-frame representations to realistic, shaded-solid representations in full color.

Verification of Drawings and Models

Verification of drawings and models includes the tasks required to verify that design parameters meet design specifications. Design work is completed under sets of specifications that provide design criteria and constraints for the end product. Consequently, a significant amount of design activity is devoted to ensuring that design concepts and intermediate products (drawings and models) meet those specifications. Because these tasks might require the completion of some basic calculations, CAD provides appropriate algorithms and calculation capabilities.

Acquisition of Data Needed for Design Tasks

Acquisition of design data encompasses tasks involved in obtaining the information needed for the solution of design problems, including the retrieval of information from CAD data bases. Given that engineering is the application of knowledge to the solution of technical problems, a part of the design effort necessarily involves the acquisition of information that is appropriate to the problem. Prior to CAD, engineers relied heavily on information contained in printed materials, such as handbooks, and on personal interaction with supervisors, specialists, and colleagues to obtain needed information. With CAD, these traditional sources of information are augmented by data bases supported by computer-based systems. Acquisition of data also encompasses data transfer from one workstation to another or to other functions, such as CAM.

INFLUENCES ON CAD PRODUCTIVITY

Typically, CAD is introduced into an engineering design organization with the expectation that it will increase the productivity of the organization by increasing the productivity of individual designers. Productivity gains are anticipated from the capabilities of CAD to automate routine functions, enhance the accuracy and efficiency of design tasks, promote the exchange of information, and facilitate the performance of sophisticated design tasks. Thus, the principal facilitator of productivity is assumed to be the technology of the CAD system itself. However, it is the interaction of the characteristics of the CAD

Influences on CAD Productivity

- Specialization of Design Work
- Isolation of Design Work
- Time-Sharing of Workstations
- Transitional Technology
- Organizational Complexity
- System Design and Support
- Exchange and Control of Information
- Mode of Supervision

FIGURE 10-1 Possible influences on CAD productivity.

system with the specific characteristics of the personnel and the work domain that appears to facilitate or inhibit potential productivity gains.

The principal output of a design effort is a set of design products (drawings, models, descriptions, and lists) that meet agreed design objectives, guidelines, and constraints. The principal resource consumed in producing this output is labor—designer, support, administrative, and so on. Thus, regardless of the level of analysis (individual, group, department, organization), the core definition of productivity within this domain is the ratio of design output to labor input.

Within the framework defined by the four types of design activities described above, my colleagues and I examined system and domain characteristics for factors that might facilitate or inhibit the productivity of the design organization. Our interviews and surveys of designers produced 3,929 specific comments on various aspects of CAD effectiveness. Analyses of these comments produced 145 issues that we then categorized into 43 principal factors associated with CAD performance. From these results, we identified characteristics of the CAD domain that might influence, positively or negatively, the design productivity of individuals, teams, and organizations. These potential influences on productivity linkages in the CAD domain are presented in Figure 10-1 and discussed below.

Specialization of Design Work

The work of individual designers in the aerospace company appeared to be relatively specialized in terms of the four principal design activities described earlier. Many designers concentrated on just one or two of the four activities. For example, more than 60 percent of those who reported doing any three-dimensional modeling spent at least 80 percent of their time on that activity. Nearly 40 percent of those who reported doing any design verification spent at least 80 percent of their time on that activity. The levels of specialization for two-dimensional drawing tasks and for data acquisition tasks were also within these ranges. Design work was specialized, therefore, not only by what was being designed (e.g., landing gears, cockpit instrument panels) but also by the types of design activities performed. Specialization of design work can facilitate the productivity of the individual designer because it encourages the more rapid development and application of design skills. However, it might inhibit the realization of productivity gains at the team and organizational levels because of the greater administrative burdens required for coordination and communication. These burdens were discussed in Chapter 9 relative to the software development domain.

Similar findings were reported by Liker et al. (1991) in their survey of firms using CAD. They found that a high degree of specialization was characteristic of the design organizations they studied, and that a high degree of fragmentation and segmentation existed in the application of knowledge and skills to the design process. They found that, commonly, the design process was divided into many little pieces and that each piece was delegated to a separate designer.

Isolation of Design Work

A relatively common complaint voiced by CAD designers in the aerospace company was that their work was too isolated from their supervisors and their senior associates and that it suffered as a consequence. The relatively frequent, informal, personalized guidance and feedback that designers had become accustomed to while working at drafting boards were reported to be lacking with CAD. Perhaps the utilization of a CAD workstation is not conducive to the provision of the kind of guidance, communication, and feedback designers consider important. The productivity of the individual designer, as well as that of the design team and organization, may be inhibited because of these difficulties. Use of CAD may require special efforts and methods to overcome the potential handicap of designer isolation.

Time-Sharing of Workstations

Within the aerospace company many more designers used CAD workstations than there were workstations for them to use—about 1,500 designers to 300 workstations. This finding is consistent with observations reported by others to the effect that, particularly in larger organizations, resources tend to lag the need for them. For example, Liker and Fleischer (1989) reported that CAD is typically phased in gradually over an extended period of time because of the extensive investment required in workstations and the cost of transferring pre-CAD designs to CAD.

Although nearly all of the 1,500 designers in the aerospace company had received the basic training required to qualify them to use CAD, about half of them seldom if ever used a CAD workstation. Excluding the infrequent users, on the basis that their need was not great, approximately 750 designers had to time-share among the 300 workstations. Among those 750, the distribution of time spent on CAD was highly skewed. The 250 most frequent users reported averaging 27.8 hours a week at a CAD workstation, which left an average of 10.1 hours per designer to be distributed to the remaining 500 during a typical work week (5,050 workstation-hours available divided by 500 designers equals 10.1 hours per designer).

The need to time-share workstations is a potential inhibitor of productivity gains. The 250 designers surveyed reported that they spent an average of 3.5 hours a week waiting for a workstation to become available. Because of the serial nature of many design tasks, waiting time is likely to be only marginally productive. Other possible inefficiencies associated with time-sharing include those associated with the additional effort required by the individual, team, and organization for scheduling workstations, and the nonproductive time and effort involved in moving and transporting working materials between two locations (e.g., non-CAD computer terminal on the desk, CAD facility down the hall).

Transitional Technology

As with other computer-based systems, the technology that supports CAD has been evolving rapidly and is expected to continue to do so for many years to come. In turn, a company's efforts to maintain or improve its competitive position force older technology to give way to the new. As a consequence, the technology employed in CAD is typically in a state of transition. One assumption, of course, in introducing new technology is that it will result in further productivity gains for the enterprise.

The introduction of new hardware and software is also a potential source of productivity loss due to the turbulence it generates in the CAD working environment. In the aerospace company, the pool of 300 workstations was not uniform in terms of the technology offered. Workstations consisted of newer and older models from the same vendor, as well as newer models under evaluation from other vendors—all differing in important ways in the features and the interfaces they provided for the designers.

As discussed in Chapter 2, changes in hardware and software can be particularly devastating to productivity in activities in which skills are not easily acquired. Computer-aided design is one of those activities. In the aerospace company designers estimated that, on average, 9.4 months of combined formal training and on-the-job practice were needed to reach an adequate level of proficiency on CAD. Additional time was required to reach an adequate level of proficiency on tasks that they previously were unable to perform manually, such as three-dimensional modeling. These estimates are higher than those obtained by other investigators, probably because of differences in the nature of the design tasks. For example, Beatty (1986) obtained an estimated average of 4.7 months for designers at a sample of 25 industrial sites in Canada. Even when the lower estimate is used, it must be concluded that a relatively lengthy period of specialized training and experience is needed to reach an adequate level of proficiency in CAD skills.

A system change with great negative impact on the designers surveyed was the introduction of new or updated applications software. Several months before the study, a major updating of the CAD software had been introduced. The change itself created a substantial burden associated with unlearning parts of the old system and learning the new versions. These difficulties were intensified, however, by problems in the software itself. Inevitably, it seems, newly released or updated software does not function exactly as it is supposed to, even when subjected to extensive pretesting. These software development difficulties can combine with long proficiency-development lead times and transfer-of-training problems to have a negative impact on designer productivity.

Organizational Complexity

The technology of CAD imposes requirements that can lead to increased complexity in the organization of the design effort. In contrast to the relatively simple line management that previously sufficed for engineering design organizations, CAD requires the involvement of a variety of specialists in addition to designers—computer specialists, computer maintenance personnel, software engineers, programmers, system support consultants, training specialists, liaison personnel, special study committees, and others. As a consequence, almost any structural solution to the organization of CAD will be more complex than that required for the organization of pre-CAD engineering. The number and complexity of linkages among individuals and groups are likely to be greater simply because of the large number of interdependencies. The aerospace designers interviewed and surveyed reported many continuing difficulties of an intraorganizational nature that affected their design effectiveness, which suggests that these issues are not easily resolved. These findings are consistent with those reported in Chapter 4, which examines organizational complexity and inertia relative to the introduction of automation into office work.

System Design and Support

The CAD workstation provides the designer with direct access to a variety of computer-based tools with which to perform design tasks. A tool consists of some combination of hardware and software that performs a function for the designer. The principal components are hardware display and control devices, through which the designer interacts with the computer system, and software application programs that perform various functions at the command of the designer. The central role of these tools in CAD suggests that individual productivity can be facilitated or inhibited by the degree of compatibility between the designer and the tools provided. In the aerospace company, there were wide-ranging differences among the principal CAD tools in terms of their perceived effectiveness. Some were rated highly (positioning objects in three dimensions and checking the fit of parts), but others were given very low ratings (dimensioning, performing calculations, and filling and shading).

The verbatim comments that accompanied the overall ratings of the CAD tools indicate that the ratings were based primarily on the ease and consistency with which the tools could be used. The highly rated tools were characterized by comments such as "smooth and reliable response to control actions," "consistent presentation of geometry," and "ease and clarity in locating contacting surfaces and analyzing clearances between surfaces." Tools that received the lowest overall ratings were characterized by comments such as "dimensioning procedures are cumbersome and confusing," "calculation functions are not sufficiently complete or versatile," and "manipulations are difficult, inflexible, and slow."

Closely linked to the usability of the system is the effectiveness of the support provided to the designer. The support can be in the form of features incorporated into the system itself or can be provided external to the system. Examples include design features that facilitate the learning and use of the system, timely and appropriate feedback from the system regarding the results of actions and errors made, opportunities for expert consultation on system problems, appropriateness and quality of training on the system, and adequacy of on-line and off-line documentation. Design productivity can be facilitated or inhibited by the effectiveness with which these types of support are provided to designers.

Exchange and Control of Information

Allen (1977) reported, prior to the widespread introduction of CAD, that informal, interpersonal communication was the primary way in which information flowed in engineering organizations. He estimated that fully half of the information that engineers used came from personal contacts, rather than from any written source. Moreover, he found that communication declined exponentially with distance, so that engineers were half as likely to talk to a colleague two offices away as they were to talk to one next door. Harris and Casey's (1987) findings indicated that the need, or at least the desire, for informal technical communications continues in the CAD domain.

Kraut and Streeter (1990) also concluded recently that, within the context of software engineering, the need for informal, designer-initiated information acquisition continues despite the use of computer-based workstations. They recommended the construction of discretionary data bases and computer-based systems that support this type of information acquisition. Clearly, what they recommend is something that CAD is capable of providing.

Several of the more senior aerospace designers interviewed contended that CAD actually had greater productivity potential as a communication tool than as a drawing tool. If CAD provided appropriate data bases and communications media, they argued, the primary sources of information could be immediately available to the designer. Easy, rapid access to needed information and the enhanced capability of interacting with colleagues on design issues could be very positive characteristics of CAD.

A potentially negative influence on productivity involves the rules imposed to control the flow and handling of CAD information. For example, modification procedures are intended to protect products of design efforts, such as drawings and specifications, from unauthorized or inadvertent changes during their use and transmission. Although necessary, these rules add a burden to the process of gaining access to and proceeding with work in progress. The nature of these rules is not likely to facilitate productivity; however, the manner in which rule making is conducted and implemented might minimize the negative impact on productivity.

Mode of Supervision

Several of the characteristics of the CAD domain discussed above have implications for supervision of the design effort. The modes of supervision required for a design effort characterized by high degrees of designer specialization and isolation, time-sharing of workstations, high levels of technology that is transitional in nature, and organizational complexity are likely to differ from the traditional pre-CAD modes. Realizing the potential gains in productivity from CAD might depend, in part, on the extent to which appropriate modes of supervision are developed and employed. Effective modes of planning, scheduling, and coordinating the design effort might facilitate CAD productivity, whereas ineffective modes will certainly inhibit the potential gains from CAD.

PRODUCTIVITY LINKAGES

The central question in this chapter is, when CAD technology increases the productivity of individual designers, under what conditions will those increases lead to increased productivity of the design organization? The answer is derived from an examination of the productivity linkages that exist among the individuals, groups, and organizations in the design process and from an examination of the factors and processes in the CAD domain that facilitate or inhibit those linkages. This discussion is consistent with the theoretical framework for linkages and influences provided in Chapter 3.

The Designer-Team Linkage

The extent to which the productivity of a design team is increased as the consequence of the increased productivity of its members depends on influences in the CAD domain that facilitate or inhibit the coordination of individual design efforts and the exchange of information that supports those efforts. As shown in Figure 10-2, potential influences include isolation of the designer, degree of specialization among members of the design team, modes and skills of team supervision, and controls that are imposed on the flow of information. The important questions to be addressed about these influences are, how have the traditional modes of operating been changed by CAD? What impact are those changes likely to have on design productivity? What facilitates or inhibits the transformation of increases in individual productivity to

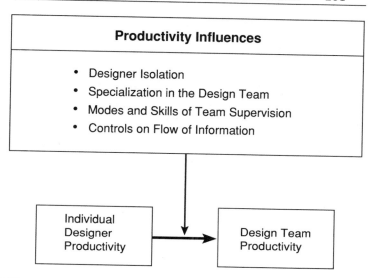

FIGURE 10-2 Possible influences on the designer-team productivity linkage.

increases in team productivity? The answers provided below were derived from an examination of influences in the CAD domain that relate specifically to the designer-team linkage.

Designer Isolation

One important characteristic of CAD work, as noted above, is the relative isolation (or insulation) of designers from one another. In contrast to working at a drawing board in the company of other designers at surrounding drawing boards, working at a CAD workstation is likely to result in more physical and psychological separation from other designers. Contact with others is reduced by computer display monitors and other equipment that block interactions beyond the immediate workstation, by the need to attend carefully to the displays and controls of the workstation, and by the reduction of ambient illumination in order to enhance the contrast ratio of displayed information. Moreover, the workstation, if time-shared, might be in a location some distance from that of other designers in the immediate work group at the time information exchange is desired.

The isolation of design work has potential implications for the linkage between designer and team productivity to the extent that the linkage depends on information sharing. As mentioned earlier, studies of pre-CAD engineering organizations revealed that about half of the information that designers used came from personal contacts that were close at hand. Informal, personal communications were found to be the primary way that information flowed in pre-CAD organizations. Because the studies were completed prior to the widespread introduction of CAD, the results apply principally to designers who were less insulated from each other.

What might happen to information sharing as designers become more insulated from one another in the CAD working environment? One possibility is that designers will necessarily switch to other modes of communication, such as electronic mail (email). If so, what is likely to be the impact on communication and the exchange of information? Greater formalization of communication might reduce the amount of information exchanged and slow the speed of needed communication, as discussed in Chapter 2. The consequence could be that increased levels of individual productivity might not be fully realized in the output of the design team.

On the other hand, CAD could provide the technology for enhancing designer-team communication. Kraut and Streeter (1990), recognizing that the introduction of computer aiding in other settings has led to more formal, impersonal communication, argued that the promotion of informal, personal communication can actually be enhanced through the construction and maintenance of discretionary data bases and computer-based communication systems. They envision systems that help identify relevant experts by providing lists of individuals, based on the relevancy of past work to the inquiry; by broadcasting requests for information to other designers by means of email; and by providing project alerts, such as changes or pointers to information that might be needed.

Kraut and Streeter have argued convincingly that informal communication, as mediated by personal contact, cannot be the major mechanism for coordination and information exchange because the transaction costs are too high. Moreover, physical proximity really does not meet today's information needs because the productivity of the designer and the design team depends on information from other groups and organizations. Communications must, necessarily, be spread across the organization and even across different sites. They suggest that the solution involves replacing physical proximity with electronic proximity. Electronic communication can be made to emulate the more informal, personal communication that designers desire. With this approach, the isolation of the individual designer by CAD need not be a productivity problem, and the technology provided by CAD might be the means to provide productivity enhancements through better communication.

Specialization in the Design Team

A relatively high degree of specialization can also mark the activities of individual CAD designers. Recall that significant specialization was found in the design problems addressed in the aerospace company. This was a function of the sophistication of the design effort and the degree of experience required to become proficient in addressing any specific type of design problem. A relatively high degree of designer specialization was also found in the type of CAD activity—three-dimensional modeling, two-dimensional drawing, verification of models and drawings, and acquisition of data. A possible explanation is that these activities differ in the skill and experience they require, and that skill differences among designers tend to drive task assignments. For example, the aerospace designers interviewed estimated that it took, on average, about 6 months to become proficient in verifying models and designs, but almost twice as long to become proficient in three-dimensional modeling.

The high degree of individual specialization in CAD activities places a premium on coordination of the design effort. The scope and product of an individual effort must fit explicitly into the scope and product of other designers and of the entire design team. Moreover, the completion time of the individual effort must match the time at which the product is needed by another designer or the design team. Team productivity, then, depends on fitting specialized individual efforts into the overall team effort through work planning and coordination. However, planning and coordination add to the costs of the design effort, which has the effect of reducing team productivity. Thus, an important challenge in capitalizing on increases in individual productivity is to arrive at an appropriate trade-off between gains realized from specialization and the costs that specialization imposes in the form of planning and coordination. Perhaps the needed planning and coordination could be made more efficient, and less costly, by applying CAD technology to those functions.

Team Supervision

In their study of how CAD technology had been integrated into engineering organizations, Liker et al. (1991) found that none of the companies in their sample had made any major changes in their organizational design when they implemented CAD. The typical approach was to replace old tools with new tools, leaving the old organizational structure and the old ways of managing the design process in place. Thus, the design group continued to be supervised in the same manner after the introduction of CAD as before the introduction of CAD. As suggested above, continuing the traditional mode of supervision can lead to problems and can inhibit the realization of potential productivity gains at the team level.

The team supervisor could be an important mediating factor in translating individual productivity into team and organizational productivity, since planning and coordination are principal supervisory functions. The traditional supervisor, however, is likely to be at a distinct disadvantage in performing these functions in a CAD environment. Resolution of many of the issues and problems that face individual designers in completing tasks and meeting schedules requires a thorough knowledge of the computer-based design tools. Unfortunately, the supervisor may have great difficulty in acquiring this knowledge and keeping up to date on tool technology while meeting various nontechnical supervisory responsibilities.

The problem is intensified by the phenomenon of transitional technology, discussed earlier, which is characteristic of CAD. In the aerospace study, designers reported considerable frustration with the quality of guidance obtainable from their supervisors. More worrisome, however, is their expressed lack of confidence that their supervisors knew enough about the technology to plan and coordinate the design effort effectively. New modes of supervision may be required before the potential productivity gains of CAD can be realized at the team and organizational levels. What has been learned about the impact of empowerment, job enrichment, and implementation of decision rules on group performance might be applicable to team supervision in this domain. An alternative to traditional modes of supervision, for example, might be self-managing teams. Goodman and associates (Goodman et al., 1988) have presented the concept and underlying theory of self-managing teams and have identified factors that are likely to facilitate productivity. Self-managing teams appear to meet some of the needs imposed on engineering teams by CAD.

Controls on Information Flow and Access

A special designer-team linkage issue in CAD is that of controlling access to and modification of information, including the drawings and specifications that are products of the design effort. A problem arises because of the need for various members of the design group to access drawings and other documentation that serve as their common products. Obviously, rules are needed to specify which designers are authorized to have access to work in progress and who can do what to it. The problem is intensified somewhat by the degree of task specialization that exists in CAD.

The rules governing access to work in progress help define the designer-team linkages and are also likely to influence the individual-to-team translation of productivity. The rules necessitate the imposition of extra steps to be taken by individual designers in gaining access to their work and in documenting the results of their efforts. While the rules, in the long term, might contribute to team productivity by avoiding the introduction of costly errors by individual designers, in the short term they place an additional burden on the designer that inhibits team productivity. Opportunities might exist here to enhance coordination of the efforts of individual designers through the exploration of more collaborative approaches to the control of information.

The Team-Organization Linkage

As a consequence of the technology required by CAD and the need for integrating design efforts into the overall industrial process, the design team works within the context of organizational complexity. Within the engineering hierarchy, the team is subject to specific organizational structures, policies, and procedures that define and govern its operations. These rules might either facilitate or inhibit the realization of productivity gains made at the team and individual levels.

The design team must also interact with groups and organizations outside the engineering hierarchy—organizations that provide computer maintenance support, software applications consulting, training, workstation allocation and scheduling, and other services. Productivity gains realized at the organizational level thus depend also on the factors that exist in the CAD domain to facilitate or inhibit these various interactions. Potential influences on the team-organization productivity linkage are illustrated in Figure 10-3 and addressed below.

The Burden of Design Support

Technology and the associated organizational complexity it spawns can inhibit CAD productivity gains by adding to the support burden of the overall design effort. That is, design teams might increase their productivity, but the gain is balanced by an increased burden of support costs. As discussed earlier, the introduction of CAD technology is accompanied by the need for various supporting functions and services, such as programming, maintenance, training, consultation, scheduling, and so on. When assessing the productivity of the design organization, therefore, one must add the costs of the various supporting functions to

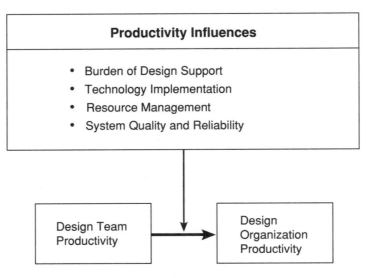

FIGURE 10-3 Possible influences on the team-organization productivity linkage.

the costs of the design effort in order to arrive at the true costs of the designs produced.

The assumption of CAD is that the additional burden imposed by support functions is more than offset by the increased efficiency and effectiveness of the resulting design process. This can certainly be true. But to arrive at an accurate assessment of productivity, one must also add the administrative costs in designer and supervisor time of interacting with the various support organizations. On the positive side, successful efforts to increase the efficiencies and reduce the costs of the support functions, and to streamline the interactions of design teams with those that provide these functions, can be avenues to enhancing productivity at the organizational level. An important issue to be addressed here is the trade-off between centralized and decentralized administration of support functions.

Technology Implementation

The policies and procedures an organization employs during CAD implementation can sow the seeds for inhibiting the actual gains in productivity expected from CAD at the organizational level. The implementation of new CAD technology has traditionally been completed as a top-down process. That is, managers and management committees develop plans for implementation, select the CAD technology, design the organizational structure, and determine and arrange for the support functions. This all takes place with little or no input from the designers who will be affected by these actions. In the companies studied by Liker and Fleischer (1989) and by Salzman (1989), there was virtually no involvement of designers in the selection or implementation of CAD, or even in decisions about hardware or software upgrades. They also found that the problem of the company's selecting inappropriate hardware and software was exacerbated by the provision of only minimal training on new systems; training was typically limited to short introductory courses.

The results of such approaches to technology implementation have been technology that does not match the requirements of users, high levels of turbulence within design organizations during technology implementation, and organizational climates that have not been conducive to productivity. One measure of the impact of this approach is the extent to which designers use the tools they have been provided. Liker et al. (1991) found that high-level features of CAD technology—those that held the greatest promise for increases in productivity—were consistently underutilized. Thus, design teams might be highly productive on tasks performed with low-level tools, but not on tasks for which the high-level tools were provided. The result would be an apparent productivity increase in design teams that is not reflected in the productivity of the organization.

Resource Management

As discussed above, the traditional top-down approaches to the acquisition and management of resources can ultimately inhibit the productivity linkages from design teams to design organizations. A related influence might be less than optimal decisions by management in the allocation of resources. An example is a decision that leads to the need to time-share workstations at a relatively high ratio of designers to workstations. The many negative consequences of time-sharing on individual and team productivity were discussed above. Time-sharing is likely to add to costs at the organizational level because of the administrative burden associated with allocating workstations to designers. For example, a system that efficiently establishes priorities and assigns workstations according to the individual needs of 750 designers, and the project needs of a major engineering organization, requires a significant effort. Minimal efforts that result in relatively inefficient allocations will further inhibit any increases in team productivity that might be realizable at the organizational level.

The management of resources during change so as to minimize turbulence in the organization should facilitate the realization of productivity gains. As discussed earlier, design organizations face frequent changes in hardware and software. In the aerospace company studied, several different models of workstations were in place in the engineering organization as older versions were being replaced by newer versions and other models were being introduced on an experimental basis. The change process was complicated by the high demand for the limited number of available workstations, which led to many of the older models being kept in place longer than the transition would usually require. In addition, issues of centralized versus distributed data processing were being addressed by introducing alternative concepts into the workplace on an experimental basis, which significantly modified previous procedures for gaining access to and controlling information in data files. Without effective planning and coordination, such changes could cause sufficient turbulence in an organization to inhibit the realization of productivity gains made by design teams.

System Quality and Reliability

The findings discussed here are consistent with those of other investigators regarding the importance to the design organization of maintaining the quality and reliability of the technical system. Gutek et al. (1984) studied the implementation of office automation in 55 work groups and concluded that technical problems with the system were key impediments to its use in office tasks. Similarly, Liker et al. (1990) reported that designers in companies in the United States and Japan considered system factors to be highly important to their productivity. Factors in system quality and reliability include maintenance and repair, consistency of operations, safeguards against data contamination, recovery from failure, system response time, and system reliability.

System quality and reliability will have direct impacts on the productivity of individual designers and design teams. These system factors, however, are also indicators to designers of the focus of attention and the problem-solving capabilities of management. Deterioration or continual neglect of these system factors at the organizational level could lead to lower levels of motivation due to reduced confidence in management. One aspect of lowered motivation by individuals and teams could be their reduced efforts to compensate for chronic system problems, which would intensify the amount of effort needed to resolve the problems at higher levels in the organization. Thus, although team productivity might actually increase, the costs of additional problem-solving efforts could eliminate any potential gains in productivity at the organizational level.

CONCLUSION AND RESEARCH RECOMMENDATIONS

When CAD technology leads to increases in the productivity of individual designers, a number of influences in the CAD domain determine whether those individual gains will also be realized in the productivity of the design team and, in turn, the design organization. The influences might facilitate or inhibit the translation of individual productivity to higher levels of analysis. Although some studies have examined the integration of CAD into engineering organizations and the impact of certain variables on CAD performance, relatively little is known about the conditions under which increases in individual productivity lead to increases in organizational productivity.

At the outset of this chapter, I noted the potentially important interface between CAD and CAM. A conclusion of a study by the National Research Council (1984) was that the full productivity potential of CAD would not be realized in an enterprise until CAD was successfully integrated with CAM. Although the discussion in this chapter was confined to productivity linkages that operate within the CAD domain, the issues of productivity linkages and influences are likely to be no less important to the successful integration of CAD with CAM.

This examination of productivity in the CAD domain resulted in the identification of several hypotheses about how the linkages among individual, team, and organizational productivity might be facilitated or inhibited. The research needed to test those hypotheses must necessarily differ from previous research conducted in this domain, which has consisted mainly of cross-sectional interview and survey approaches.

Longitudinal studies are required in which productivity measures are obtained and tracked over time at each level of analysis—individual, team, and organization. Linkages can then be defined and assessed on the basis of those measures. Concurrently, measures of potential influences on productivity linkages can be obtained and correlated with linkage measures. Because some influences cannot easily be manipulated for research purposes and must therefore be taken as found in specific settings, it will probably be necessary to collect data in several settings and make cross-comparisons to assess important facilitators and inhibitors of linkages. The following hypotheses should be tested using the longitudinal research approach:

• The relative isolation of individual designers in CAD teams can reduce the strength of the linkage between individual and team productivity. The development and use of techniques that promote informal, designer-initiated communication directly from the workstation to other team members, and to others in and beyond the immediate organization, can strengthen the linkage.

• The costs of planning and coordinating design activities at the organizational level can offset individual productivity gains realized from extensive specialization. Developing and using better models and procedures for making the specialization-coordination trade-off can strengthen productivity linkages.

• The strength of productivity linkages is diminished by the transitional nature of the CAD system technology. Minimizing turbulence during the phasing-in of new technology and the phasing-out of old technology can strengthen productivity linkages.

• Traditional modes of team supervision are not appropriate to CAD. New approaches to team supervision, such as self-managing teams, can strengthen productivity linkages.

• More efficient rules for controlling access to work materials and for documenting work results can strengthen productivity linkages. Collaborative approaches to rule making and to the implementation of rules can serve to strengthen the individual-team linkage.

• Efforts to reduce the organizational complexity within which individual designers and design teams work, and thereby reduce the burden of design support, can strengthen productivity linkages. Models that provide an appropriate trade-off between centralized and decentralized design support can strengthen productivity linkages.

• The policies and procedures employed during technology implementation can weaken productivity linkages. Approaches other than the traditional top-down management of implementation, such as providing for more user input during the process, can strengthen the linkages.

• The management of resources can influence productivity linkages. Less-than-optimal allocations are likely to reduce the productivity of the organization by increasing administrative burdens. The development of better models and procedures to support resource management can strengthen the linkages.

• Maintaining a high level of system quality and reliability will strengthen the linkages between individual and organizational productivity.

REFERENCES

Allen, T.T.
1977   *Managing the Flow of Technology: Technology Transfer and the Dissemination of Technological Information Within the R&D Organization.* Cambridge, Mass.: MIT Press.

Beatty, C.A.
1986   The Implementation of Technological Change: A Field Study of Computer Aided Design. Doctoral dissertation, The University of Western Ontario, Canada.

Beatty, C.A., and J.R.M. Gordon
1988   Barriers to the implementation of CAD/CAM systems. *Sloan Management Review* 29:25-34.

Goodman, P.S., R. Devadas, and T.L. Griffith
1988   Groups and productivity: Analyzing the effectiveness of self-managing teams. Pp. 295-327 in J.P. Campbell and R.J. Campbell, eds., *Productivity in Organizations.* San Francisco: Jossey-Bass.

Gutek, B.A., T.K. Bikson, and D. Mankin
1984   Individual and organizational consequences of computer-based office information techniques. Pp. 231-254 in S. Oskamp, ed., *Applied Social Psychology Annual,* Vol. 5. Beverly Hills, Calif.: Sage.

Harris, D.H., and S.M. Casey
1987   Organizational effectiveness of computer-aided design. *Proceedings of the 31st Annual Meeting of the Human Factors Society* 214-217. Santa Monica, Calif.: Human Factors Society.

Kraut, R.E., and L.A. Streeter
1990   Satisfying the Need to Know: Interpersonal Information Access. Unpublished manuscript, Bell Communications Research, Morristown, N.J.

Liker, J.K., and M. Fleischer
1989   Implementing computer-aided design: The transition of nonusers. *IEEE Transactions on Engineering Management* 36:180-190.

Liker, J.K., M. Fleischer, M. Nagamachi, and M.S. Zonnevylle
1990   *Designers and Their Machines: User Assessments of CAD and CAD Use in the U.S. and Japan.* Ann Arbor, Mich.: Industrial Technology Institute.

Liker, J.K., M. Fleischer, and D. Arnsdorf
1991   *Fulfilling the Promises of CAD: Integrating Technology and Organization.* Ann Arbor, Mich.: Industrial Technology Institute.

Majchrzak, A., T.C. Chang, W. Barfield, R. Eberts, and G. Salvendy
1987   *Human Aspects of Computer-Aided Design.* London: Taylor & Francis.

National Research Council
1984   *Computer Integration of Engineering Design and Production: A National Opportunity.* Washington, D.C.: National Academy Press.

Salzman, H.
1989   Computer aided design: Limitations in automating design and drafting. *IEEE Transactions on Engineering Management* 36:252-261.

11

Organizational-Level Productivity Initiatives: The Case of Downsizing

David A. Whetten and Kim S. Cameron

Taken together, the preceding chapters have shared two distinctive features: (1) They have examined the productivity paradox from a bottom-up perspective. That is, they have examined various explanations for the observed fact that increased productivity at the job or unit level does not readily accumulate into productivity gains at the firm level. (2) They have examined this form of the productivity paradox primarily within the context of information technology (IT) applications.

This chapter focuses on alternative forms and contexts of the productivity paradox. Specifically, it examines a top-down form of the productivity paradox—organizational downsizing—in a broad range of settings, primarily in the manufacturing sector. The intent is to urge a broader examination of this troubling organizational phenomenon.

Throughout this chapter we use the traditional definition of productivity: output divided by input. Our observations about downsizing apply to partial factor productivity (the only input is labor) and total factor productivity (inputs include labor, capital, energy, and so on). Cameron and colleagues (1991, 1993) have found that managers involved in downsizing tend to plan in terms of partial factor productivity (most downsizing plans focus only on projected labor savings). The most successful downsizing they found, however, involved total factor productivity; that is, downsizing tended to be associated with a wide array of cost factors, as well as an aspiration to regain the nimbleness and spontaneity typical of younger, smaller organizations. Because no conclusive evidence exists that downsizing alone improves an organization's culture, our discussion centers on the widely shared belief that downsizing will generate cost and labor savings.

DOWNSIZING AS A PRODUCTIVITY INITIATIVE

As noted in Chapter 1, between 1973 and 1990, the hourly output of U.S. workers grew only 0.7 percent. In contrast, hourly output had grown at a rate of 2.5 percent from 1948 to 1973 (Sawhill and Condon, 1992). This slowdown in productivity significantly affected the quality of life of the American work force.

A major cause of the decline in productivity in the United States has been the "bigger is better" ethic that permeated management thought from the end of World War II until the mid-1980s. Alfred P. Sloan, Jr. (1963:xxii), the legendary former chairman of General Motors, argued that "growth is essential to the good health of an enterprise. Deliberately to stop growing is to suffocate." It is telling that the *Fortune* ranking of companies (Fortune 100, 500, 1000) is in terms of size, not profitability. Given this passion for growth, it is not surprising that in many large firms, the unrelenting pursuit of large size has often exceeded that which can be justified by economies of scale. "The biggest companies are the most profitable—on the basis of return-on-equity—in only 4 out of 67 industries in the Top 1000 firms. Well over half the time, the biggest corporate player fails to attain even the industry average return on invested capital" (*Business Week*, March 27, 1989:92). This pattern is a product of a number of important liabilities of size (Cameron et al., 1993), among them the cumbersomeness with which new products are developed and new market opportunities pursued. For example, Compaq Computer, less than half the size of the International Business Machines (IBM) Corporation, can develop a new computer three to five times faster than can IBM, and Bethlehem Steel produces a ton of steel with one-third the labor its larger competitors use (Henkoff, 1990). Unfortunately, it has been traditional for more employees and larger units to be used as rewards for successful managers, and they became treated as measures of managerial power and status (Whetten, 1980a).

As a result of the prevailing view of growth, organizational downsizing traditionally was treated as an aberration from the norm. Shrinking, retrenching, or consolidating the organization was viewed as a last-ditch effort to thwart organizational demise or to adjust temporarily to cyclical downturns in sales. It was almost always targeted at blue-collar or hourly employees, and it was customarily defined negatively (Hirshorn et al., 1983). For example, of all the firms that eliminated blue-collar jobs in the first half of the 1980s, 90 percent did not eliminate a single white-collar job (Thurow, 1986). The seriousness of this strategy is highlighted by the fact that across all U.S. manufacturing firms, the percentage of nonproduction employees (i.e., managerial overhead) grew from 19 percent in 1950 to 32 percent in the mid-1980s (Tomasko, 1987). The recent economic recession, coupled with the decade-long deterioration in global competitiveness among American businesses, exposed a serious weakness in U.S. organizations, namely, that many firms had become overstaffed, cumbersome, slow, and inefficient. At the beginning of the 1990s, for example, American automakers had more than twice the number of hierarchical levels in their organizations as their Japanese counterparts. Moreover, it became clear that American businesses had developed a significant cost disadvantage compared to their Asian competitors in almost every head-to-head product competition (Cameron et al., 1993). Swollen managerial overhead rates, for example, are an important contributing cause of U.S. auto manufacturers carrying a cost disadvantage in excess of $1,000 per car compared to their Japanese rivals.

The newly recognized weakness in U.S. organizations led managers and theorists to consider downsizing in a different light. In order to increase productivity, enhance competitiveness, and contain costs, fundamental ways of organizing and managing had to be reexamined. A transition was made from merely reacting to downturns in the economy to trying to improve internal efficiency. Whereas downsizing had been synonymous with blue-collar layoffs, it became an overhead reduction strategy affecting mainly white-collar employees. Instead of focusing on job redesign, working harder, and tightening up rules and procedures, downsizing became more focused on bottom-up participation by empowered employees, team coordination, and working smarter through redesigned work processes. In brief, downsizing was redefined as a productivity improvement strategy rather than as a last-ditch survival effort. These changes in the definition of downsizing in the 1990s are reflected in Table 11-1.

The recent change in philosophy about downsizing is evidenced by the fact that nearly all the Fortune 1000 firms engaged in downsizing between 1985 and 1990, and a majority indicated that they would engage in downsizing in the future (Henkoff, 1990). In 1990, for example, three times more employees were laid off in the United States than in 1989. Large reductions in work force have occurred in virtually every large, name-brand firm in North America in the past 5 years, and not a single week in 1992 passed without an announcement in the business press that some firm had initiated a downsizing program. Between one-third and one-half of all medium- and large-sized firms have downsized each year since 1988 (Henkoff, 1994). Cameron et al. (1991)

TABLE 11-1 Alternative Approaches to Productivity Improvement

	Organizational Goal	
	---	---
	Recovery	Performance Improvement
Organizational environment	Downsizing (1970-1980s)	Downsizing (1990s)
	Reaction to downturns	Reaction to inefficiency
	Blue-collar layoffs	White-collar layoffs
	Elimination of plants or units	Organizational restructuring or realignment
Alignment focus	Job redesign (individual) Specialization of work (group)	Automation of work (individual) Coordination of work through teams (group)
	Increase work hours and effort (work harder)	Improve processes (work smarter)
	Adherence to policies and rules	Empowerment and participation (e.g., suggestion systems)

reported that more than half of the managers displaced from 1989 through 1991 took pay cuts of 30 to 50 percent to obtain new jobs.

Overall, it is clear that organizational downsizing (focused on employee headcounts and hierarchical levels) has been one of the major initiatives undertaken during the past decade to increase the productivity of American firms. Unfortunately, however, there is mounting evidence that the anticipated effects have not been realized. In a 1990 survey of 909 downsized U.S. firms, Right Associates, an outplacement firm interested in downsizing, found that 74 percent of senior managers in downsized companies thought that morale, trust, and productivity suffered after downsizing (Henkoff, 1990). A survey by the Society for Human Resource Management found that more than half of the 1,468 firms that downsized indicated that productivity had deteriorated as a result of downsizing (Henkoff, 1990). This conclusion is further substantiated by a survey conducted by the Wyatt consulting firm and published in the *Wall Street Journal* (Bennett, 1991). The survey found that 71 percent of the firms involved in downsizing did so to increase productivity, but only 22 percent of those firms thought that goal had been accomplished. The director of research for Wyatt, John Parkington, succinctly summarized the experience of downsizing during the 1980s, "Lots of bullets were fired, but few hit their targets. Sometimes companies did it three, four, and five times, but still didn't hit their expense-reduction targets. Something is wrong" (quoted in Bennett, 1991:B1). It should be noted that limited amounts of systematically gathered or published financial data are available to support these retrospective, subjective assessments. Nonetheless, the consistency of these observations regarding the fate of downsizing initiatives is sobering.

The several investigations revealing that downsizing initiatives frequently do not yield commensurate gains in productivity appear to have identified another form of the productivity paradox. Indeed, this is an especially troublesome version of the paradox because it would naturally be expected that removing sizable amounts of overhead or slack from an organization's balance sheet would lead to increased organizational productivity. The optimistic view that a reduction in organizational capacity will not result in a proportionate reduction in organizational productivity is simply not substantiated by the experience of many firms.

One primary purpose of this chapter is to explore alternative explanations for the downsizing form of the productivity paradox. Specifically, we address two questions: (1) Given a substantial downsizing initiative, what factors might account for the apparent lack of anticipated productivity gains? (2) To what extent are the attenuating factors embedded in organizational linkage issues? Before proceeding to address these questions in detail, we briefly point out how downsizing fits into the broader discussion of organizational linkages and productivity in this report.

Most examples of the productivity paradox discussed in earlier chapters are based on the assumption that by increasing the productivity of the constituent elements of an organization, the organization as a whole will become more productive. Such an assumption is not necessarily embedded in commonly practiced downsizing. Like other change efforts, downsizing can be applied at any level of analysis—from subunit to organizational network. But the downsizing initiatives most frequently pursued by organizations in the hope of affecting productivity are at the organizational level. Specifically, the approach is to cut costs (the denominator in the productivity equation) by reducing the size and configuration of the overall organization. These "demassing" decisions affect people at all levels in the organization, but the intent of most downsizing programs is not to increase the productivity of a specific individual or work unit so much as the entire organization. Thus, the role of organizational linkages in this form of the productivity paradox is different from that discussed in previous chapters.

When productivity enhancements are initiated within subunits of an organization, there is generally an implicit assumption (and often an explicit declaration) that local gains in productivity will benefit the organization as a whole. Consistent with the well-known justification, "What is good for General Motors is good for the U.S.," internal organizational improvements are often justified on the basis that, "What is good for the finance department (e.g., increased productivity) is good for General Motors."

In the case of downsizing, cross-level organizational effects play an equally important role in determining the long-term "success" of the initiative. However, in the typical cost-cutting-oriented, top-down-initiated downsizing program, insufficient attention has been paid to the effects (intended or unintended) of downsizing on the productivity of individuals and work units. Questions about whether (and if so, how) aggregate cost savings can be disaggregated into subunit productivity gains are seldom considered by downsizing strategists.

We believe that this lack of attention to cross-level effects helps explain why organizational productivity typically suffers from downsizing. When an organization cuts costs but does not realize an overall productivity gain, we suspect that the organization's ability to transform inputs efficiently into outputs has been seriously diminished. Figure 11-1 provides a sample of commonly occurring, unintended dysfunc-

Personal	Organizational
Priority: self-protection, self-absorption	Loss of innovation
Uncooperativeness (lack of teamwork)	Loss of long-term vision
Erosion of commitment	Loss of company loyalty
Secretiveness	Increased conflict
Skepticism and cynicism	Politicized decision making
Mourning of losses—preoccupation with	Resistance to change
past guilt feelings	Inaccessible, unavailable leaders
Loss of self-confidence	Sabotage
Anxiety and apprehension	Increased bureaucratization
Increased burnout	Destruction of informal networks
Blaming—search for scapegoats	System slowdown
	Rise in invisible (unmeasured) costs

FIGURE 11-1 Unintended negative consequences of downsizing.

tional outcomes from flawed downsizing initiatives that can reduce the productivity of individuals, work units, and the organization as a whole.

EXPLANATIONS FOR THE DOWNSIZING PRODUCTIVITY PARADOX

Several plausible explanations exist for the lack of productivity gains from downsizing efforts. First, consistent with the American preference for the "one-minute quick fix" (Blanchard and Johnson, 1983; Kilmann, 1984), many firms may have had unrealistic expectations regarding the productivity gains to be realized from downsizing. The requisite patience and broad-based approach to downsizing have often been replaced by announcements of quick headcount reductions in the hope that immediate results will accrue. Yet, the fact is that the overhead rates and cost structures for most U.S. firms continue to remain significantly above those of their best global competitors (Cameron et al., 1993). Thus, U.S. executives may be administering the right medicine, but at insufficient dosage or without sufficient duration to produce the desired results.

Second, the downsizing process may not have been managed competently in many firms, and thus the intended productivity gains have not been achieved (Whetten, 1981). In fact, in one set of studies the *process* by which downsizing programs were implemented was found to be more important than the actual downsizing strategies applied (Cameron et al., 1991). That is, unanticipated dysfunctional outcomes may result from poor implementation. Implementation mistakes include removing the wrong people, levels, or functions from the firm; eroding trust and morale to the point that employees lose loyalty and commitment to the firm and reduce their work efforts; restricted communication from top management, lack of information sharing, and poorly communicated plans that cause confusion and misunderstanding, which results in wasted or uncoordinated efforts; and an escalation of long-term costs because a crisis mentality emanates from pressures to achieve immediate bottom-line results.

It is our experience that both obstacles to increased productivity have plagued most downsizing efforts. Indeed, they are interrelated factors. In many firms, downsizing has been managed so poorly that managers have encountered enormous resistance and hostility from internal and external constituencies. A pattern emerges of plans conceived at the top being derailed at lower levels. As a result, downsizing programs must be repeated, escalated, and revised over and over again. One large company we studied, for example, has initiated 18 downsizing programs in the past four decades (Cameron et al., 1993).

Downsizing Implementation Mistakes

One of our intentions in this chapter is to identify implementation mistakes commonly made by organizations engaged in downsizing. Our concern is that these mistakes are so pervasive they represent the norm. Further, it appears that this is more than a statistical norm, in the sense that lots of managers independently have made poor downsizing choices. Instead, we believe that a pattern exists in these mistakes that reflects three fundamental social dynamics.

First, we believe these mistakes are buttressed by an underlying belief system regarding the central role of management in problem-solving settings. Our concern is that this paradigm is both anachronistic and dysfunctional in downsizing situations. Second, evidence exists that the managers of poorly performing firms are highly susceptible to social contagion. That is, because of the extreme pressures and erosion of credibility they often experience, they are likely to adopt readily available and accepted problem-solving processes and options. Third, the nominal decision-making process in such organizations is truncated during a period of decline by the strong pressure to act quickly. This time constraint limits the search for alternatives and reduces the time allocated for planning and implementing changes. We briefly discuss each of these underlying causes of downsizing management mistakes in turn.

Paternalistic Management

The ineffective downsizing initiatives we have observed are indicative of a paternalistic management paradigm that was repudiated during the expansion era of the 1960s and 1970s, but that appears to be reemerging during the period of contraction that began in the 1980s. Our research suggests that the highly participative approach to managing "positive" organizational change (i.e., expansion) has been replaced with a much more closed, authoritarian approach to managing "negative" change (i.e., contraction). Information acquired and monitored by managers that may portend a downsizing decision tends not to be shared with lower-level employees when the implications are negative. This restricted information flow from the top, however, often leads to rumor, fabrication, and faulty decision making at lower organization levels. This dynamic is based on the assumption that sharing bad news with lower-level employees will produce resistance and self-protection instead of enhanced participation and commitment. This philosophy may reflect an underlying, even unconscious, lack of trust, a high level of suspicion, and a skepticism regarding the motives and skills of subordinates.

This conclusion is consistent with the threat-rigidity effect observed by Staw et al. (1981). When an organization is threatened by a major crisis, managers tend to restrict the flow of information. This action is supported by the belief that current practices and routines are sufficient to handle the problem, so additional information is not only unnecessary but costly in terms of impeding response time. The belief that the organization's existing repertoire of responses is capable of handling a crisis is paternalistic in the sense that management's deference to institutionalized definitions, philosophies, and problem-solving routines drives out novel inputs from subordinates.

Following Accepted Practice

It is a well-established fact that decision makers are susceptible to social influence (Deutsch and Gerard, 1955). They are as likely to select solutions on the basis of their perceived social acceptability as their inherent merits (e.g., cost, speed of implementation; Scott, 1987). Organizations require two forms of support in order to be successful: resources and legitimacy (Aldrich, 1979). Common resource needs include revenues, personnel, technology, and physical space. Legitimacy stems from the perception that the organization's actions are congruent with accepted norms and social values. Another term for legitimacy is reputation. Resources and legitimacy are interrelated in that when an organization's resource stream (e.g., sales revenues) significantly decreases, its legitimacy often suffers. Put simply, cash-flow crises are generally associated with confidence crises (D'Avani, 1990).

Thus, it is quite natural for managers of poorly performing organizations to prefer remedies that enhance legitimacy. Their goal is to prevent further erosion of their organization's reputation by using problem-solving processes and solutions that have the stamp of "accepted practice" (Galaskiewicz and Wasserman, 1989).

Truncated Decision Making

The tendency to mimic the behavior of other highly visible downsizing firms is reinforced by the extreme time pressure generally associated with a performance crisis. Managers think they simply do not have the time to experiment with new options and, instead, opt for off-the-shelf packages. They rely heavily on problem-specific consultants (e.g., experts in fighting off unfriendly acquisitions, downsizing, increasing productivity or quality), who strengthen the credibility of their recommendations by identifying other organizations that have adopted their programs.

Linkage Insensitivity

The three social dynamics often combine to create a decision-making process that is "linkage insensitive." That is, top-level executives make decisions about the whole, without adequately considering their effects on the parts. This oversight results in implementation problems in most downsizing programs that substantially inhibit or diminish the anticipated productivity gains. Indeed, some downsizing initiatives are so disruptive at lower levels that organizational productivity is impaired (Cameron et al., 1993).

How is it possible that such practice can occur, much less become the norm? Why is it that downsizing programs are particularly afflicted by flawed decision-making processes? It has been our observation that the social dynamics identified above create a decision-making climate dominated by "myth." A myth is a belief that may or may not be true but whose truth, or reality, is accepted uncritically. It constitutes the prevailing commonsense practice.

Common Myths About Downsizing

In the case of downsizing, decision makers appear to rely heavily on prevailing myths regarding common practice because (1) the myths are congruent with an underlying management paradigm, (2) they reduce the time necessary to announce a crisis management plan, and (3) they bestow badly needed legitimacy on the proposals. Top management teams understand that credibility is a key to overcoming resistance to painful downsizing proposals. Thus, they shroud their plan in the espoused virtues of "making a timely response," "doing what's best for the organization as a whole," "rising above self-interest," "having the courage to make tough decisions," and "following the lead of highly reputable firms."

From our research we have identified seven common myths about the best way to design and implement a downsizing program (Cameron et al., 1993). We have found that these myths about accepted practice create a socially constructed reality that entraps managers in faulty decision-making processes. These defective premises produce a common outcome: linkage-insensitive decisions. We briefly discuss each of the seven common downsizing myths and point out why it frequently produces dysfunctional outcomes. We then examine the combined set of strategies and contrast it with a more effective approach to downsizing.

We illustrate the prevalence of the seven myths with findings from the survey of 909 U.S. businesses by Right Associates (Henkoff, 1990).

Myth 1: Act Quickly—Don't Prolong the Agony of Downsizing

According to this myth, uncertainty and anxiety are reduced and organizational life can return to normal if downsizing is done with dispatch. It is quite natural for managers to want to minimize the disruptive effects of downsizing. Change is inherently stressful, and negative changes are especially traumatic. In their haste to minimize pain, however, managers often inadvertently prolong and intensify it by inadequate planning and forced execution. In the Right Associates survey, for example, 35 percent of the firms that downsized announced and implemented downsizing in less than one week. More than 50 percent announced and implemented downsizing in less than a month.

A broadly published comparison between decision making in U.S. and Japanese firms (Imai, 1986) shows that Japanese managers spend more time making a decision than their American counterparts. The American penchant for action, however, actually lengthens the overall time required to plan and implement a program because the truncated planning (decision-making) cycle leads to a protracted implementation process often marred by multiple false starts.

The contrast between Japanese and U.S. firms is especially pronounced under crisis conditions. Eastern philosophy argues that crises contain two elements: threat and opportunity. Those who subscribe to this perspective are less likely to rush the downsizing process in hopes of minimizing its pain. Instead, they are more likely to take a longer-term, more holistic, approach to solving the problem—accepting pain and inconvenience as a necessary, but acceptable, element. This approach obviously requires more time up front. But the resulting increase in understanding and acceptance of the proposal substantially speeds the implementation process. This leads us to myth 2.

Myth 2: Minimize the Involvement of Subordinates

One of the most widely held tenets regarding the management of downsizing is that, as potential targets of cutbacks and reductions, subordinates cannot make objective decisions and will not initiate cost-saving ideas that negatively affect their own jobs and functions. Many managers argue forcefully that their subordinates are not in a position to decide what is best for the organization because their self-interests will cloud their judgment. They further argue that it is an abrogation of responsibility for managers to share decision making—"We're paid to make the tough decisions."

This myth is inconsistent with sound decision-making principles and observed practice in effectively downsizing organizations. One of the general guidelines in the literature is that the quality of decisions reflects the knowledge and judgment of the decision makers (Hogarth, 1987). Recognizing the importance of these conditions, top management would find it unthinkable to plan a major reorganization during a period of growth without extensive consultation throughout the organization. Myth 2 reflects managers' willingness to sacrifice the quality of knowledge brought to bear on a downsizing decision on the false premise that threatened subordinates cannot, categorically, exercise good judgment. In only 4 percent of the firms surveyed by Right Associates was the affected employee population represented in the downsizing decision process. Yet, in firms in which employees were involved, commitment to the organization, perceptions of fairness, and optimism regarding the firm's future were significantly higher than when no representative participation occurred.

Our research on effectively managed downsizing operations indicates that subordinates can, in fact, make objective decisions about eliminating their jobs if the organization creates a "win-win" environment (Cameron et al., 1991; Whetten and Cameron, 1985). Research on factory closings also supports this position. Effective management of plant closings involves employees throughout the various stages of closure. As counterintuitive as it may seem, involved employees remain committed and productive to the end (Sutton, 1984).

Myth 3: Minimize the Sharing of Information About Costs and Inefficiencies with Employees and Outside Stakeholders

This myth is an extension of myth 2. The common underlying assumption is that neither subordinates nor outside stakeholders (e.g., suppliers and customers) can be trusted to act in the best interests of the firm if they are worried about the longevity of their relationship with the firm. Thus, the less information they have about the company's status, the less likelihood there is that they will be distracted from their work by rumors and speculation, become demoralized, abandon ship prematurely, or withhold commitment and resources. Most managers in charge of downsizing, therefore, share much less information than they should. Right Associates found, for example, that only 74 percent of the downsizing firms surveyed communicated information to employees about the reasons for downsizing, and less than half of the firms provided crucial details about the downsizing, such as timing and decision criteria. However, Cameron et al. (1993) found that one of the most powerful predictors of successful downsizing is the involvement of internal and external constituencies in the planning and execution of downsizing strategies. We believe this occurs for the following three reasons.

First, if top management has any chance of securing the commitment of internal and external stakeholders to a potentially threatening course of action, it must be forthright from the beginning. The character of a firm is reflected in how its management deals with crises. During periods of tranquility, purchased with the coin of steady growth, it is not difficult for managers to espouse a partnership philosophy. Unfortunately, many firms abandon this perspective when hard times set in. This relativistic value system breeds cynicism and distrust among suppliers, customers, and lower-level employees.

Second, the presumption that information about threatening events will result in damage through speculative discussions is not consistent with our observations. In fact, in our experience the lack of information is far more likely to stimulate nonproductive distractions. Change, especially threatening change, creates uncertainty (the difference between the amount of information one has and the amount one thinks is needed). Uncertainty, in turn, creates stress, which beyond a certain level, fosters counterproductive behaviors. Information theorists have pointed out that the best way to break this negative cycle is to increase the flow of information (Mansuripur, 1987). Further, they argue that the more massive and/or negative the change, the more information people require. Because there are few changes that are more massive or negative than downsizing, massive amounts of information are required.

These observations about the need of potentially affected stakeholders to acquire information are supported by research on "procedural justice" (Lind and Tyler, 1988). This work has shown that people are as concerned about the fairness of the process used to render a verdict affecting them, as they are about whether they received a favorable ruling. One criterion individuals use to judge procedural justice is the availability of information. Decisions that are shrouded in secrecy are automatically suspected of being procedurally flawed. Thus, one requirement for gaining commitment to a potentially threatening course of action is open sharing of information, especially about the supporting "whys."

Third, when firms restrict the information dissemination process, they invariably receive less feedback. Such information from a variety of internal and external sources is critical for fine-tuning a downsizing operation, especially in a large, diversified organization. Downsizing, by its very nature, is an iterative process. It is impossible to foresee all possible contingencies, obstacles, and legitimate objections. Thus, restricted two-way flows of communication will significantly reduce the effectiveness of a downsizing program.

Myth 4: To Enhance the Organization's Image of Fairness, Equity, and Legitimacy, Pay Special Attention to the Casualties

In most downsizing organizations, considerable time and money are focused on meeting the needs of terminated employees. Elaborate early retirement incentives are crafted, outplacement services are provided, and personal counseling is arranged. Executives in downsizing organizations report feelings of guilt, regret, and remorse. They are sensitive to criticisms that poor management of the company has resulted in the violation of employment contracts. Consequently, it is natural for them to provide at least partial restitution to terminated employees (Hirsch, 1987).

Many executives, unfortunately, overlook the negative effects of the downsizing process on the remaining work force. They erroneously assume that the relief of avoiding a pink slip will overshadow any negative feelings ongoing workers have about the consequences of the downsizing process. In slightly more than half the downsizing firms in the Right Associates survey, the reasons for downsizing were communicated to the surviving employees. Less than half the firms, however, shared other details—including reorganization plans and employee assistance benefits—with surviving employees prior to downsizing. Moreover, more than 80 percent of surviving employees received no training in new work processes or how to operate in the downsized environment.

This stinginess with information is harmful to firm performance for several reasons (Cameron et al., 1993). First, entire functions are seldom removed during downsizing. As a result, the remaining work force must do more work with fewer resources. Unless other productivity tools (e.g., automation) are phased in following downsizing or processes are redesigned to remove work, remaining employees often feel that the terms of their contract have been violated. Many are simply not prepared to handle the increased work demands or the additional knowledge required. Employee burnout following downsizing is a common complaint.

Second, if the firm's downsizing program was implemented according to the prevailing myths, the remaining workers are likely to harbor feelings of resentment toward upper levels of management. They perceive that they have been systematically excluded from decision-making processes and given mere crumbs of information about why actions have been taken.

Third, remaining employees tend to feel insecure about their jobs and their psychological contract with the organization. Employees traditionally have assumed that if they displayed loyalty to their employing organization, showed up at work each day, performed their work competently, and contributed to the success of the company, they would be rewarded with continued employment, pay increases, and some degree of security. Downsizing destroys this psychological contract and, with it, the loyalty and commitment of employees to the organization. The traditionally valued attributes of good employees—loyalty, hard work, and personal competence—no longer count in the firm because individuals who displayed those traits still lost their jobs. This is especially the case if the company does not couple downsizing with a major strategic realignment. That is, if the company only treats the symptoms of poor performance, employees are likely to expect that further layoffs will be necessary.

The importance of attending to the needs of remaining employees has been convincingly supported in research by Brockner (1988). They observed that white-collar employees who remained with a downsized firm were likely to experience what they called "survivor guilt," characterized by increased anxiety about loss of job, decreased loyalty to the firm, and guilt feelings about lost coworkers. Survivor guilt occurred when the remaining employees felt guilty about working overtime, for example, or receiving a paycheck when their friends and former coworkers were out of work. On the other hand, Cameron and his colleagues (1991) found the reverse phenomenon, "survivor envy." That is, they found that after downsizing, many survivors were faced with restricted promotion opportunities, salary caps, lost cost-of-living increases, and an overloaded work schedule. Those who took early retirement or buy-out packages (i.e., who lost their jobs), however, were viewed as having opportunities for new jobs, new challenges, and an improvement of their lot in life. This led to demoralization resulting from envy. Both survivor guilt and survivor envy are likely to operate among employees in downsized firms.

Myth 5: Spread the Pain—Don't Target Specific Areas for Disproportionate Reductions

The Right Associates survey indicated that most organizations simply hand down a mandate to downsize or cut costs. In only about half the firms surveyed were line managers, chief financial officers, or chief operating officers involved in planning for decisions about where to cut costs. The information needed to identify where prioritized cutbacks should be made is not even available in a substantial number of firms that downsize.

Many managers embrace this myth for at least three reasons. First, they believe it is easier to make across-the-board cuts than to cut differentially. More time and effort must be devoted to crafting a selective retrenchment plan because it is more likely to be challenged as inequitable. Units that receive a disproportionate cut can be expected to charge that the decision was either politically motivated or poorly informed. Consequently, the decision maker must prepare more extensive justifications for the proposed actions prior to their announcement.

Second, selective cuts are more likely to encounter strong political resistance. Internal and external constituencies are likely to interpret disproportionate cuts as threats to the viability of their entrenched interests in the firm. For example, they are likely to charge that large cutbacks in the advertising budget signify upper management's lack of commitment to a strong marketing program. Threats to business functions encounter stronger resistance because it is inherently easier for the opposition to get organized. This opposition can slow, or in extreme cases, derail (through legal means) the implementation process.

Third, many managers are unwilling to invest the time, or simply do not have the time, the necessary information, or the political good will, to defend what is seldom a cut-and-dried decision to administer cutbacks disproportionately. To justify selective downsizing adequately, managers must have access to data on sources of redundancy, slack, fat, non-value-adding activity, wasted time, inadequate skills, and so on. However, those kinds of data are often not collected in organizations, not measured in comparable ways across different subunits, and held secret by threatened employees.

On the other hand, when substantial reductions are anticipated, nontargeted cuts can also be interpreted by organization members as a failure either of nerve or of vision. This presents a catch-22 situation. If top managers do not gather adequate data, assiduously analyze it, and prepare a rationale for prioritized downsizing, whether they administer it selectively or across the board will create defensiveness and criticism.

The major problem with the across-the-board approach to downsizing is that cutbacks, by themselves, are generally an inadequate response to a deteriorated competitive position. They miss the opportunistic function of downsizing, namely, to engender organizational improvement. This introduces myth 6.

Myth 6: Cost Cutting and Cost Containment Are the Best Ways to Reduce Overhead

It is clear that many U.S. firms must undergo massive cost-restructuring programs. They are bloated hierarchically and numerically. However, it is just as obvious that for most such firms, excessive overhead is a symptom, not the problem. The overarching problem is poor performance, characterized not only by poor productivity, but also by poor production and service quality, inferior product design, insensitivity to customer needs and preferences, lack of accountability among top managers, lack of a global strategy, and so on (Drucker, 1988). To focus merely on improving the short-term balance sheet by reducing overhead, without simultaneously addressing a broader range of issues, would be shortsighted.

Firms that have adopted the balance-sheet view of downsizing appear to be characterized by an overall passive orientation. Specifically, they see downsizing as a temporary, protective mechanism for helping them weather the storm until more normal environmental conditions return. Or, they view downsizing as an admission of weakness or failure, which sets in motion highly defensive, reactive processes characterized by scapegoating and blaming. Managers in these firms are so preoccupied with analyzing the causes of the problem (in order to assign responsibility precisely) they neglect the need for forging aggressive remedies. In the Right Associates survey of downsizing organizations, 75 percent said they undertook downsizing in order to improve the financial well-being of the firm, but only 32 percent said they downsized in order to add new business products (Henkoff, 1990). Most were defensive rather than offensive in their orientation. Moreover, less than half of the downsizing organizations revised or updated human resource, communications, reporting, administrative, or production systems in connection with downsizing.

We have observed at least two unintended, dysfunctional consequences of this approach to downsizing. First, it fosters a cynical reaction to the downsizing initiative. Internal and external constituencies lose confidence in the senior management team because of its unwillingness to address long-term, systemic problems. This often results in resistance to the downsizing plan, not because it is not necessary, but because it is obviously piecemeal and uncoordinated, and because the pain of poor performance is focused on only one element of the organization: the employment contract.

Second, critical functions or skill bases may become eroded to the point that the organization's capacity to implement new initiatives is severely hampered. Because it is necessary for downsizing organizations to continue addressing broader strategic issues, remain innovative, and maintain competitive strength, treating downsizing as merely an overhead reduction tactic often undermines the organization's ability to reposition itself for new challenges to be faced in the future. A common experience among those who follow this sequential process (short-term downsizing followed by long-term planning) is that the strategic plan they evolve involves resource requirements that are incompatible with the outcomes of the downsizing operation.

The case of early retirement incentives illustrates this problem. More than 85 percent of firms in an American Management Association survey of 1,005 companies reported the loss of their star performers when early retirement packages were offered (Bennett, 1991). Firms found that this undifferentiated approach to saving costs resulted in the wrong people leaving the system. The skills and experience levels of such individuals are so vital to the firm's operations, however, that the firm often ends up trying to hire these people back as consultants or having to recruit new managers from the outside to replace the lost expertise. In personal interviews with corporate executives, we learned that Hughes Aircraft spends an estimated $500,000 in recruiting costs to replace a manager. At IBM, executives estimate that it costs between $2 million and $3 million to replace a manager whom they did not want to leave the firm. The point is that hidden costs can escalate substantially when defensive or passive cost cutting occurs.

Myth 7: When Radical Change Is Required to Avoid the Demise of the Organization, Adopt a Revolutionary Model of Change— Beginning with Top Management.

Studies of strategic change in response to poor organizational performance have identified five commonly used steps: (1) the methods and orientations sponsored by the "old guard" are challenged, (2) the old leaders are replaced, (3) the new executives introduce new methods and orientations, (4) the firm's performance improves and the improvement is attributed to the revolutionary change, and (5) the new leaders institutionalize their new approach through their own reward system, hiring criteria, and so on (Dyer, 1985).

This approach reflects a compelling premise: Problem causers have low credibility as problem solvers. Given the propensity to blame problems experienced by a group on the inadequacies of its leaders, it follows logically that replacing top management, along with its methods and orientations, is the key to restoring internal and external confidence in the capability of a poorly performing organization. It also follows logically that the more serious the organization's performance problems, the broader and deeper the decapitation process will be.

While a radical approach to change has apparently been successful in several cases (e.g., Bankamerica, Columbia Broadcasting System, USF&G, Chrysler, UNISYS), it also appears to have failed in even more organizations (Wilkins, 1989). One reason is that radical change frequently shakes the foundations of organizational culture and core corporate competencies. Wilkins (1989) argued against such revolutionary approaches, citing numerous examples in which the failure to "honor the past" stripped a firm of its distinctive character and thereby created confusion, alienation, and cynicism. His research supports an incremental, evolutionary approach to change, in which managers of poorly performing organizations return to the past for inspiration and instruction, find current examples of success within the company, and promote hybrids (combinations of old and new approaches). This is consistent with the "small wins" approach to change advocated by Weick (1984) or the "logical incrementalism" change promoted by Lindblom (1959). These noted scholars have argued that the most effective organizational change occurs as a result of the cumulation of tiny changes built on the foundation of current organizational culture. Building momentum to accomplish broad-scale change and establishing a climate that can tolerate transformation best occur by accomplishing small changes, advertising their success, and then building on the energy they create.

Our research corroborates this viewpoint. In the successful downsizing firms we have observed, it is clear that they have not confused a timely response with a radical response. One of the best predictors of whether declining firms can be successfully turned around is the length of the delay between a significant performance downturn and the initiation of remedial action (Whetten, 1980b). While in some cases, current management's unrelenting commitment to an unsuccessful course of action is the cause of the delay (requiring it to be replaced before any change can be initiated), premature removal of the top management team can also cause a substantial delay in the firm's response. Our concern is not that the revolutionary approach is never warranted, only that it is too often invoked as a myth without sufficient consideration of the long-term consequences.

Two Approaches to Downsizing

The core argument thus far has been that prevailing myths about downsizing represent not ideal, but flawed, practice. The purpose of the downsizing initiatives characterized by these myths is too narrowly focused on cutting costs. Efforts to increase efficiency are proposed without sufficient consideration of their implications for effectiveness. Moreover, the accompanying process for planning and implementing downsizing programs is too narrowly focused on top management's perspective. Downsizing is treated as something that management is doing "to" subordinates, rather than "with" subordinates.

The result of flawed purposes and processes is that a downsizing program yields myriad decrements in productivity as the effects of downsizing "trickle down" through the organization. Each of these decrements is small enough that it can easily be dismissed as an unfortunate specific outcome of an important general initiative. However, their cumulative effects are often so great that the anticipated gains in organizational productivity fail to materialize.

What we have characterized as the flawed approach can be summarized as top management treating "subordinates as victims" of a massive cost-cutting plan. This perspective is portrayed as model A in Table 11-2, where it is contrasted with model B, which we have observed in highly successful downsizing firms. Model B can be characterized as top management treating "subordinates as partners" in an organizational improvement program.

An examination of the differences between model A and model B leads to the paradoxical conclusion that the more management concen-

TABLE 11-2 Comparisons Between Two Models of Downsizing

	Model A	Model B
Purpose of downsizing	Cost Containment	Performance Enhancement
Process	Subordinates treated as victims	Subordinates treated as partners
Speed of implementation	Immediate	Immediate; continuous long-term
Scope of involvement	Limited	Extensive
Extent of communication	Minimal	Substantial
Target	Spread pain	Maximize gain
Scope of decisions	Focused on costs	Focused on costs and performance
Model of change	Revolution	Evolution and revolution
Organizational redesign	Structure	Structure and processes

trates on using downsizing to accomplish the objective of increasing productivity, including using a highly resource-efficient design and implementation process (low involvement, low communication, and so on), the less likely it is to achieve its goal.

Although Table 11-2 is useful for representing the general contrasts between the two models, it does not do justice to the dualistic philosophy underlying model B. That is, model B's purpose is to improve performance and cut costs. Its process is neither mandated by top management nor driven by involved employees from the bottom up. It is neither exclusively short term in focus nor exclusively long term. In other words, instead of simply selecting a set of polar opposites, managers of effective downsizing programs combine seemingly opposing elements into a hybrid strategy. Specifically, effective downsizing is characterized by four seemingly incompatible practices (see Cameron et al., 1991, for an elaboration).

First, effective downsizing is implemented from the top down and also from the bottom up. Effective downsizing is managed and monitored by top managers; it requires hands-on involvement and energy that originate at the top of the organization. This top-down direction, however, is augmented by bottom-up recommendations and suggestions from lower-level employees. In effective downsizing, employees themselves analyze the operations of the firm job by job and task by task. This can be done by cross-functional groups, blue ribbon committees, or self-designed task forces. Members identify redundant jobs and official tasks, find ways to eliminate organizational fat and to improve efficiency, and help plan ways in which changes can be implemented with minimal disruption.

This win-win approach to problem solving was evident in one firm we observed. Employees were told that if their jobs were eliminated, they would still receive full pay for a year. If they required retraining in order to find a new job (either inside the firm or outside the firm), it would be paid for, but they would have to justify the expenditure in a proposal. Employees were encouraged to find ways to begin new businesses or to improve current products and processes within the firm (i.e., to add to the bottom-line revenue stream). Some employees used the time to find jobs outside the firm, others found ways to try out ideas that improved bottom-line (cost control) and top-line results (new processes or products). A large number voluntarily recommended the elimination of their own jobs because they were treated as resources for organizational improvement, not liabilities to the bottom line.

A second paradoxical characteristic of effective downsizing is that across-the-board downsizing processes are used in conjunction with selective downsizing processes. Both approaches to downsizing have merit.

Across-the-board cuts are an effective way to highlight the seriousness of conditions facing the firm and mobilize the energy of all the organization's members. Broad cutbacks make it clear that the status quo is no longer acceptable. In successful firms, however, deep cutbacks are made using a selective approach. One such approach is a "value analysis" of all tasks in the organization, in advance of any downsizing. The question asked is, what value does this task provide for the final product or service for which we are in business? In one firm, the employees themselves identified the individuals, tasks, and jobs that needed not only to be protected, but to be strengthened. Following this value analysis, investments were increased in some areas, but in areas adding less value, jobs were redesigned or eliminated and individuals were reassigned or let go.

One very successful firm eliminated the quality control and work area maintenance functions. This work was reassigned to operating employees as part of a job enrichment program. Investment in advanced training for all employees focused on preparing them for the changes that were to take place. Discussions were held regarding a proposal to change the work week from five 8-hour days to four 10-hour days to generate savings in maintenance, security, and energy costs (Cameron et al., 1993).

A third paradoxical characteristic of effective downsizing is that the transition is managed for employees who lost their jobs as well as for survivors. The best downsizing practices include outplacement services, personal and family counseling, relocation expenses, and active sponsoring of employees whose positions have been eliminated. They also provide generous severance pay, extended benefits, and retraining opportunities. Several top managers in the firms we have studied have proudly announced that none of their white-collar employees was without a position someplace else. In short, these firms took responsibility for the transition created by loss of employment.

Successful downsizing firms pay equal attention to the transition experienced by the survivors. For example, one company held regular "forums" in which data were shared on the performance of the company and its major competitors, and it conducted sessions with blue- and white-collar workers. In addition, the company posted data that were previously confidential in several locations so that employees felt included in downsizing planning and implementation. It also held special events to signal the end of the degeneration phase and the beginning of the regeneration phase of the company's turnaround plan. The latter included "launch lunches," a new company logo, new signs, and new colors in the production areas. Finally, the company involved survivors in redesigning and rationalizing the firm's new work processes, and it gave teams of employees input on the front end of major decisions and planning exercises. In short, it made the survivors feel trusted, valued, responsible, and involved.

The fourth paradoxical characteristic is that downsizing is defined as a means to an end as well as an end in itself. The most successful firms treat downsizing as an opportunity to accomplish multiple objectives. They simultaneously strive to cut costs and bolster performance. "Taking out headcount" and "trimming the fat" are clear, consensual objectives. Top management uses cost figures to demonstrate that this is essential, not elective, surgery. At the same time, management focuses members' attention on proposed constructive improvements.

In the midst of a severe headcount reduction period, for example, one organization instituted a "Build with Pride Week." Family members were invited to the firm on one day, customers on another, suppliers on another, local government officials on another, and so on. Special events, refreshments, and decorations were used throughout the week to signal the beginning of a new era in the firm. Nonmanagement employees served as hosts and guides, and outsiders were permitted to question and observe workers as they performed their jobs. Dramatic improvements in productivity, product quality, and a sense of corrective teamwork were outcomes of this event. Other firms have used name changes to spur improvements, such as renaming the quality control department the customer satisfaction department, or generated names and slogans for subunit teams (e.g., one product design team became Delta Force: "Seek and destroy errors before customers catch them").

The intent of such novel, even playful, initiatives is serious: To create a different mind-set among employees about downsizing and redesign efforts—to define downsizing as an opportunity, as well as a threat. This philosophy is reflected in one manager's comment to us, "We're not getting smaller, we're getting better. It just happens that having fewer employees is a way to accomplish that."

Relationship Between Model B and Productivity

To date, few studies have investigated the relationships between the ways in which downsizing is implemented and organizational performance, and organizational-level productivity has not been included in any such assessments. The question is as yet unaddressed, therefore, regarding whether model B represents a superior method of downsizing as supported by rigorous scientific analysis. That is, the question remains, do model B strategies have a more positive impact on productivity than model A strategies?

Cameron and colleagues (1993) conducted an investigation of the strategies implemented by manufacturing organizations when downsizing and the impact of those strategies on organizational effectiveness. They chronicled firms over a 4-year period in terms of how downsizing was implemented and how it affected organizational performance. Many of the observations made in this chapter were drawn from that work. In a related study, Freeman (1992) investigated the extent to which certain patterns could be identified in the strategies used by firms engaged in downsizing. She also investigated the relationship between those patterns and indicators of organizational performance. In neither study was productivity measured as an outcome variable, however. Instead, both studies assessed perceptions of organizational effectiveness and compared the performance of each firm with that of its competitors (i.e., was the firm performing better or worse than its competitors?). In both studies, model B downsizing strategies were associated with superior organizational performance compared to model A.

The most important predictors of effective downsizing in the Cameron et al. study were multifunctional coordination and teamwork among managers and between managers and lower-level employees; a combination of gradual and immediate execution of strategies; broad participation in the formulation and execution of downsizing strategies by employees and outside stakeholders; a high degree of communication and information sharing; and systematic analysis in advance of downsizing so that the downsizing strategies could be applied differentially. In each case, these predictors are consistent with the attributes of model B. On the other hand, factors that were negatively associated with organizational effectiveness (i.e., led to declines in effectiveness as a result of downsizing) included failure to redesign the work being done in conjunction with downsizing, top-down mandated downsizing with little chance for input by employees, limiting downsizing to eliminating employees to cut costs without supplemental improvement strategies, and the failure to include organizational advancement as a strategic outcome of downsizing. Each of these variables is consistent with the attributes associated with model A.

In the Freeman study, two major approaches to downsizing were identified in 30 manufacturing organizations. In one approach downsizing took precedence over organizational redesign (a "downsizing drives redesign" strategy). In the other approach organizational redesign took precedence over downsizing (a "redesign drives downsizing" strategy). Freeman found that a cluster of managerial actions and downsizing strategies characterized each approach to downsizing. That is, managers tended to engage in a predictable set of strategies when pursuing one of the downsizing approaches. The two approaches differed from one another in the following ways: compared to the former approach (downsizing drives redesign), the latter approach (redesign drives downsizing) was characterized by more communication, more extensive organizational changes, more emphasis on improving effectiveness (doing the right things) in addition to efficiency (doing things right), more involvement of internal and external constituencies, more changes in technology and structure, and more challenges to the status quo and current operating procedures in the downsizing organizations.

In analyzing the relationship of these two approaches to organizational performance, the organizations typified by the redesign-drives-downsizing strategy performed significantly better in terms of productivity, quality, and competitive position than those typified by the downsizing-drives-redesign strategy. Once again, model B is closest to the most effective approach (redesign drives downsizing) and model A to the less effective one (downsizing drives redesign).

The findings of these two studies imply that organizational-level productivity is also likely to be associated with the downsizing approach characterized by model B. It is reasonable to assume that high organizational productivity is closely associated with assessments of organizational effectiveness and with competitive superiority. Hence, it does not require a large leap of faith to make at least an indirect connection between model B downsizing strategies and enhanced productivity. This suggests that when organizations downsize, paradoxical management strategies, as typified by model B, help resolve the productivity paradox discussed elsewhere in this volume.

Implications for Research

As downsizing becomes increasingly accepted as an essential productivity improvement tool in American industry, a greater understanding of the relationship between the process of downsizing and its effects is needed. Our contention is that faulty design and implementation of downsizing often result in unintended, dysfunctional outcomes (e.g., diminished organizational productivity).

Although the observations and propositions in this chapter are based on our examinations of many downsizing and downsized organizations, we believe that more information is needed on the following research questions:

• Are the effects of downsizing on organizational productivity the same as those on organizational profitability, or on quality? Do effective downsizing strategies differ depending on the primary organizational outcomes targeted (Cameron and Whetten, 1983)?

- Why are the myths of downsizing management so pervasive? In what circumstances, with what types of managers, and in what kinds of organizations are they more or less pervasive? Which of them are true more or less of the time (Cameron et al., 1991)?

- Do our observations about effective downsizing strategies apply equally to all organizations? Or, do organizations that downsize effectively differ fundamentally from other downsizing firms in terms of their culture, structure, size, age, industry, history, and so on (Cameron et al., 1987)? What combinations of across-the-board and selective downsizing strategies work best in various circumstances (e.g., degree of cutback required, type of work force, form of technology)?

- Is downsizing inevitable for most mature organizations? To what extent is downsizing the natural consequence of imprudent management during earlier expansion phases of organizational development? If downsizing is inevitable, can lessons be gleaned from examining the contraction phase of the "organizational life cycle" that can inform better management practice during the expansion phase (Whetten, 1987)? In what ways can organizations prepare for continuous downsizing as they grow and expand through early stages of their life cycle (Quinn and Cameron, 1983)?

- What specific defects in the downsizing process contribute most to the unintended outcome of unrealized increased productivity? What are the effects of employees not understanding the need to cut back and, therefore, resisting the downsizing initiatives; the lack of lower-level involvement in planning who and what to downsize; and regulatory and union contract constraints?

- To what extent are flawed downsizing purposes and processes linked empirically as well as logically? While some evidence exists to suggest that the model A and model B purposes and processes cluster together (Cameron et al., 1993; Freeman, 1992), that should not be treated as a definitive conclusion but as a hypothesis to be tested in a wider array of organizations and circumstances. Subsequent research should systematically examine the conditions under which purposes and processes are more or less likely to occur together.

CONCLUSION

The purpose of downsizing has evolved over the past three decades. Initially instituted primarily as a strategy for enhancing lagging performance, more recently, downsizing has been added to the tool kit for enhancing productivity. Current research indicates, however, that downsizing very often does not produce the anticipated productivity gains. Given the fact that downsizing efforts, by definition, directly reduce costs, this form of the productivity paradox is both practically disconcerting and intellectually challenging.

We have proposed an explanation for this form of the productivity paradox based on the premise that faulty management practice results from faulty assumptions. Specifically, we have argued that the dominant approach to downsizing is based on seven prevailing myths about ideal practice. The attractiveness of these institutionalized beliefs is that they add an aura of legitimacy to management decisions that are inherently uncomfortable and unpopular. The disadvantage is that they represent an inherently flawed perspective on the appropriate purposes and implementation processes for downsizing initiatives. The purpose is narrowly defined as cost cutting, and the process is very much top-down—with limited employee involvement.

In contrast, we have proposed an alternative perspective that incorporates a broader set of purposes and processes. This dualistic approach is less disruptive to organizational productivity and more likely to produce desired organizational outcomes. It requires not merely a different set of managerial actions but an entirely new model for approaching the process of downsizing on a continuous basis.

REFERENCES

Aldrich, H.E.
    1979   *Organizations and Environments*. Englewood Cliffs, N.J.: Prentice Hall.
Bennett, A.
    1991   Downsizing doesn't necessarily bring an upswing in corporate profitability. *The Wall Street Journal* (June 6):B1, B4.
Blanchard, K., and S. Johnson
    1983   *The One-Minute Manager*. New York: Morrow.
Brockner, J.
    1988   The effects of work layoff on survivors: Research, theory, and practice. In B.M. Staw and L.L. Cummings, eds., *Research on Organizational Behavior*, Vol. 10. Greenwich, Conn.: JAI Press.
Cameron, K.S., and D.A. Whetten
    1983   *Organizational Effectiveness: A Comparison of Multiple Models*. New York: Academic Press.
Cameron, K.S., M.Y. Kim, and D.A. Whetten
    1987   Organizational effects of decline and turbulence. *Administrative Science Quarterly* 32:222-240.
Cameron, K.S., S.J. Freeman, and A.K. Mishra
    1991   Best practices in white-collar downsizing: Managing contradictions. *Academy of Management Executive* 5:57-73.
    1993   Organizational downsizing and redesign. In G. Huber and W. Glick, eds., *Organizational Change and Redesign*. New York: Oxford University Press.
D'Avani, R.
    1990   Top managerial prestige and organizational bankruptcy. *Organizational Science* 1:121-142.

Deutsch, M., and H.B. Gerard
   1955   A study of normative and informational social influences upon individual judg-
           ment. *Journal of Abnormal and Social Psychology* 51:629-636.
Drucker, P.F.
   1988   The coming of the new organization. *Harvard Business Review* 66:45-53.
Dyer, W.G., Jr.
   1985   The cycle of cultural evolution in organizations. In R.H. Kilmann, M.J. Saxton,
           R. Serpa, and Associates, *Gaining Control of the Corporate Culture*. San Fran-
           cisco: Jossey-Bass.
Freeman, S.J.
   1992   Organizational downsizing and redesign: A case of appropriated interpreta-
           tion. Doctoral dissertation, School of Business, University of Michigan, Ann
           Arbor.
Galaskiewicz, J., and S. Wasserman
   1989   Mimetic processes within an interorganizational field: An empirical test. *Ad-
           ministrative Science Quarterly* 34(3):456-479.
Henkoff, R.
   1990   Cost cutting: How to do it right. *Fortune* (April 9):17-19.
   1994   Getting beyond downsizing. *Fortune* (January 10):58-64.
Hirsch, P.M.
   1987   *Pack Your Own Parachute*. Reading, Mass.: Addison-Wesley.
Hirshhorn, L., and associates
   1983   *Cutting Back: Retrenchment and Redevelopment in Human and Community
           Services*. San Francisco: Jossey-Bass.
Hogarth, R.M.
   1987   *Judgement and Choice: The Psychology of Decision*. New York: John Wiley &
           Sons.
Imai, M.
   1986   *Kaizen: The Key to Japanese Competitive Success*. New York: Random House.
Kilmann, R.
   1984   *Beyond the One-Minute Quick Fix*. San Francisco: Jossey-Bass.
Lind, E.A., and T.R. Tyler
   1988   *The Social Psychology of Procedural Justice*. New York: Plenum Press.
Lindblom, C.E.
   1959   The science of muddling through. *Public Administration* 20:79-88.
Mansuripur, M.
   1987   *Introduction to Information Theory*. Englewood Cliffs, N.J.: Prentice Hall.
Quinn, R.E., and K.C. Cameron
   1983   Organizational lifecycles and shifting criteria of effectiveness: Some prelimi-
           nary evidence. *Management Science* 29:33-51.
Sawhill, I., and M. Condon
   1992   Bidding war—or growth? *The Washington Post* February 27.
Scott, W.R.
   1987   *Organizations: Rational, Natural, and Open Systems*. Englewood Cliffs, N.J.:
           Prentice Hall.
Sloan, A.P., Jr.
   1963   *My Years with General Motors*. Garden City, N.Y.: Doubleday.
Staw, B.M., L.E. Sandelands, and J.E. Dutton
   1981   Threat-rigidity effects in organizational behavior: A multilevel analysis. *Ad-
           ministrative Science Quarterly* 26:501-524.

Sutton, R.I.
1984   Organizational death. Doctoral dissertation, University of Michigan.
Thurow, L.C.
1986   White-collar overhead. *Across the Board* 23:234-242.
Tomasko, R.M.
1987   *Downsizing: Reshaping the Corporation for the Future.* New York: AMACOM.
Weick, K.
1984   Small wins: Redefining the scale of social problems. *American Psychologist* 39:40-49.
Whetten, D.A.
1980a   Organizational decline: A neglected topic in the organizational sciences. *Academy of Management Review* 4:577-588.
1980b   Sources, responses, and the effects of organizational decline. Pp. 342-374 in J. Kimberly and R. Miles, eds., *The Organizational Lifecycle.* San Francisco: Jossey-Bass.
1981   Organizational responses to scarcity: Exploring the obstacles to innovative approaches to retrenchment in education. *Education Administration Quarterly* 17:80-97.
1987   Organizational growth and decline processes. *Annual Review of Sociology* 13:335-358.
Whetten, D.A., and K.S. Cameron
1985   Administrative effectiveness in higher education. *Annual Review of Higher Education* 9:35-49.
Wilkins, A.
1989   *Developing Corporate Character.* San Francisco: Jossey-Bass.

12

Conclusions

In this chapter, the panel presents the key findings that emerged from its analyses and deliberations. The discussion is centered on the broad themes and conclusions that have implications for research policy and program development and for future directions for research in the behavioral sciences—particularly human factors, industrial engineering, and industrial and organizational psychology. Specific research recommendations can also be found in individual chapters.

ORGANIZATIONAL LINKAGES EXPLAIN
THE PRODUCTIVITY PARADOX

Processes at and across individual, group, and organizational levels intertwine and affect one another such that productivity improvements at one level do not translate simply into productivity improvements at higher levels. The introduction of an intervention, such as technology, designed to improve productivity creates a series of trade-offs at different levels of the organization. As discussed by Attewell in Chapter 2, the potential benefits of the intervention might be channeled into one of two alternative directions—either in a direction that is productivity enhancing, that is, enabling the original work to be done more efficiently, or in a direction that is not productivity enhancing, such as improving some attribute of the product, expanding the work to be done, or inhibiting the productivity of other entities in the organization.

Most of the evidence in this report, however, indicates that even when productivity improvement is realized at a lower level (e.g., the individual), there are influences that might inhibit improvement from being realized at a higher level (e.g., the organization). We have examined those influences from the individual to the organization and from the organization to the individual. The concepts that aid in the understanding of these dynamics were presented by Goodman, Lerch, and Mukhopadhyay in Chapter 3. Examinations of those concepts and of how they operate in specific work domains were reported for office automation by Schneider and Klein in Chapter 4, for software engineering by Kiesler, Wholey, and Carley in Chapter 9, and for computer-aided design by Harris in Chapter 10.

Another form of the productivity paradox is provided by the practice of downsizing. Organizational downsizing has been one of the major initiatives undertaken by U.S. firms during the past decade to increase productivity. It is an initiative that is assumed to lead directly to increased productivity by increasing the ratio of output to input. However, according to the evidence summarized by Whetten and Cameron in Chapter 11, this intervention (similar to the introduction of technology) has not had the anticipated effects. They concluded that this productivity paradox is explained by the use of downsizing approaches that typically ignore the effects of organizational linkages.

The concept of organizational linkages provides a useful framework for examining the productivity paradox. It has led the panel to conclude that a major contributor to the paradox has been the common attempt to initiate change through the introduction of a single intervention (technology) at a single level in the organization (the individual). As suggested by Schneider and Klein in Chapter 4 and by Sink and Smith in Chapter 6, changing a single aspect of an organization almost never results in a substantial change in organizational performance. Organizations are too complex, their performance is too multidetermined, and their inertia is too great for a single innovation at the individual level to have a substantial impact on organizational performance. Even if an intervention does in fact augment individual productivity, there may be no resulting improvements in organizational productivity. Multiple, congruent interventions are needed to achieve the desired impact. This leads to the requirement for an organizational systems framework to clarify the multiple reciprocal linkages that determine organizational productivity.

As discussed by Sink and Smith in Chapter 6, making an improvement intervention in one entity and projecting positive performance linkages to other entities at the same or different levels require profound knowledge. *Profound knowledge* encompasses a theory of systems, variation, psychology, and knowledge itself. It equates to a sufficient understanding of the organizational system to identify and predict cause-and-effect relationships. When interventions are made without profound knowledge, they are not likely to have their intended effect—subsystem performance may be enhanced, but the performance of the larger system will not be because the linkages are not understood. The consequence is the productivity paradox—extensive investments in enhancing the productivity of individuals and groups that do not lead to expected improvements in larger organizations or in the enterprise.

ORGANIZATIONAL STRUCTURES AND PROCESSES CAN INHIBIT OR FACILITATE LINKAGES

In our examination of linkages, we identified structures and processes that inhibit increases in individual productivity from increasing organizational productivity. These structures and processes are common to organizations engaged in varied activities—office work, software development, postal services, manufacturing, computer-aided design, and others.

A structural inhibitor, for example, can be found in the existence of core and peripheral activities in most organizations. Core activities, such as the production of engineering design specifications, are directly related to the process of transforming inputs into outputs. Peripheral activities, such as updating computer-aided design software, are only indirectly related to this process. Thus, as a consequence of this structure, increases in individual productivity in core activities will be more likely to contribute to organizational productivity than increases in peripheral activities.

Process operates as an inhibitor when an intervention that increases productivity in one set of activities cancels the gain by decreasing productivity in a related set. For example, the introduction of a computer system resulted in increased productivity on routine tasks by individual customer service representatives. However, the change had negative consequences for the functions of supervisors of the customer service representatives. It reduced the visibility of the operations they supervised and thereby reduced their ability to solve problems and coordinate activities. The net result was no gain in the productivity of the work group, even with the intervention of new technology and the improvement in the productivity of the customer service representatives.

Facilitators are equivalent in importance to inhibitors. Facilitators are processes that can function either to remove conditions that impede linkages or to create conditions that facilitate linkages. Several critical facilitative processes were defined and examined in various chapters of the report. Examples include coordination, problem solving, focus of attention, organizational evolution, and motivation. These facilitators were examined and illustrated by Goodman, Lerch, and Mukhopadhyay in Chapter 3.

At a somewhat more specific level, the following facilitators were defined for the domain of software engineering: coordination through team design and coordination through communication. Team design is the development of appropriate structure and procedures that provide built-in solutions to coordination—task decomposition, lines of authority, centralization of control, and standard operating procedures. Communication is the process provided to permit team members to interface with each other, to permit the negotiation of goals and processes by people of different skills and perspectives, and to share information and integrate work outputs. These facilitators might become inhibitors if they are misapplied and lead to costs that outweigh benefits. Coordination issues in software engineering were addressed by Kiesler, Wholey, and Carley in Chapter 9. Additional examples of inhibitors and facilitators, along with descriptions of how they operate in other work domains, were provided by Schneider and Klein in Chapter 4 and Harris in Chapter 10.

There is much to be learned about organizational structures and processes and how they inhibit or facilitate linkages. For example, how do different linkage situations generate inhibitors? What types of interventions or productivity changes will more likely evoke negative consequences under different linkage situations? We have emphasized the role of processes in facilitating individual-organizational linkages. However, in our analyses, processes such as problem solving and organizational evolution were treated as though they were independent of other variables. This gives rise to the question, will these processes affect linkages in the same manner and to the same degree under conditions of complexity and uncertainty as under conditions of stability? In the specific area of software development, a large portion of the variance in the productivity of technical teams is known to derive from how the teams coordinate their work. However, there are many unknowns and questions in this domain alone, such as, what are the side effects and outcomes of linkages over time? The research direction required to provide answers to these and related questions will provide valuable insights into how to realize productivity gains from technology and other organizational interventions.

LINKAGE INFLUENCES ARE SUBJECT TO LEVEL OF ANALYSIS AND DIFFERENTIAL SCALING

Many linkage explanations are likely to be specific to the level of analysis. That is, what accounts for the relationship between individual and group productivity might be different from what accounts for the relationship between group and organizational productivity. For example, the role of the supervisor might be more influential in transforming increases in individual productivity to group productivity than in transforming group increases to organizational increases.

Researchers must also recognize that explanations might scale differentially for different dimensions of an organization. Differential scaling is analogous to the problem faced in designing boats. Estimating hull performance by using a small but accurate scale model may not accurately predict the performance of a full-size version. Differential scaling will occur because different features or dimensions of a hull scale up at different rates, causing relationships between features found for a small hull to be different when scaled up for a large one.

Translated into an organizational setting, this analogy suggests that a change in scale of one feature of a firm may lead to unexpected effects because other dimensions of the organization will not change proportionately. In downsizing, for example, a retrenching firm might shrink its managerial staff by 10 percent. An unintended consequence of this action might be an increase in managerial work load, because each manager now has, on average, a larger number of units reporting than before. Differential scaling occurs because it is unlikely that the number of units reporting to managers will decrease as fast as the number of managers, even if employment in the firm as a whole is cut by an equivalent 10 percent. Thus, span of control does not scale down at the same rate as number of managers, which has potentially negative consequences for organizational productivity. This and other problems associated with attaining productivity gains from downsizing were addressed by Whetten and Cameron in Chapter 11.

HORIZONTAL AND VERTICAL LINKAGES DO NOT NECESSARILY OPERATE IN THE SAME MANNER

In this report, influences on organizational linkages have been invoked as both inhibitors and facilitators of the spread of productivity from one work unit in an organization to other work units. The point has been made in Chapter 9, for example, that coordination and communication mechanisms are important determinants of the extent and degree of this spread. It is less clear whether horizontal and vertical linkages operate in the same manner—horizontal linkages being between units at the same level and vertical linkages being between units at different levels.

Differences between horizontal and vertical linkages might be viewed as inhibitors to the transfer of productivity gains from one unit to another. For example, if horizontal and vertical linkages require different coordination modes, that degree of specialization might be difficult or impossible to provide. On the other hand, an understanding of the differential characteristics might be a key to the development and implementation of successful coordination and communication mechanisms. In Chapter 4 Schneider and Klein introduced the concept of open systems and discussed the principle of differentiation, integration, and coordination within this context. They summarized previous research that indicates the need to counterbalance organizational movement toward differentiation with integrating and coordinating mechanisms that bring the system together for unified functioning. An understanding of the differential effects of horizontal and vertical linkages may be required to develop the appropriate mechanisms.

METHODS AND MEASURES ARE NEEDED FOR TRACING LINKAGES

A principal focus of our study has been on methodological and measurement issues surrounding the linkage question. These issues were addressed specifically by Ruch (Chapter 5), Sink and Smith (Chapter 6), Pritchard (Chapter 7), and Campbell (Chapter 8). A principal theme of each of these chapters is that methods are needed to determine, analytically, whether specific productivity changes in one work unit are passed through to others. That is, methods are needed for tracing changes through the system from individual to group to organization.

Empirical research is needed to identify the significant linkage variables and their relative importance. To do such research, multiple links within multiple organizations must be studied using longitudinal research designs. First, improvements in outputs at the most molecular level must be shown to have occurred because of an intervention and those improvements must then be traced through the various linkages to the broadest organizational level. The idea would be to measure each explanatory factor (slack, conflict in objectives, and so on) along with the amount of loss of output across the linkage. Then, the importance of each could be assessed empirically. Ideally, the data would be collected so that the variance accounted for by each factor could be estimated.

The macro models now used to assess the effect of information technology on productivity are informative but not very precise. They do not do a good job of capturing the nature of the specific form of information technology, determining the degree to which this technology has an impact on individual performance, or revealing the structure of linkages and their influences. Consequently, there are a number of challenges in conducting research on linkage questions. First, one has to develop a reasonable representation of the production function of a firm. Second, one needs a model that can capture changes at different levels of analysis. Third, one needs a strategy to identify the lag structure between changes at the various levels. The lag structure is likely to be a critical issue and to be influenced by the specific technology and by many of the variables discussed earlier.

LINKAGES SHOULD BE EXAMINED RELATIVE TO OTHER CRITERIA OF PERFORMANCE

The performance of an organization is a function of at least seven interrelated criteria: effectiveness, efficiency, quality, productivity, innovation, quality of work life, and profitability. A complete picture of organizational performance over time requires measures of these criteria. Operational definitions of each of these criteria were provided by Sink and Smith in Chapter 6. Productivity has been our main criterion as we have focused on understanding how changes in one work unit might lead to changes in other work units. We have examined factors that facilitate or inhibit the transfer of changes. An important challenge is to extend this type of analysis to the other criteria.

As an example, suppose the introduction of information technology improved quality at the individual level. Are the nature of linkages, and the factors that facilitate and inhibit quality changes at the organizational level, the same as would have been predicted for changes in productivity? Would the analysis of linkages be different if one looked at other performance criteria, such as effectiveness, quality of work life, innovation, or customer satisfaction? An underlying theoretical question is whether there is similarity or dissimilarity in the structure of the criteria. That is, given an understanding of the factors that facilitate linkages between individual- and organizational-level productivity, will those same factors predict linkages for other criteria? The practical issue is that a more complete understanding of facilitators and inhibitors will require the examination of linkages relative to the complete set of performance criteria, not just productivity.

In our study, we did not explore how changes in individual productivity might affect these other criteria of organizational performance. For example, the conditions that enable changes in individual productivity to increase organizational productivity might actually decrease other organizational criteria, such as quality, innovation, or quality of work life. Ultimately, it will be necessary to address the functional or dysfunctional consequences of how other criteria change as individual and organizational productivity are more strongly linked.

A THEORY OF ORGANIZATIONAL LINKAGES IS NEEDED

A theory of linkages is required and should be developed. We have focused on the productivity paradox and have suggested explanations and solutions. However, the paradox is only an example of the importance of studying and understanding the linkages among organizational subsystems. What is needed at this point is a better understanding of how outputs get combined and transformed across organizational levels, the identification of important factors that facilitate and inhibit those linkages, and the determination of conditions under which facilitators and inhibitors operate.

Panel members agree that a theory of linkages is an important goal. However, they are not all in agreement on the direction to take to reach that goal. Some members (see Chapters 5 and 7) propose to develop a composition theory of linkages—an explication of the variables that affect the translation of outputs from one unit or level of the organization to the next. They claim several advantages for such a theory. First, it would provide an integration of all the factors, as argued in the previous chapters of this report, that define and influence linkages. Second, it would provide a description of how those factors are combined and an explanation of how the factors interact. Finally, if valid mathematical functions could be developed to describe the relationships, one could predict the effects that changes at one unit or level would have on changes at other units or levels. They point out, however, that attempts to aggregate individual productivity measures or to disaggregate organizational measures are thwarted by the dissimilarity in measures of output. At the individual level, for example, output is often counted in units of product produced or service provided. At higher levels of analysis, however, different outputs from different sources are combined by means of some form of accounting scheme that is incompatible with measures at the individual level.

Other panel members (see Chapter 6, for example) conclude that composition approaches would not be fruitful. They would emphasize the application of systems theory and statistical approaches to the measurement of total system performance. Rather than pursuing the aggregation or disaggregation of measures at various levels, they would attempt to construct cause-and-effect relationships among measures. For example, they claim that modeling organizational linkages and analyzing the productivity paradox for a selected set of specific examples could generate tangible theories about cause-and-effect relationships and permit the framing of the problem in a manner susceptible to a solution. Their view is that the paradox of unrealized productivity improvements is an example of incomplete systems thinking and failure to understand the nature of organizational linkages. Their approach would provide answers to such questions as, at which level would one expect performance to improve as a result of an intervention? What aspects of organizational performance will be quantifiable, and which will not? To what extent has what is known versus what is believed about cause and effect relative to linkages been clarified? Thus, an important issue to be resolved is which direction to take in developing a theory of organizational linkages.

IMPLICATIONS

We believe that the findings presented in this report have significant implications for policy and research. Our study has focused on the widely reported productivity paradox—successful interventions at individual and group levels have not led to increased productivity at higher organizational levels. We have studied this paradox by examining linkages among individuals, groups, and organizations and have found that those linkages can not only explain the paradox, but also provide the systems framework necessary for determining much of what needs to be learned about improving organizational performance. A key implication of our study is that organizational change, from the introduction of information technology to the downsizing of the enterprise, is an extremely complex endeavor. Recognizing this complexity and addressing it by means of systems thinking are the first steps in successful intervention programs. A successful intervention to increase performance requires that a number of actions be taken at different organizational levels and that they be congruent in their goals, strategies, actions, and measures. As stated earlier, organizations are too complex, their performance too multidetermined, and their inertia too great for a single innovation at the individual or group level to have any substantial impact on organizational performance.

We have described in this report many of the inhibitors and facilitators that influence the extent to which changes in the productivity of one entity result in corresponding changes in the productivity of another entity. We have also identified specific organizational structures and processes that can inhibit or facilitate linkages. Moreover, we have examined and illustrated, in detail, how those structures and processes affect organizational linkages in several specific domains—office operations, software engineering, and computer-aided design.

The major contribution of our effort, however, lies in our identifying what is known about organizational linkages and in providing a framework for designing and conducting needed research. Although most of our specific research recommendations have been provided in the individual chapters in which the issues related to them were introduced, we complete our report by listing what we consider to be the three most compelling research opportunities.

1.   Theory and methods are required for the measurement of performance across work units of different sizes at different levels in an enterprise. For example, methods are needed that will permit changes to be traced through the system, from individual to group to organization. Because the tools now available are at such an immature stage of development, research on organizational linkages and their influences is difficult to conduct at the level of precision required.

2.   Much more needs to be learned about how structures and processes inhibit and facilitate organizational linkages. The dynamics of these interactions are very complex, and enhancing linkages is likely to be more than simply a function of removing inhibitors and activating facilitators. At this point, possible inhibitors and facilitators have been identified, but a theory is lacking for relating the structures and processes involved to organizational linkages. For example, it is not known when certain structures will inhibit the transfer of productivity gains and when they will not. Nor is it known under what conditions certain processes will facilitate productivity gains and under what conditions they will not.

3.   The analysis of productivity linkages should be expanded to encompass other aspects of organizational performance—effectiveness, efficiency, quality, quality of work life, innovation, and profitability. Focusing on a single performance criterion, productivity, does not provide a complete and true picture of the effects of an intervention, even if the goal of the intervention was solely to improve productivity. Do the conditions that increase productivity also increase or decrease product quality or the level of innovation in the organization? A different question to be addressed by an expanded analysis is, will a theory of organizational linkages developed for productivity apply as well to other criteria of organizational performance?

As we look ahead, we cannot help but conclude that attaining a more productive society and higher overall standard of living will require a better understanding of organizational linkages. The United

States and the rest of the world will inevitably continue to invest more heavily in technological solutions. However, as this report has demonstrated, implementation of new technology is not enough. Organizational linkages must be understood well enough to permit the creation of conditions that will ensure that investments in technology provide the returns of which they are capable.

Index

A

Accounting practice
  cost-center analysis, 137
  information technology and, 22-23
  productivity assessment of, 127
  in traditional performance evaluation,
    144-145
Aerospace industry, 240, 241, 245, 248
Aggregation of data, 119, 120, 128, 171-
    172, 176-177, 184
  theory of composition, 185, 298
American Hospital Supply Corporation,
    43-44
Automated teller machines, 46, 89-90, 202
Automobile industry, 2, 56, 61, 232, 264

B

Banking/finance industry, 17, 18-20, 21,
    23, 56
  automated teller machines, 46, 89-90,
    202
Behavior modification
  measurement of productivity and, 107-
    108, 110-111, 139-140
  principles of, 108-109
Biotechnology, 2
Bottlenecks, 117, 144, 155-156, 165, 175

C

Clerical productivity, 20
  information technologies and, 33-36,
    86
Communications
  in computer-aided design, 249-250,
    251-252, 260
  in downsizing efforts, 269-270, 273-275
  formalization of, 28-29, 252
  in gain-sharing plans, 70-72
  indexicality of, 27
  individual skills, 197
  in lean production systems, 66-67, 68
  negative effect on productivity, 166,
    225
  social effects, 230
  in software development, 10, 221, 222,
    223-225, 226-228, 294
  speed of, 26-27
  team design and, 221, 226-228
  threat-rigidity effect, 270
Communications industry, 18
Competency multiplier effects, 219-220
Competition
  international, 1-2
  managerial overhead and, 264
  strategic information processing, 43-44
Composition theory, 185-188, 190, 298-299

Computer-aided design
  assessment methodology, 141-142
  computer-aided manufacturing and,
    241, 259
  data collection and management in, 243
  definition of productivity in, 10, 244
  designer-team linkage, 250-255, 259-260
  expectations for, 10-11, 241, 243
  implementation, 256-257
  information flow in, 249-250, 251-252,
    254-255, 260
  isolation of workers in, 245, 251-252,
    259-260
  organizational complexity in, 247-248,
    255, 260
  principal activities in, 242-243
  productivity determinants in, 243-250
  productivity linkages in, 11
  research needs, 259-260
  resource management in, 245-246,
    257-258, 260
  role of, 240, 241
  specialization in, 244-245, 253, 260
  supervision, 250, 253-254, 260
  system support, 248-249, 255-256, 260
  team-organization linkage, 255-259, 260
  tools, 248
  training, 247
  as transitional technology, 246-247,
    254, 258, 260
  workstation time-sharing, 245-246,
    257-258
Computer-aided manufacturing, 241, 259
Computer-aided software engineering, 221*n*
Computer industry. *See* Software
  development
Conceptual Schematic Productivity
  model, 111-114
Continuous improvement, 70-71, 107,
  147, 150
Core activities, 61-62, 293
Corporate investments, 2-3, 15, 17-18, 46
Customer service, 44-46
  automation in, 62
  subtask productivity analysis, 59-60

D

Document preparation
  document revisions in, 34-35
  quality vs. quantity trade-offs, 29-30

spoken communication vs., 26-27
  See also Information technology
Downsizing
  attitudes of retained workers, 275-276,
    283-284
  compensation for casualties of, 275, 283
  as cost reduction tactic, 278-279, 281
  as crisis management, 269, 270, 271, 274
  cross-level effects, 267-268
  decision-making processes, 270-271, 273
  early retirement incentives in, 279
  employee targeting in, 263-264, 276-
    277, 282-283
  implementation, 268, 269, 272
  information flow in, 269-270, 273-275,
    285
  level of application, 266-267
  linkage insensitivity in, 271
  mistaken beliefs in, 271-280, 288
  obstacles to productivity gains in, 268,
    281-284, 285, 295
  organizational productivity and, 284-
    286, 292
  partial factor productivity in analysis
    of, 262
  participants in design of, 272-273, 276-
    277, 282, 283-284, 285
  as productivity initiative, 11, 263-268
  removal of top management in, 279-280
  simultaneous restructuring, 278, 284,
    285-286
  successful model of, 281-286, 288
  total factor productivity in analysis of,
    262
  trends, 263-266
  value analysis in, 283

E

E-mail, 35, 225, 252
  speech vs., 27, 28
Educational system, 141
Effectiveness, as assessment criterion, 8,
  106, 134-135
Efficiency
  coordination in groups, 230
  as organizational assessment
    criterion, 8, 106, 134, 135
Employee compensation
  bonus plans, 70, 71, 86-87
  in downsizing, 275

gain-sharing plans, 69-72
in lean production systems, 68
productivity and, 48
response to change and, 85
stock participation, 83
subtask focus of, 86-87
wages, 2, 48
work behavior and, 108-109
Employee evaluation
misuse of productivity assessments,
127-128
motivation in, 140, 168, 171
in Productivity Measurement and
Enhancement System, 178, 182-
183
productivity measurement for, 107,
127-128
productivity vs. performance, 126-127
unit cost analysis, 127
Employee participation
in downsizing decisions, 272-273, 282,
283-284, 285
employee ownership and, 83
in innovation process, 136-137
in office automation decisions, 85
organizational congruence and, 140-
141
in Scanlon plan, 70
in technology implementation, 257
trends, 207

F

Focus of attention, 65, 70, 75
Food service industry, 21, 108

G

Gain-sharing plans, 69-72
Goal alignment, 9, 107-111, 119, 139-141,
174, 183-184, 187, 202
Group functioning
communications in, 223-225
in composition theory, 185
in computer-aided design, 11, 250-255
coordination in, 10, 215, 225
in decentralized environments, 207,
260
degree of interdependence in, 185-187
entrainment process in, 228-229
experimental modeling, 230-232

in Goal Alignment model, 109-110, 119
individual performance and, 82, 117-
121, 214, 218-219, 229-232, 250-
255
in information technology, 33-36, 48
in innovation process, 137
input factors, 118
as measure of individual performance,
197
in organizational performance, 118,
187, 232, 250-255
performance measurement system for,
178-184
productivity determinants, 205
productivity linkages in, 122-123, 129
productivity measurement of, 117-119
public goods problem, 226n
research, 4, 229-232
role accuracy in, 187
in software development, 10, 214-215,
216-217, 218-229, 231-233
supervision, 185, 253-254
team design, 220-223
types of group structures, 120-121
worker isolation as productivity factor,
251-252, 259-260

H

Hiring practices, 95, 188
for software development teams, 220
Hourly output, 2, 263
Human factors research, 3-4

I

Individual performance/productivity
aggregation of data, 119, 120, 128
behavior modification in measurement
of, 107-108, 139-140
communication skills, 197
components of job performance, 195-
197, 199
in composition theory, 185
in computer-aided design, 250-255
Conceptual Schematic Productivity
model, 111-114
in context of total performance, 126-127
in core vs. peripheral tasks, 61-62, 64-
65, 293
demonstrated effort as factor in, 197

determinants of, 197-198, 204-206
direct observation for assessment of, 200-201
discipline as factor in, 197
downsizing effects, 267-268
effects of measurement on, 193
facilitative processes in organizations, 65-72
financial measures in assessment of, 127
gain-sharing plans and, 69-72
group performance and, 117-119, 128, 218-219, 250-255
information technologies and, 26-33, 35, 206
input measures, 124-125, 129
job-specific task proficiency, 195-196, 199
leadership skills, 197
management skills, 197
measurement of, 9
misuse of assessments, 127-128
model for IT assessment, 194-198
motivation in, 197, 198
non-job-specific task proficiency, 196
obstacles to measurement of, 128-129
obstacles to organization-level change, 58-64, 65, 73
organizational linkages, 56-64, 65, 72-76, 297-298
output determinants, 185
output measures, 123-124, 128, 168-170
peak vs. typical, 199-200
process determinants, 5-6, 58, 65-66
Productivity Servosystem model, 114-117
quality as assessment factor, 125-126
rating method, 200
research in, 4, 105-106
research needs, 77-79, 123-129
role linkages in, 57, 59-64
in software development team productivity, 215, 218-219
standardized sample for assessment of, 200
subtask relationships in, 57, 58-61, 86-87, 94-95
system determinants, 82
uncontrollable factors, 112-113
variables in, 111, 112
Industrial engineers, 4

Industrial/organizational psychology
behavior modification, 108-109
productivity research, 4
Information technology
administrative overhead in, 36-38
case studies, 211-212
clerical productivity and, 20
corporate investment in, 2-3, 15, 17-18, 46
corporate strategic applications, 43-44
customer service and, 44-46
ease of use and overuse of, 35, 41-42, 86
equipment obsolescence issues, 31
increases in workload related to, 33-36
interindustry comparisons, 16, 20-21
interrole effects, 62
intraindustry comparisons, 16, 21-24
labor productivity in, 145
latent structure, 195, 210
macro modeling of, 296-297
management control-seeking behavior, 40-41
management information systems, 21-22, 40-42, 48
multilevel analysis, 16-17
operator skills, 31-33
opportunity for profitability, 44-46
organizational communication and, 26-29
organizational structure and, 205-206
planning for implementation, 148
in poorly run vs. well-run firms, 25-26
productivity and, 47-49
productivity assessment, 194, 202, 207-208, 209
productivity components, 203-204, 210
productivity determinants, 205-206, 210
productivity improvement strategies, 206-208
quality vs. quantity trade-off in, 29-30, 48, 125
research needs in, 49, 158, 209-212, 297
sectoral analyses, 16, 17-20
socioeconomic impacts, 13, 14-15
spiraling investment in, 46-47, 90-91
subtask productivity analysis, 59-60, 86-87
See also Office automation
Innovation
international comparison, 137, 222
as organizational assessment criterion, 8, 106, 134, 136-137

Insurance industry, 17, 23-24, 46
Internal Revenue Service, 30
International linkages, 1-2
IT. *See* Information technology

J

Job classification, 68
Just-in-time manufacturing, 28

L

Labor costs, 91, 124-125, 129

M

Management/supervision
    assessment activities, 138-139
    assessment of, 197, 263
    in computer-aided design, 250, 253-
        254, 260
    control-seeking behavior, 40, 150, 223
    decentralized, 207, 260
    of downsizing efforts, 268-271
    in dynamic environment, 143-144
    as group performance variable, 185
    growth trends, 264
    improvement/PDCA cycle, 139, 147
    information culture in, 40-42
    introduction of office automation, 84-85
    in IT productivity, 206-207
    knowledge of results, 140
    leadership climate, 83
    level-specific performance evaluation,
        141-143, 153, 168
    by numbers, 41, 42, 48
    optimal production technique strategy,
        155-156
    as organizational subsystem, 88
    as overhead in IT, 36-38
    participants in downsizing efforts,
        272-273, 276-277
    paternalistic style, 269-270
    performance measurement needs, 145-
        146, 147-149, 167
    productivity analysis for, 107
    in productivity assessment, 129
    as productivity determinant, 131-132,
        205, 206
    removal of, in crisis, 279-280
    resource allocation issues, 257-258

    role of, 138
    social context of decision-making, 270
    in software development teams, 222,
        223
    strategic planning, 147-148
    of successful downsizing, 281-284, 285
    systems model, 133, 134, 146-147
    total quality management, 93-94
    traditional measures of success in, 263
Marketing activities
    customer service, 44-46
    growth in, 38
    information technology in, 22-23, 44-46
Material velocity management, 143-144,
    155-156
Measurement of productivity outcomes,
    136
    administrative/managerial factors in,
        129
    aggregation of data, 176-177, 184
    analysis of variance in, 208
    as behavior modifier, 107-108, 139-140
    comparison across units, 183, 184, 188
    in computer-aided design, 244
    in context of total performance, 125-
        126, 297-298, 300
    contingencies concept, 179-181
    cultural aspects of organizations, 99
    data sources, 24-25
    defining linkages in, 132-133, 139
    definition of productivity in, 8-9, 202,
        209
    design variables, 153-155
    in engineering design, 10
    errors in, 127
    financial measures in, 127
    flexibility in, 139, 143-144, 151, 189
    goal alignment in, 139-141
    goals of, 128
    good qualities in, 142-143, 150-152, 201
    group level, 117-119, 129
    hierarchical model, 9
    inadequacy of, 131, 133-134, 157-158
    individual level, 9, 106-107, 195
    in information technologies, 14, 15-16,
        194, 195, 209
    as input/output ratio, 55, 244
    input units in, 124-125, 129
    knowledge of results in, 140
    latent variable vs. observed measure, 194
    in management system model, 147,
        148-149

methods in, 200-201
misuse of results, 127-128
natural phenomenon, 166-172
new thinking in, 150-152, 158-159
obstacles to, 128-129
organizational conflicts as obstacle to, 166, 173-174, 177, 183-184
organizational goal alignment in, 9, 107-111, 119, 174, 202
at organizational level, 59
output units in, 123-124, 128, 168-171, 175, 185, 187, 190, 296
peak vs. typical performance, 197-198
performance components, 195-197, 199
performance determinants, 197-198
problems in, 24-26, 207
as productivity determinant, 193
productivity determinants, 204-206
Productivity Measurement and Enhancement System, 177-184, 211
profit impact of market strategies approach, 21
profound knowledge in, 133, 292-293
quality issues in, 125-126
research needs, 145-146, 209-212, 296-297, 300
role of, 106-107, 156, 167-168
scaling in, 193, 230-232, 295
selection of measures in, 152-153, 168-171
self-reported data in, 30
side effects of interventions in, 175-176
as source of productivity paradox, 7-8, 166, 171, 174-177
in strategic planning, 148
substantive theory, 193
task classification in, 120
taxonomy of linkage problems, 189
time lag effects, 7, 31, 157, 165, 175, 207
traditional measures, 139, 144-145
unit of analysis in, 202-203
user needs in, 139, 141-143, 154
welfare economics framework for, 18-19
Motivation, 66, 68-69, 71, 76
employee ownership and, 83
equipment problems and, 258-259
measurement of, 176, 178
operant psychology, 108-109
performance evaluation systems and, 140, 168, 171, 197, 198
productivity measurement as, 110-111

O

Office automation
definition, 84
employee response, 84-85, 97-98
generalizability of productivity outcomes, 91
implementation, 84-85
individual productivity and, 86-87, 94-95
labor costs and, 91
maintenance investments, 90-91
negative productivity effects, 86, 90, 91
obstacles to productivity improvement, 7
organizational subsystem interactions, 89-93, 95-96
symbolic values in, 97-98
technical problems in, 258
training, 91
See also Information technology
Organizational culture, 92-94, 97, 100
Organizational productivity
administrative overhead and, 36-38
analysis of variance in, 208
benefits of, 48
communications technologies in, 26-29
in computer-aided design, 255-259
conditions for improvement in, 72-76
coordination systems in, 65, 66-67, 68, 71-72, 74-75
core vs. peripheral tasks in, 61-62, 64-65, 293
defining linkages in, 132-133
determinants of, 205-206
downsizing and, 11, 284-286, 292
effects of measurement on, 193
equifinality of interventions for, 89, 93-94
facilitative processes, 65-72, 293-294
focus of attention in, 65, 70, 75
gain-sharing plans and, 69-72
goal alignment in, 173-174, 183-184, 187, 202
group functioning in, 33-42, 118, 187, 232, 255-259
horizontal linkages in, 295-296
implementation of interventions, 94
individual productivity and, 26-33, 57, 59-61
industry productivity and, 43-44

information technology in, 26-42, 43-47, 48-49, 205-206
in lean production systems, 68-69, 72
management functions in, 40-42, 48, 206
motivation processes in, 66, 68-69, 71, 76
office automation and, 6-7, 84, 86-87, 90, 91
in open system theory, 94-96
organization-specific measures of, 9, 107-111, 119, 139-141
organizational evolution and, 65-66, 70-71, 75-76, 78
in poorly run vs. well-run firms, 25-26
problem-solving systems in, 65, 67-68, 69, 71-72, 75, 78
process determinants, 5-6, 58, 65-66, 293-294
research needs, 76-79
role linkages in, 57, 59-64
side effects of interventions, 7, 165-166, 175-176
social linkages in, 77
sources of intervention failure, 207
system determinants of, 82, 83, 293-294
in systems model, 8, 99-100
as target of downsizing initiatives, 266-267
theory of aggregation for, 185
theory of composition for, 185-188, 190, 298-299
types of organizational linkages in, 56-58
vertical linkages in, 295-296
wages and, 48
See also Productivity
Organizational structure
company size, 263
complexity of linkages in, 57-58, 299
in computer-aided design, 247-248, 255, 260
degree of interdependency in, 58, 88
design activities in, 11, 162-164
dynamic homeostasis in, 89, 92-93
effects of office automation in, 89-93
employee compensation, 68-72
group structure in, 119
information needs at different levels of, 141-143, 153, 168
in IT productivity, 205-206

lean vs. mass production systems, 66-69, 72
linkages in, 162-165
as obstacle to productivity growth, 7, 293
as open system, 87-89, 94-96
organizational evolution and, 76
organizational subsystems in, 88, 162-164
political context, 97, 98-99
as productivity factor, 165, 175, 293-295
project teams, 10
specialization in, 88, 89-90
subsystem linkage as source of paradox, 184-185
subsystem reverberations, 88, 90-91, 95
system-wide intervention, 81, 95-96
taxonomy of linkage problems, 189
team design, 220-223
types of linkages in, 55-56, 189
See also Downsizing
Organized labor, 63-64

P

Partial factor productivity, 55, 262
Postal Service, U.S., 60-61, 62, 63, 64
Problem-solving systems, 65, 67-68, 69, 71-72, 75, 78
in Scanlon plan, 70
Product development, 263
Productivity
capital/labor, 19-20, 21, 145
company size and, 263
in computer-aided design, 10-11, 241, 243-250, 260
computer security measures and, 249-250, 254-255, 260
corporate investment in, 2-3
definitions, 8-9, 55, 106, 136, 202, 209, 244, 262
determinants, 204-206, 209
downsizing effects, 265-268
importance of growth in, 1-2
information technology components, 203-204, 209
partial factor productivity, 55, 262
profitability and, 43, 44
resource management issues, 246, 260
software/hardware upgrades and, 246-247, 258, 260
strategic planning for, 147-148

supervision issues, 253-254, 260
systems support in, 255-256, 260
task specialization in, 245, 253, 260
technology implementation in, 256-257
technology problems and, 258-259
throughput, 13-14
total factor productivity, 55, 262
trends, 2, 14-15
See also Individual performance/
    productivity; Measurement of
    productivity outcomes;
    Organizational productivity
Productivity Measurement and
    Enhancement System (ProMES)
aggregation of data, 184
conceptual base, 177
definition of productivity, 177
feedback report, 178, 182-183
linkage issues, 183-184
process, 178-181, 211
role of, 177-178
Productivity research
case studies in, 211-212
decentralized management, 207
downsizing effects, 284-287
individual level, 105-106
information technology, 14, 16-24
large group performance, 229-232
level of analysis, 3-4, 105, 161-162,
    292, 295
linkages in software development, 218-
    219
multidisciplinary approach, 5
needs, 123-129, 145-146, 157, 185,
    189-190, 259-260, 286-287, 294,
    300
organizational linkages, 4-5, 162
software development teams for, 215
theory development, 74, 298-299
Productivity Servosystem model, 114-117
Profitability
company size and, 263
new technologies and, 44-46
as organizational assessment
    criterion, 8, 106, 134, 137
productivity and, 43, 44
Profound knowledge, 133, 292-293
Public goods theory, 226n
Purchasing procedures
computerization of, 43-44
corporate software, 32
organizational politics in, 98

Q

Quality
checkpoints, 135-136
information technologies and, 29-30,
    48
as organizational assessment
    criterion, 8, 106, 134, 135-136
in productivity assessment, 8, 125-126
productivity rewards for employees, 87
total quality management, 93-94
Quality of work life, 8, 68-69, 106, 134,
    136

R

Resource management, 245-246, 257-258
Retail settings, 92
Retirement incentives, 279
Robotics, 2

S

Scaling issues, 193, 230-232, 295
Scanlon plan, 69-72, 77
Security measures, 249-250, 254-255, 260
Shipbuilding industry, 2, 230-231
Side effects of interventions, 7, 165-166,
    175-176
Size of companies, 263
Slack, 7, 11, 60-61, 63-64, 67, 73, 77, 78,
    165, 188
Social linkages, 77
Software
in information technology
    productivity, 203, 246-247
product obsolescence as productivity
    issue, 31-32
spreadsheet modeling, 41-42, 90
Software development
analysis phase, 215
authority structure, 222, 228
coding operations, 216
communications in, 221, 222, 223-225,
    226-228, 294
competency multiplier effects, 219-220
complexity of, 216
computer-aided, 221n
coordination in, 215, 216-226
design phase, 215-216
documentation of, 216

entrainment process in, 228-229
individual-group linkages, 10, 218-219
in information technology
    productivity, 203
infrastructure costs, 223
interdependence of components, 217-218
object-oriented design, 221*n*
process, 215-216
productivity determinants, 214-215,
    233, 294
reassignment of members, 229
research on linkages, 218-219
role of teams in, 214
team design in, 10, 214, 219, 220-223,
    226-228, 294
uncertainty in, 217
as unit of analysis, 215
unit of output in, 124
Specialization, 11, 88, 89-90, 244-245,
    253, 260
Spreadsheet programs, 41-42, 90
Steel industry, 2, 263
Strategic planning, 147-148
Systems theory
    analysis of decision-making, 96
    in design of measurement systems, 154
    human resources assessment in, 96-97
    limitations of, 96
    of management, 133
    open systems, 87-89
    organizational functioning in, 133-137
    in productivity interventions, 94-96, 299
    subsystem interactions in
        organizations, 88-94

T

Tank crew performance, 232
Task classification, 120
Textile industries, 2
Throughput productivity, 13-14
Time lag effects, 7, 31, 157, 165, 207
Total factor productivity, 55, 262
Total quality management, 93-94, 136,
    147
Training
    after downsizing, 275, 283
    competency multiplier effects, 219-220
    in computer-aided design, 247
    hardware/software obsolescence and,
        31-33, 246-247
    office automation, 85, 91
    in problem-solving, 68
    software development teams, 219-220
    system interactions in, 83

V

Valve-manufacturing industry, 22-23

W

Wages, 2, 48
Warehousing/inventory activities
    information technology in, 43-44
Warehousing operations, 23
Waste, 190